THE FATHERS ACCORDING TO RABBI NATHAN

THE FATHERS

ACCORDING TO

RABBI NATHAN

TRANSLATED FROM THE HEBREW BY

JUDAH GOLDIN

SCHOCKEN BOOKS · NEW YORK

First SCHOCKEN PAPERBACK edition 1974

Copyright © 1955 by Yale University Press
Library of Congress Catalog Card No. 74–9638

This book was originally published as Volume X of the Yale Judaica Series
and is reprinted by arrangement with Yale University Press.

Manufactured in the United States of America

Library of Congress Cataloging in Publication Data

Aboth de-Rabbi Nathan. English.
  The Fathers according to Rabbi Nathan.

  Reprint of the ed. published by Yale University Press, New Haven, which was
issued as v. 10 of Yale Judaica series.
  Includes bibliographical references.
  1. Ethics, Jewish. I. Goldin, Judah, 1914-   tr. II. Title. III. Series: Yale
Judaica series, v. 10.
[BJ1287.A22E5 1974]   296.1   74-9638

For Grace

EDITOR'S NOTE

İT IS almost exactly ten years since Judaica Research at Yale University was founded for the purpose of promoting studies and publications in the various fields of Hebrew lore and literature.

Those charged with putting the plan into effect were by no means unaware of the manifold difficulties and obstacles they were likely to encounter. They were mindful, in fact, not to permit their enthusiasm for the project to render them unduly sanguine about its realization. As the work continued to evolve, their enthusiasm did not diminish, but their consciousness of the crucial responsibility they had taken upon themselves increased with each book approaching completion, with each manuscript submitted, with each volume published.

Seen in retrospect, the work so far done is not inconsiderable and its quality has been found to be not inadequate; but it was accomplished at a very high cost of human effort and scholarly labor. Ten years is not too long a period in which to advance the cause of a greatly specialized and, in many ways, neglected branch of scholarship. But even half of such a period is a dire price in the life of the productive scholars who have shared in the work of the series.

From the beginning, the principle guiding the editorial policy of the series has been that of combining accuracy of philological analysis with complete independence from the style and idiom of the Semitic texts that were to be made available in translation. It has often been demonstrated—more often in negative than in positive terms—that philological accuracy is a sine qua non for safeguarding the stylistic independence of a translator of ancient and medieval works against the hazard of license, misinterpretation, or unnecessary exegesis.

Even within the relatively limited scope of the two cycles envisioned in the report on the first year of work, the series was designed to embrace a rather wide range of subjects, of cultural background, of literary species, of linguistic variability. The works already published have been translated, mostly for the first time, from Ethiopic, Arabic, Aramaic, and several kinds and periods of Hebrew. In literary subject matter they represent Apocrypha, Agada, liturgy, philosophy, polemics, and a wide sphere of sacred and civil law. As it often happened in the preparation of our volumes, a given phrase or vocable, especially when used as a standing locution or technical term, might be found listed in the standard dictionaries as bearing a variety of connotations. To make the proper choice or to provide a connotation that was not listed but had to be deduced from the context in which it occurred, the translator often found it necessary to consider the literary, cultural, and historical area out of which the work he translated had grown.

Most of our volumes are bound to assume the nature of text books or works of reference. Some of them have already found their way onto the shelves of university libraries and seminar rooms to stand side by side with the classic originals which they have made available in translation. Lacking in philological precision and accuracy, they would be condemned as untrustworthy witnesses to those classics. But failing to replace the idioms of the originals by the idiom of modern literary English, they would have failed to render the classic monuments accessible to non-Semitist scholars—historians, theologians, philosophers, jurists—and would be of even less service to the general reader, for both of whom they have been primarily intended.

In the initial report the belief was expressed that it might be advantageous to find, for the works selected, translations already made by scholars on their own initiative. It may now be said that the advantage has been found to lie in the opposite direction. In fact, in cases where a manuscript submitted for publication contained work which the translator had done at his own discretion, such work had virtually to be done over again in order to adjust it to the essentially popular nature of the series and, in particular, to the principle of its editorial policy.

As a rule, however, our translations have been prepared by scholars for the specific purpose of submitting them for publication in the present series. This has made it possible for translator and editor to cooperate in the task on hand from beginning to end: from the time the work got under way until its completion, and from questions bearing on details of the translation and annotations to those concerning the nature of the introduction, the make-up of the index, and often even the exact wording of the title. This close progressive cooperation has given the published volumes inner cohesion, as well as outer uniformity, despite their great divergence in subject matter and cultural-literary species.

By contrast, another belief expressed in the initial report has crystallized into firm conviction: that the enormous range of hitherto untranslated Jewish classics should be made available to the humanistic sciences and the general public. What has been brought out in the present series represents but a small segment of that range. Even if only the most vital desiderata be considered, the work remaining to be done would be enough to occupy many generations of students.

JULIAN OBERMANN

New Haven
December, 1954

CONTENTS

Torah study. Temple service and the world's blessings. Acts of loving-kindness and atonement. Daniel's acts of loving-kindness. The war with Rome. Johanan ben Zakkai escapes Jerusalem; meets Vespasian. Jamnia granted as a refuge for scholars. Destruction of Jerusalem; the Temple in flames; the priests and the Temple keys. Mourning for the Temple. Three distinctions between men

CONTENTS

to all of creation. What God showed Adam. The Torah created before the world. Man as microcosm

INTRODUCTION

THE FATHERS ACCORDING TO RABBI NATHAN—or, as the work is generally referred to by its Hebrew title, *'Aḇoṯ dĕ-Rabbi Naṯan*—is one of the so-called extracanonical Minor Tractates of the Talmud.[1] Briefly it may be described as a commentary and amplification of the renowned mishnaic tractate—more accurately, as we shall see, of an early form of that tractate—called *'Aḇoṯ* (*Fathers*) or *Pirḳe 'Aḇoṯ* (*Chapters of the Fathers*). For the sake of convenience we shall refer to *'Aḇoṯ dĕ-Rabbi Naṯan* and *Pirḳe 'Aḇoṯ* in the following pages as ARN and PA respectively. And since a full understanding of ARN is possible only by studying it in close conjunction with PA, it is important to recall several principal facts about the mishnaic tractate before proceeding with the detailed discussion of ARN.

PA is the only tractate of the Mishnah devoted exclusively to Agada, to that unlimited range of contemplative themes and teachings which are of a religious-ethical-folkloristic character. As such, PA stands in sharp contrast to all the other sixty-two tractates of the Mishnah, which deal with Halakha, that is, with matters of law, with legal discussions concerning civil, criminal, ritual, ceremonial, marital, agricultural, and similar questions.[2] Another distinctive feature of PA is that its contents are in the form of sayings and maxims; each of these, as a rule, especially

1. On the Minor Tractates at the end of the fourth division of the Babylonian Talmud, see Strack, pp. 73 f. Although in the first edition of the Minor Tractates (Giustiniani, 1550) ARN is put last, in the regularly printed editions of the Talmud it is placed first—perhaps because the works are arranged according to size, and ARN is the longest of them all; perhaps too because of all the Minor Tractates, ARN alone is related to a canonical tractate of the Mishnah, indeed to a tractate in the fourth division. For a general orientation on the terms related to rabbinic literature —such as Mishnah, Tosefta, Midrash, Agada, Halakha, Talmud, Tannaite, etc.— cf. Strack and JE under the corresponding headings.

2. Because of its agadic nature there is reason to suggest that although at present PA is one of the tractates at the end of the fourth division, it was intended originally as a peroration for the Mishnah as a whole. Note indeed its position in the Munich manuscript of the Talmud.

in the first four chapters, is transmitted in the name of a particular Sage; and the succession of authorities—in part drawn up
in chronological order—reaches, on the one hand, as far back as
the Men of the Great Assembly and Simeon the Righteous (*ca.*
200 B.C.E.), and on the other, down to Rabbi Judah the Prince, the
redactor of the Mishnah (d. *ca.* 220 C.E.), and his immediate suc-
cessors. Thus the material gathered together in PA constitutes a
kind of repository for the thinking and teachings of the Tannaite
Fathers, for the spiritual, moral, and practical values emphasized
by Israel's Sages during the first five centuries of talmudic
Judaism.[3]

In subject matter ARN is the same as PA, that is to say, it too
is entirely devoted to Agada, it too is a compilation of the wisdom
of the Fathers, of their reflections, ideals, disciplines, and above
all the expression of their singular commitment to "the study of
Torah."

As for its literary character, the bulk [4] of ARN consists of commentary on the sayings and maxims of PA, now interpreting and
elucidating their meaning, now expanding their import and implication, now illustrating by means of parable, now again dwelling on the lives of the authorities quoted and other distinguished
personalities referred to in passing. The interpretations of the PA
text in ARN are not merely of literal meaning but of what might
be called their larger intent. In effect, therefore, the relation of
ARN to PA is that of the Midrash to the Scriptures: a verbal
peculiarity or suggestive phrase may become the cue for homiletical, imaginative interpretation. And like the Midrash, ARN will

3. In one more respect PA is unique: it is the only talmudic treatise to have been
included in its entirety in the Prayer Book (cf. n. 6 below) and for this reason
has been reprinted more frequently than any other rabbinic works. For additional
discussion of PA see the introduction in R. T. Herford, *Pirke Aboth*, New York,
1925.

4. The exegetical character of ARN (that is, of Version A of ARN; see further below, p. xxi) is manifested chiefly in its first twenty-one chapters, and to a somewhat lesser degree in the last ten. Chapters 22–30, however, are more like PA in
style. Here, by and large, there is little or no comment on the sayings. Authorities
are simply quoted, once or several times, and nothing is added to or derived from
their statements.

frequently offer not one but several explanations of a saying, so that when we are done with one, "another interpretation," and often still "another," will be forthcoming. Again like the Midrash, discussion in ARN lends itself easily to digression, winding from one theme to the next, to expound a biblical verse previously cited as proof text or to enlarge upon what may have been no more than casual allusion or to round out discussion of a topic or person mentioned in connection with the primary subject. To be sure, some of the discursiveness is due to interpolation, for the compiler or compilers of ARN apparently drew on numerous sources in which comments were made on PA passages. Nevertheless, the apparent ease with which the additions have been assimilated points to an initial elasticity of structure. As a result, we get in ARN what we get in the Midrash too: not a systematic theological or ethical treatise devoted to abstract argumentation, but homilies and comments revolving around the sayings and concepts interpreted, and reinforcing what rabbinic literature as a whole assumes: "God as a reality, Revelation as a fact, the Torah as a way of life, and the hope of Redemption as a most vivid expectation." [5]

It is because of its exegetical character and discursiveness that ARN is so much larger in volume than PA, consisting of forty-one chapters, as compared with the six (originally five) [6] chapters of PA.

Students have long since observed that ARN is based on an early form of PA differing in organization and important details from the form of this tractate in the Mishnah as redacted by Judah the Prince.[7] Thus it frequently happens that the order of sayings

---

5. *Aspects*, p. 12; cf. L. Ginzberg, *Students, Scholars and Saints* (Philadelphia, 1928), p. 92.

6. The so-called sixth chapter of PA, *Ḳinyan Torah*, was originally not part of the Mishnah. It was added to PA for liturgical purposes, so that there would be a chapter for every Sabbath between Passover and the Feast of Weeks, when PA was recited. Cf. L. Zunz, *Die Ritus des synagogalen Gottesdienstes* (Berlin, 1859), pp. 85 f.

7. On the redaction of PA, the original core of its composition, and the early form of many of its sayings as preserved in ARN, see the critical study by D. Hoffmann, *Die erste Mischna* (Berlin, 1881–82), pp. 26 ff.

occurring in both PA and ARN differs; [8] the chronological arrangement of some early authorities quoted is more strictly adhered to in ARN than in PA; [9] so too a number of sayings in the "canonical" PA are wanting in ARN; [10] often sayings common to both PA and ARN differ in their wording and even in the Sages to whom they are attributed. Yet despite these variants the degree of agreement between the readings in PA and ARN, and even the similarity of their general organization,[11] is so overwhelming as to suggest that ARN would hardly have differed essentially from its present form if it had been based on the PA of the Mishnah before us. Along with many scholars, therefore, we may look upon ARN as a Tosefta to PA, for in style and composition it often supplements the material of PA in the same manner that treatises in the Tosefta supplement their respective counterparts in the Mishnah.

Nothing can be said with certainty about the identity of the "Nathan" in the title of ARN or about the exact nature of his relation to this work. The fact that a Rabbi Nathan is one of the authorities quoted in the opening paragraphs is in no way instructive, for the authority almost certainly intended at that point is Rabbi Jonathan; moreover, in another version of our work, to which we shall refer shortly, the name Nathan does not appear until the thirty-fourth chapter. The most plausible suggestion remains that ARN is based on a rescension of PA by the Babylonian Rabbi Nathan who was an older contemporary of Judah the Prince. There is still the possibility, however, that

8. Cf. e.g. PA 3–4 with ARN, chs. 19–30.

9. Note how in PA 1: 15–2: 7 chronological sequence is interrupted in order to list the heads of the Jewish community in Palestine, while in ARN 13 ff. the chronological order is retained without regard to the official status of the Sages quoted.

10. The following PA passages do not occur in ARN: 1: 18; 2: 1–2, 3 (nevertheless, see below, Ch. 11, p. 63; and cf. ARNB, p. 47), 4a, 5b; 3: 2 (on 2b, however, see below, Ch. 8, p. 50), 3, 4 (but see below, Ch. 29, p. 120), 5 (but see below, Ch. 20, p. 94), 6 (but see below, Ch. 8, p. 50), 7–8, 10a, 12; 4: 4, 5b, 7–8, 10a, 11a, 13a, 15a, 16–17, 19, 20 (on 20a however, cf. below, Ch. 23, p. 102), 21–22; 5: 6, 9b, 11, 12–14 (on 5: 12 and 5: 14, however, cf. below, Ch. 40, p. 164), 19, 21. It should be added that ARNA closes with the statement of R. Hananiah ben ʿAḳaŝya (M. Makkot 3: 16), with which each of the PA chapters is customarily concluded in the liturgy.

11. Cf. e.g. Mabo, p. ix.

our Rabbi Nathan is an otherwise unknown sage who is responsible for ARN itself rather than for the alternative PA on which it is based.

It has been frequently suggested that in its present form ARN was probably compiled some time between the seventh and ninth centuries, when the other Minor Tractates seem to have been redacted. But date of compilation must not be confused with date of composition. Since no authority quoted in ARN is later than the Tannaite period, that is, later than the early part of the third century, and since, furthermore, the language [12] and the teachings and the idiom [13] are typical of what we find in Tannaite sources, the composition of the contents of ARN cannot be much later than the third or following century, or at the utmost shortly thereafter. According to one scholar who has meticulously analyzed all the variant readings and the pattern of ARN,[14] different parts of our treatise were composed at different times, and the earliest part he would assign to a date as early as the first century.

A particularly significant fact about ARN is that it has come down to us in two versions, the one regularly printed in our editions of the Talmud and the other, consisting of forty-eight chapters, published in full for the first time by Solomon Schechter: he designated the two versions as A and B respectively. In the main, what has been said about ARN applies to Version B no less than to Version A. But a comparative study of the two versions reveals a number of differences between them—in readings, in substance, in arrangement, and in the extent of PA material.[15] Especially noteworthy are the following: on two occasions ARNB attributes to certain early Sages what both ARNA and PA attribute to their colleagues; again, unlike ARNA, in the course of inter-

12. I.e. Hebrew. Some sayings of Hillel and another half dozen or so words are in Aramaic; but occasional Aramaic clauses or expressions occur also in Tannaite sources. So too, the few Greek and Latin loan words are in no way unusual.

13. It is occasionally suggested that some phrases in ARN reflect a later age; but even this must be regarded with extreme caution, in the light of what S. Lieberman points out in DR, pp. xxii–xxiii.

14. Cf. Mabo, pp. 18 ff. and see p. 38.

15. The following PA passages do not occur in ARNB: 3: 7, 8, 10a, 12; 4: 3, 5b, 19; 5: 11, 21. On differences between the two versions cf. ARNS, pp. xx ff.

preting a PA passage ARNB does not tend to go out of its way to associate "the study of Torah" with other themes; [16] finally, where ARNA and PA often refer simply to "the world" ARNB reads "this world and the world to come."

Schechter believed that originally there was only one text of ARN, from which the different versions developed in the course of time and transmission; ARNA he regarded as the older of the two, but he felt that ARNB remained closer to the original. Other scholars, however, maintain that the two versions are independent not only of each other but of "any written proto-ARN." [17]

That ARN was always regarded as a valuable source of rabbinic teachings is evidenced by the number of posttalmudic authorities who quote from it or refer to it in their own writings.[18] The importance of our treatise lies, of course, in what it has preserved for students of Jewish literature, especially for students of Agada. Specifically, and by way of summary: ARN provides us with the oldest commentary on PA. It discloses a rescension—or at least parts of a rescension—of PA which makes it possible for us to perceive the steps in the composition and final redaction of that unique mishnaic tractate. In its interpretation and expansion of PA sayings it has brought down to us a wealth of homiletical, legendary, biographical, and historical material, of which some appears in an early form in ARN and was later taken over by compilers of other works, and some is available to us only here.[19] It has

16. Cf. HUCA, *19*, 97 ff.

17. Cf. L. Finkelstein in JBL, *57*, 16, 39.

18. In addition to the 36 medieval authorities whom Schechter lists, there might be added the Karaite Abu'l Faraj Furkan (wrote about 1050; cf. J. Mann, *Texts and Studies in Jewish History and Literature*, *2*, 36) and Rabbi Jacob bar Hananel of Sicily (14th cent.; cf. OD, *2*, 624 f.). For still others cf. N. Bruell in *Jahrbuecher fur Juedische Geschichte und Litteratur*, Frankfurt a.M., *9*, 134 f. Professor Lieberman calls my attention to the fact that the earliest quotation from ARN, ch. 19 of ARNB, occurs in the Šě'eltoṭ (ed. Berlin, Pt. 3, p. 212), the oldest work of Geonic times.

19. Of particular interest e.g. is the story of the origin of certain famous sects during the period of the Second Commonwealth, and a whole chapter devoted to sayings by Elisha ben 'Abuyah, the second-century sage who broke away from the tradition. It is perhaps significant that in one of these sayings Elisha seems to be echoing a Roman proverb and quoting from Sirach.

recorded points of view which reflect ancient, more conservative attitudes that were later modified along the liberal lines of "normative Judaism."[20] According to one scholar ARN has frequently preserved the original, conversational idiom of many PA sayings before these were edited by the redactor of the Mishnah.[21]

Above all, the importance of our treatise lies not merely in its various literary properties but in the nature of its content, the wisdom taught by the Fathers of the Synagogue, a wisdom which they strove themselves to exemplify, pre-eminently through the study of Torah, and which they tried to inculcate in their contemporaries and those who would follow after.

The present translation of ARN in its traditional form is based on the text edited by Schechter.[22] This text form, as we have seen, he called Version A as distinct from Version B, and his edition offers both versions in parallel columns. Both versions are copiously annotated, principally for the purpose of supplying readings from unedited manuscripts, cross-references to rabbinical literature, some textual emendations, and occasional suggestions for interpretation. Schechter's edition is prefaced by a searching, pioneering, highly informative study touching on the many problems offered by the text and the history of ARN. Additional critical text material and comments Schechter furnished in four appendices to his work, of which the second is particularly significant, for it reproduces a rather extensive, though poorly preserved, fragment of yet another version of ARN containing material not found in either of the other two versions.

A new edition, accompanied by a concise, philologically oriented apparatus, is very much needed today; for since Schechter's time not only have the methods of critical editing of Semitic texts been refined, but there have come to light sources which were either accessible to him in manuscript form only or entirely unknown to

20. Cf. e.g. the statement of "the Sages," below, p. 16, with R. 'Aḳiba's view in B. Šabbaṭ 64b; note the attitude in the commentary below, Ch. 8, p. 50, and n. 14, *ad loc*. In this connection see also *Mabo*, pp. 21 ff.

21. See *Mabo*, p. 1 of the Hebrew Introduction (unpaged).

22. Salomon Schechter, *Aboth de Rabbi Nathan*, Vienna, 1887; reprinted New York, 1945.

him, and as a result many of his annotations are by now anti-
quated.[23] Nevertheless, in the history of modern rabbinical
scholarship Schechter's work on ARN remains a milestone: it
was the first classical rabbinic text prepared with painstaking care
on the basis of all extant manuscripts.[24] Until a new edition appears, no serious study of ARN is possible without constant reference
to Schechter's text and notes and his introduction; any new edition
will have to lean heavily on his findings.[25]

In 1654 a Latin translation of our work was published by
Francis Tayler. A German translation by Kaim Pollak appeared
in 1905. Apart from a questionable paraphrase by L. M. Rodkinson,[26] this is the first attempt to furnish a complete English
translation of *The Fathers according to Rabbi Nathan*.[27]

Where the text of ARN is intact, its language is for the most
part simple and lucid and offers no major difficulties to the
translator. Unfortunately, however, the text does suffer from a
number of smaller or larger lacunae, defective readings, scribal
errors—the whole assortment of enigmas familiar to a student of
ancient Jewish literature. Occasionally the translation is based on
better readings of our text preserved in certain medieval works or
in the manuscripts used by Schechter, or on emendations offered
by scholars. Every advantage was taken of whatever assistance
ARNB could provide. Where the translation departs from Schechter's edited text, the notes call attention to the fact.

As a rule an attempt has been made to translate all Hebrew terms
into their English equivalents, even where the equation is not
entirely satisfactory, as when *yeṣer* is rendered "impulse" and
maḳom is translated "God." Some technical words remain untrans-

23. For a list of relevant sources published since Schechter's time cf. *Mabo*,
p. 3, n. 3.

24. On an additional ARN MS, unknown to Schechter, cf. *Mabo*, p. 2.

25. Professor Louis Finkelstein is now preparing a new edition of ARN.

26. Francis Tayler, *Tractatus de patribus Rabbi Nathan auctore*, London, 1654;
Kaim Pollak, *Rabbi Nathans System der Ethik und Moral*, Frankfurt a.M., 1905;
M. L. Rodkinson, *Babylonian Talmud* (New York, 1900), *1*, 9. An earlier version
of the first chapter of the present translation of ARN appeared in MMKJV, pp. 263 ff.

27. This rendering of the Hebrew-Aramaic title of ARN was suggested by Professor Obermann.

lated and are explained in the notes. The terms Torah and Shekinah can now be found in standard English dictionaries: translation does them violence, explanation is not easily compressed in a
footnote.

For biblical quotations—which are frequently given in full
even when they appear in abridged form in the text—the version
of the Jewish Publication Society of America has been used. However, where the context demands otherwise—where there is a play
on words or where interpretation departs from the literal meaning
—the translation has departed from the usual rendering.

English idiom at times required an addition or contraction of
clauses or words, or similar deviations from the Hebrew original.
But an effort was made to retain as much as possible of the
quality or flavor of the original whenever this did not sacrifice
intelligibility.

The punctuation and transliteration adopted by this series of
Judaica Research publications govern the present volume also.
Quotations from PA are set off from the commentary of ARN by
capitalization, and scriptural passages are indicated by italics.
Quotation marks have been used in narrative involving direct
discourse. A colon with no quotation marks is employed to introduce the sayings and maxims of the Sages. For the sake of
economy, titles of works referred to in the notes have been given
in abbreviated form; the full titles are reproduced in the List of
Abbreviations. In the text, parentheses have been used to indicate
words or phrases which have been added for the sake of correct
English idiom; brackets indicate words or phrases missing in the
original but restored on good authority.

At the suggestion of the editor of this series, the text of PA in
the translation by the late Herbert Danby has been added as an
appendix.[28] I want to take this opportunity of thanking the heirs
and publishers of Canon Danby for the permission to reprint his
translation in this volume.

In preparing this translation I constantly drew upon the works
of the traditional commentators of PA and ARN. I have been

28. Herbert Danby, *The Mishnah* (Oxford, 1933), pp. 446 ff.

particularly fortunate in being able to turn to my late teacher, Professor Louis Ginzberg, for advice and guidance ever since I began the study of ARN. He went through an earlier form of this translation and lavishly contributed of his learning. Though he is no longer here, his memory continues to be a blessing. To Professor Louis Finkelstein I must express gratitude for urging me many years ago to undertake the translation of ARN, and for his sustained interest in the work. It has been a unique privilege to be able to come again and again to Professor Saul Lieberman with passages I could not understand and to benefit from his consummate erudition and insight. To Doctors Max Kadushin and Zalman Dimitrovsky I am grateful for the opportunity to discuss various concepts and ideas encountered in the study of ARN. Many suggestions by Grace Goldin are incorporated in the pages that follow. For help and encouragement in the publication of this manuscript I am indebted to Professor Erwin Goodenough and Mr. Louis M. Rabinowitz. Ruth S. Stern prepared the typescript and helped with the work on the indexes. Without the staffs at the libraries of the State University of Iowa and the Jewish Theological Seminary of America it would have been impossible to get all the sources I needed; to the library of the Hebrew Union College I am grateful for the loan of the first edition of ARN. Last but not least I wish to express my appreciation to Professor Julian Obermann, Editor of this Series, for his sustained counsel and helpfulness in the preparation of this book.

These good people to whom I am grateful are of course not responsible for errors or shortcomings in what follows. Such are wholly my own.

THE FATHERS ACCORDING TO RABBI NATHAN

CHAPTER 1

MOSES was sanctified by the cloud and received the Torah at Sinai; [1] as it is said, *And the glory of the Lord abode upon Mount Sinai, and the cloud covered him six days* (Exod. 24:16), that is, it covered Moses, in order to purify him. This occurred after (the proclamation of) the Ten Commandments. Such is the view of Rabbi Yose the Galilean. But Rabbi 'Akiba says: *And the cloud covered it* [2] *six days* refers to the mountain and not to Moses, (the *six days* being counted) from the beginning of the month; *And the seventh day He called unto Moses out of the midst of the cloud* (ibid.), (merely) to pay honor to Moses. [3]

Rabbi Nathan said: "Why was Moses made to wait all these six days before the Word came to rest upon him? [4] So that he might be purged of all food and drink in his bowels, before he was sanctified and became like the ministering angels." Said Rabbi Mattiah ben Ḥeresh to him, "Master, (this waiting) was intended only to fill him with awe, so that he would receive the words of the Torah with awe, with fear, with dread, and with trembling; [5] as it is said, *Serve the Lord with fear, and rejoice with trembling*" (Ps. 2:11).

The following once occurred with Rabbi Josiah and Rabbi Mattiah ben Ḥeresh, who had been sitting together engaged in the study of Torah. Rabbi Josiah went off to attend to some worldly matters. Said Rabbi Mattiah ben Ḥeresh to him, "Master, why forsake the words of the living God and let thyself be carried away by worldly matters? Now, although thou art my master and I am thy disciple, (I declare) it is not good to forsake the words of the living God and be carried away by worldly matters."

It was said of them: So long as they sat studying Torah, they acted as though they were jealous of each other; but when they parted, they were like dear friends of old. [6]

By [7] the hands of Moses was the Torah given at Sinai, as it is said, *And He wrote them upon two tables of stone, and gave them unto me* (Deut. 5:19). And elsewhere it says, *These are the statutes and ordinances and laws, which the Lord made between Him and the children of Israel in Mount Sinai by the hand of Moses* (Lev. 26:46). The Torah which the Holy One, blessed be He, gave to Israel was given by the hands of Moses only, as it is said, *Between Him and the children of Israel:* Moses merited becoming God's messenger [8] to the children of Israel.

Moses prepared the lamb of consecration and the anointing oil,[9] and with this oil he anointed Aaron and his sons during all seven days of the consecration.[10] From it (came also the oil with which) the High Priests and kings were anointed. And Eleazar burnt the (red) heifer of purification,[11] whereby the unclean were made clean throughout all generations.

Rabbi Eliezer said: So great was this rite (of anointing) that it is to be practiced throughout all generations,[12] for both Aaron and his sons were sanctified by the anointing oil; as it is said, *And thou shalt anoint Aaron and his sons, and sanctify them, that they may minister unto Me in the priest's office* (etc.) [13] (Exod. 30:30 f.).

Joshua took over from Moses,[14] as it is said, *And thou shalt put of thy honor upon him, that all the congregation of the children of Israel may hearken* (Num. 27:20).

The Elders took over from Joshua, as it is said, *And the people served the Lord all the days of Joshua, and all the days of the elders that outlived Joshua, who had seen all the great work of the Lord, that He had wrought for Israel* (Jud. 2:7).

The Judges took over from the Elders, as it is said, *And it came to pass in the days when (only) the judges* [15] *judged* (Ruth 1:1).

The Prophets took over from the Judges, as it is said, *And though I have sent unto you all My servants the prophets, sending them daily betimes and often* (Jer. 7:25 f.).[16]

Haggai, Zechariah, and Malachi took over from the Prophets. The Men of the Great Assembly took over from Haggai, Zechariah, and Malachi; and they said three things: BE DELIBERATE

IN JUDGMENT, AND RAISE MANY DISCIPLES, AND MAKE A HEDGE ABOUT
THE TORAH.[17]

BE DELIBERATE IN JUDGMENT: what is that? This teaches that a
man should take time in rendering judgment; for whoever takes
time in rendering judgment is unruffled in judgment. As it is
said, *These also are the proverbs of Solomon which the men of
Hezekiah king of Judah copied out* (Prov. 25:1): it is not that
they copied them out, but that they took their time.[18]

Abba Saul says: It does not mean that they took their time, but
that they interpreted.[19] Originally, it is said,[20] Proverbs, Song of
Songs, and Ecclesiastes were suppressed; for since they were
held [21] to be mere parables and not part of the Holy Writings,
(the religious authorities) arose and suppressed them; (and so
they remained) until the men of Hezekiah [22] came and interpreted them.

For (in Proverbs) it is said,

> *And I beheld among the thoughtless ones,*
> *I discerned among the youths,*
> *A young man void of understanding . . .*
> *And, behold, there met him a woman*
> *With the attire of a harlot, and wily of heart.*
> *She is riotous and rebellious,*
> *Her feet abide not in her house.*
> *Now she is in the streets, now in the broad places,*
> *And lieth in wait at every corner.*
> *So she caught him, and kissed him,*
> *And with an impudent face she said unto him:*
> *Sacrifices of peace offerings were due from me;*
> *This day have I paid my vows.*
> *Therefore came I forth to meet thee,*
> *To seek thy face, and I have found thee.*
> *I have decked my couch with coverlets,*
> *With striped cloths of the yarn of Egypt.*
> *I have perfumed my bed*
> *With myrrh, aloes, and cinnamon.*
> *Come, let us take our fill of love until the morning;*

Let us solace ourselves with loves.
For my husband is not at home,
He is gone a long journey;
He hath taken the bag of money with him;
He will come home at the full moon.

(Prov. 7: 7–20)

And it is written in the Song of Songs,

Come, my beloved, let us go forth into the field:
Let us lodge in the villages.
Let us get up early to the vineyards;
Let us see whether the vine hath budded,
Whether the vine-blossom be opened,
And the pomegranates be in flower;
There will I give thee my love.

(Cant. 7: 12–13)

And it is written in Ecclesiastes,

Rejoice, O young man, in thy youth;
And let thy heart cheer thee in the days of thy youth,
And walk in the ways of thy heart,
And in the sight of thine eyes;
But know thou, that for all these things
God will bring thee into judgment.

(Eccl. 11: 9)

And (again) it is written in the Song of Songs,

I am my beloved's
And his desire is toward me.

(Cant. 7: 11)

This proves, not that they took their time, but that they interpreted.[23]

Another interpretation. BE DELIBERATE IN JUDGMENT: what is that? This teaches that a man should be patient in his speech and not short tempered in his speech, for whoever is short tempered in his speech forgets what he has to say. For thus we find in the case of Moses our master: when he was short tempered in his speech he forgot what he was to tell (Israel).[24]

Now, where do we find of Moses our master that he forgot what he was to tell (Israel)? For it is said, *And Eleazar the priest said unto the men of war that went to the battle: This is the statute of the law which the Lord hath commanded Moses* (Num. 31:21), (which was to say:) "It is Moses whom the Lord commanded and it is not I whom He commanded; it is Moses, my father's brother, whom He commanded, and it is not I whom He commanded." And where do we find of Moses that he was short tempered in his speech? Lo, it says in regard to the officers of the host, *And Moses was wroth with the officers of the host* (Num. 31:14).[25]

And Moses said unto them: Have ye saved all the women alive (etc.) (Num. 31:15 f.). If so,[26] to what does the verse refer when it says, (*Have ye saved*) *all the women?* It refers to the counsel which the wicked Balaam offered against Israel; as it is written, *And now, behold, I go unto my people; come, and I will announce to thee what this people shall do to thy people in the end of days* (Num. 24:14). Balaam said to Balak, "This people whom thou hatest is hungry for food and thirsty for drink, and has naught to eat or drink save manna. Go, therefore, fix booths [27] for them and leave for them food and drink; and have the booths occupied by beautiful women, royal women, so that the people will go awhoring after Baal Peor and fall by the hand of God." Balak went at once and did all that the wicked Balaam advised him to do. See what the wicked Balaam brought upon Israel! For twenty-four thousand of them fell, as it is said, *And those that died by the plague were twenty and four thousand* (Num. 25:9).[28]

Now is there not an inference [29] to be drawn here? If Moses our master, the wisest of the wise, the father of the prophets, forgot what he had to say when he was short tempered in his speech, how much more so we! Which teaches that a man should be patient in his speech, and not be short tempered in his speech.

Ben 'Azzai says: Be careful in thy speech lest it come to naught.[30]

AND MAKE A HEDGE ABOUT THE TORAH. (This means): and make a hedge about thy words the way the Holy One, blessed be He, made a hedge about His words,[31] and Adam [32] made a hedge about his words. The Torah made a hedge about its words. Moses made a hedge about his words. So too Job, and also the Prophets, the Holy Writings, and the Sages—all of them made a hedge about their words.

What is the hedge which the Holy One, blessed be He, made about His words? Lo, it says, *And all the nations shall say: Wherefore hath the Lord done thus unto this land?* (Deut. 29:23). This teaches that it was manifest to Him-that-spake-and-the-world-came-into-being that future generations were to speak in this way. Therefore the Holy One, blessed be He, said to Moses, "Moses, write down the following and leave it for the coming generations: *Then men shall say: Because they forsook the covenant of the Lord . . . and went and served other gods, and worshiped them, gods that they knew not, and that He had not allotted unto them*" (Deut. 29:24–25). Thus thou dost learn that the Holy One, blessed be He, meted out the reward of His creatures to the letter.[33]

What is the hedge which Adam made about his words? Lo, it says, *And the Lord God commanded the man, saying: Of every tree of the garden thou mayest freely eat; but of the tree of the knowledge of good and evil, thou shalt not eat of it; for in the day that thou eatest thereof thou shalt surely die* (Gen. 2:16–17). Adam, however, did not wish to speak to Eve the way the Holy One, blessed be He, had spoken to him. Rather, this is what he said to her: *But of the fruit of the tree which is in the midst of the garden, God hath said: Ye shall not eat of it, neither shall ye touch it,[34] lest ye die* (Gen. 3:3).[35]

At that time the wicked serpent thought in his heart as follows: Since I cannot trip up Adam, I shall go and trip up Eve. So he went and sat down beside her, and entered into a long conversation with her. He said to her, "If it is against touching the tree thou sayest the Holy One, blessed be He, commanded us—behold,

I shall touch it and not die. Thou, too, if thou touch it, shalt not die!" What did the wicked serpent do? He then arose and touched the tree with his hands and feet, and shook it until its fruits fell to the ground.

And some say: He did not touch it at all.[36] On the contrary, as soon as that tree saw him it cried out to him in these words, "O wicked one, wicked one, do not touch me!" as it is said, *Let not the foot of pride overtake me, and let not the hand of the wicked shake me* (Ps. 36:12).[37]

Another interpretation. *Let not the foot of pride overtake me* refers to the wicked Titus, blast his bones! For wand in hand [38] he kept striking upon the altar, crying, "Lycos,[39] Lycos, thou art a king and I am a king; come and wage war with me! How many oxen have been slaughtered upon thee, how many birds have been put to death upon thee, how many wines have been poured out over thee, how much incense has been burned upon thee! Thou art he that lays waste the whole universe!" As it is said, *Ah, Ariel,*[40] *Ariel, the city where David encamped! Add ye year to year, let the feasts come round* (Isa. 29:1).

Furthermore, the serpent said to her, "If it is against eating of the fruit of the tree thou sayest the Holy One, blessed be He, commanded us, behold I shall eat of it and not die. Thou too, if thou eat of it shalt not die!" What did Eve think in her mind? "All the things about which my master admonished me at first are false"—for at first Eve addressed Adam only as "my master." Forthwith she took of the fruit and ate, and gave some to Adam and he ate; as it is said, *And when the woman saw that the tree was good for food, and that it was a delight to the eyes,* etc. (Gen. 3:6).

With ten curses [41] was Eve cursed at that time; as it is said, *Unto the woman He said: I will greatly multiply thy pain and thy travail; in pain thou shalt bring forth children; and thy desire shall be to thy husband and he shall rule over thee* (Gen. 3:16).

(*I will greatly multiply thy pain*) refers to the two kinds of blood discharges, one the blood of menstrual pain and the other the blood of virginal pain.

And thy travail refers to pregnancy pain.

In pain thou shalt bring forth children is self-explanatory.

And thy desire shall be to thy husband teaches this, that a woman longs for her husband when he is gone on a journey.

And he shall rule over thee: for man demands gratification outspokenly, but woman demands it in her heart, her head covered like a mourner [42] and as though she were bound in prison and banned from all men.

What led to Eve's touching the tree? It was the hedge which Adam put around his words.[43] Hence it has been said: If a man puts an (excessive) hedge around his words, he shall not be able to stand by his words. Hence it has also been said: Let no man add to what he hears.

Rabbi Yose says: Better (a standing fence of) ten handbreadths than (one of) a hundred cubits which has broken down.[44]

What was the wicked serpent contemplating at that time? He thought: I shall go and kill Adam and wed his wife, and I shall be king over the whole world. I shall walk with upright posture and eat all the world's dainties. Said the Holy One, blessed be He, to him, "Thy thought was, I shall kill Adam and wed Eve; therefore *I will put enmity between thee and the woman* (Gen. 3:15). Thy thought was, I shall be king over the whole world; therefore *cursed art thou from among all cattle* (Gen. 3:14). Thy thought was, I shall walk with upright posture; therefore *upon thy belly shalt thou go* (*ibid.*). Thy thought was, I shall eat all the world's dainties; therefore *dust shalt thou eat all the days of thy life*" (*ibid.*).

Rabbi Simeon ben Menasia says: Alas that a great servant was lost to the world! For had the serpent not been reduced to disgrace,[45] everyone in Israel might have had two serpents in his home, one to send toward the west and another toward the east; and they could have brought back costly sardonyx, precious stones, pearls, and every kind of precious object in the world. No creature could have harmed them. Not only that but they could have been used instead of camels or donkeys or mules to carry out fertilizer to the orchards and gardens.

Rabbi Judah ben Bathyra says: Adam was reclining in the Garden of Eden and the ministering angels stood before him, roasting meat for him and cooling wine for him. Along came the serpent and saw him, beheld his glory, and grew jealous of him.

How was Adam created? In the first hour the dust of which he was made was collected; in the second the model after which he was formed was created; in the third the soulless lump [46] of him was made; in the fourth his limbs were tied together; in the fifth orifices were opened in him; in the sixth a soul was added to him; in the seventh he stood upright on his feet; in the eighth Eve was joined [47] to him; in the ninth he was brought into the Garden of Eden; in the tenth he was commanded; in the eleventh he sinned; in the twelfth he was banished and made to leave the garden, confirming what is said, *But man doth not lodge overnight in honor* (Ps. 49:13).

What is recited on the first day [48] (of the week)? *The earth is the Lord's, and the fullness thereof; the world and they that dwell therein* (Ps. 24:1). For it is He who possessed and giveth possession of [49] the universe and He will judge it.

What is recited on the second day? *Great is the Lord, and highly to be praised, in the city of our God* (Ps. 48:2). He sundered (in two) what He had made and became King over His universe.[50]

What is recited on the third day? *God standeth in the congregation of God; in the midst of the judges He judgeth* (Ps. 82:1). He created the sea and the dry land, and the earth was unfolded [51] in its place, and room was made for His congregation.

What is recited on the fourth day? *O Lord, Thou God to whom vengeance belongeth, Thou God to whom vengeance belongeth, shine forth* (Ps. 94:1). He created the sun and the moon and the stars and the constellations which give light to the world; and He shall punish their worshipers.

What is recited on the fifth day? *Sing aloud unto God our strength; shout unto the God of Jacob* (Ps. 81:2). He created the fowl and the fish and the sea monsters who sing aloud [52] (God's praises) in the universe.

What is recited on the sixth day? *The Lord reigneth; He is clothed in majesty; the Lord is clothed, He hath girded Himself with strength; yea, the world is established, that it cannot be moved* (Ps. 93:1). He completed all His works and ascended and sat in the heights of the universe.

What is recited on the seventh day? *A Psalm, a Song. For the Sabbath day* (Ps. 92:1): For a day which is wholly sabbath, in which there is neither eating nor drinking nor trafficking, but the righteous sit with their crowns on their heads and are nourished by the splendor of the Shekinah; as it is said, *And they beheld God, and did eat and drink* [53] (Exod. 24:11)—like the ministering angels.

And what was the reason for this? [54] So that he might enter upon his Sabbath meal immediately.

Rabbi Simeon ben Eleazar says: [55] I shall tell thee a parable; to whom may Adam be likened? To a certain man who wed a proselyte. This man would sit admonishing her, saying to her, "My dear, do not eat bread when thy hands are unclean and do not eat fruits which have not been tithed; do not profane the Sabbaths and do not treat vows loosely and do not go about with other men: for if thou transgress any of these, verily thou shalt die." Now, what did that man do? He proceeded to eat bread in her presence while his hands were unclean, and he ate fruits which had not been tithed, and profaned the Sabbaths and treated vows loosely, and with his own hands put before her (what was forbidden).[56] What did that proselyte say in her heart? All the things about which my husband admonished me at first are false. Forthwith she arose and transgressed them all.

Rabbi Simeon ben Yoḥai [57] says: I shall tell thee a parable; to whom may Adam be likened? To one who had a wife at home. What did that man do? He went and brought a jar and put into it figs and nuts,[58] a definite number of them. Then he caught a scorpion and put it at the mouth of the jar. The jar he sealed with a tight-fitting lid and put it in a corner. "My dear," he said to her, "everything I have in this house is in thy hands, except this jar which thou mayest not touch at all."

What did that woman do? As soon as her husband left for the market place, she arose and opened the jar, and stuck her hand into it—and the scorpion stung her. She started back and fell on her couch. When her husband returned from the market place, he exclaimed, "What is this?" "I put my hand on the jar," she replied, "and a scorpion stung me; and now I am dying!" "Did I not tell thee so in the beginning," he demanded, "everything I have in the house is in thy hands, except this jar which thou mayest not touch at all?" Forthwith he grew angry with her and sent her away.[59]

This is what Adam was like when the Holy One, blessed be He, said to him, *Of every tree of the garden thou mayest freely eat; but of the tree of the knowledge of good and evil, thou shalt not eat of it; for in the day that thou eatest thereof thou shalt surely die* (Gen. 2:16–17). When he ate of it, he was banished; confirming what is said, *But man doth not lodge overnight in honor; he is like the beasts that perish* (Ps. 49:13).

On[60] that day was formed the model after which he was fashioned, on that day he was created: on that day was formed the model after which he was fashioned, on that day the soulless lump of him was made, on that day his limbs were tied together and orifices were opened in him, on that day a soul was added to him, on that day he stood upright on his feet, on that day Eve was joined to him, on that day he named (the animals), on that day he was brought into the Garden of Eden, on that day he was commanded, on that day he sinned, and on that day he was banished, confirming what is said, *Man doth not lodge overnight in honor* (*ibid.*).

On that day two lay down together and four arose.[61] Rabbi Judah ben Bathyra says: On that day two lay down together and seven arose.[62]

On that day three decrees were decreed against Adam, as it is said, *And unto Adam He said: Because thou hast hearkened unto the voice of thy wife . . . cursed is the ground for thy sake; in toil shalt thou eat of it. . . . Thorns also and thistles shall it bring forth to thee; and thou shalt eat the herb of the field* [63] (Gen. 3:17-18).

As Adam heard the Holy One, blessed be He, say to him, *And thou shalt eat the herb of the field,* he trembled in every limb.[64] "Master of the Universe," he cried, "shall my beast and I eat out of the same crib?"

Said the Holy One, blessed be He, to him, "Because thou didst tremble in every limb, *in the sweat of thy face shalt thou eat bread*" (Gen. 3:19).

And even as three decrees were decreed against Adam, so were three decrees decreed against Eve, as it is said, *Unto the woman He said: Greatly will I multiply thy pain and thy travail; in pain thou shalt bring forth children; and thy desire shall be to thy husband, and he shall rule over thee* (Gen. 3:16).

Greatly will I multiply thy pain and thy travail.

Greatly teaches that when a woman is menstruating, at the beginning of her period she is in pain.

Will I multiply teaches that the first time a woman cohabits it is painful for her.

Thy pain and thy travail teaches that the first three months after a woman has conceived, her face turns ugly and pallid.

When eventime came, Adam saw the world grow dark and the sun setting in the west. "Woe unto me!" he cried. "Because I have sinned, the Holy One, blessed be He, is making the world around me to grow dark"—for he did not know that this was the way of the world. The following morning when he saw the world grow light and the sun rising in the east, he rejoiced exceedingly. He arose and built altars and brought an ox whose horns extended beyond its hoofs; [65] and he offered it up as a burnt offering; as it is said, *And it shall please the Lord better than a bullock whose horns extend beyond its hoofs* (Ps. 69:32).

The ox which Adam offered up and the bullock which Noah offered up and the ram which Abraham our father offered on the altar in place of his son—all of them had horns extending beyond their hoofs, as it is said, *And Abraham lifted up his eyes, and looked, and behold, behind him a ram caught in the thicket by his horns* [66] (Gen. 22:13).

At that time [67] three groups of ministering angels came down, and in their hands were lutes and lyres and all kinds of musical instruments. And they sang the song of praise with Adam; as it is said, *A Psalm, a Song. For the sabbath day. It is a good thing to give thanks unto the Lord . . . to declare Thy loving-kindness in the morning, and Thy faithfulness in the night seasons* (Ps. 92:1-3).

To declare Thy loving-kindness in the morning refers to the world to come, which is compared to the mornings; as it is said, *They are new every morning; great is Thy faithfulness* (Lam. 3:23).

And Thy faithfulness in the night seasons refers to this world, which is compared to the nights; as it is said, *The burden of Dumah. One calleth unto me out of Seir: Watchman, what of the night? Watchman, what of the night?* (Isa. 21:11).

At that time [68] the Holy One, blessed be He, said, "If I do not punish him,[69] I will be destroying the whole universe." [70] Moreover, He exclaimed, "This one I had made king over the whole world;[71] how he degenerated and ate of the fruit of the tree!" Forthwith He turned to him and cursed him, as it is said, *And the Lord God said unto the serpent,* etc. (Gen. 3:14 ff.).[72] Rabbi Yose says: Had his curse not been included [73] after theirs,[74] he would have destroyed the whole universe.

When the Holy One, blessed be He, created Adam,[75] He formed him (with two faces), front and back,[76] as it is said, *Thou hast fashioned me in back and in front, and laid Thy hand upon me* (Ps. 139:5). Then the ministering angels came down to destroy him, but the Holy One, blessed be He, took him up and put him under His wings, as it is said, *And Thou hast laid Thy hand upon me.*

Another interpretation of *And Thou hast laid Thy hand upon me:* when Adam sinned, the Holy One, blessed be He, took away one of his faces.

Hence [77] we learn that when Adam and the Temple were created, they were created with both of God's hands. How do we know that Adam was created with both of His hands? For it is said, *Thy hands* [78] *have made me and fashioned me* (Ps. 119:73). How do we know that the Temple was created with both His hands? For it is said, *The sanctuary, O Lord, which Thy hands have established* (Exod. 15:17). And it says, *And He brought them to His holy border, the mountain, which His right hand had gotten* (Ps. 78:54). It says also, *The Lord shall reign for ever and ever* (Exod. 15:18). [79]

CHAPTER 2

WHAT is the hedge which the Torah made about its words? [1] Lo, it says, *Also thou shalt not approach unto a woman . . . as long as she is impure by her uncleanness* (Lev. 18:19). May her husband perhaps embrace her or kiss her or engage her in idle chatter? [2] The verse says, *thou shalt not approach*. May she perhaps sleep with him in her clothes on the couch? The verse says, *thou shalt not approach*. May she wash her face perhaps and paint her eyes? The verse says, *And of her that is sick with her impurity* (Lev. 15:33): all the days of her impurity let her be in isolation. Hence it was said: She that neglects herself in the days of her impurity, with her the Sages are pleased; but she that adorns herself in the days of her impurity, with her the Sages are displeased.

There was once a certain man who had studied much Scripture and had studied much Mishnah [3] and attended upon many scholars, who died in middle age. His wife took his *tefillin* [4] and kept making the rounds of the synagogues and study houses, crying aloud and weeping. "Masters," she said to the Sages, "it is written in the Torah, *For it is thy life and the length of thy days* (Deut. 30:20). My husband studied much Scripture and studied much Mishnah and attended upon many scholars. Why did he die in middle age?" There was not a person who could answer her.

One time she encountered Elijah, of blessed memory.[5] "My child," he asked her, "why art thou weeping and crying?"

"Master," she answered him, "my husband studied much Scripture and studied much Mishnah and attended upon many scholars, yet he died in middle age."

Said Elijah to her, "During the first three [6] days of thine impurity, how did he conduct himself in thy company?"

"Master," she replied, "he did not touch me, God forbid! even with his little finger. On the contrary, this is how he spoke to me: 'Touch nothing [7] lest it become of doubtful purity.'"

"During the last days [8] of thine impurity, how did he conduct himself in thy company?"

"Master," she replied, "I ate with him and drank with him and in my clothes [9] slept with him in bed; his flesh touched mine but he had no thought of anything."

"Blessed be God who killed him," Elijah exclaimed; "for thus it is written in the Torah, *Also thou shalt not approach unto a woman as long as she is impure by her uncleanness.*"

Lo, Scripture says, *None of you shall approach to any that is near of kin to him* (Lev. 18:6). Hence it was said: Let no man be alone with any woman in an inn, even with his sister or his daughter or his mother-in-law, because of public opinion. Let no man chat with a woman in the market place, even if she is his wife, and, needless to say, with another woman, because of public opinion. Let no man walk behind a woman in the market place, even behind his wife, and, needless to say, another woman, because of public opinion.

Here (Lev. 18:6) it is said, *You shall not approach* and later (Lev. 18:19) it is said, *Thou shalt not approach;* (hence,) approach nothing which might lead to transgression, keep far from what is hideous and from whatever seems hideous. Therefore the Sages have said: Keep far from minor sin lest it lead thee to grievous sin; be quick to carry out a minor commandment for it will lead thee to a major commandment.

Lo, Scripture says, *Thy belly is like a heap of wheat hedged in by lilies* (Cant. 7:3).[10]

Thy belly is like a heap of wheat refers to the congregation of Israel.

Hedged in by lilies refers to the seventy Elders.[11]

Another interpretation. *Thy belly is like a heap of wheat* refers to the minor [12] commandments that are tender.[13] *Hedged in by lilies* teaches this: when Israel put them into practice, they are led thereby to the life of the world to come. How so? One's wife in her menses is alone with him at home. If he is so minded he cohabits with her; if he is otherwise minded he does not cohabit with her. Does then anyone see him, or does anyone know to tell him aught? He fears only Him who commanded against contact with a menstruant.

(Again,) one has suffered a pollution. If he is so minded he bathes; [14] if he is otherwise minded he does not bathe. Does anyone see him, or does anyone know to tell him aught? He fears only Him who commands ritual immersion.

The same may be said of the law of dough offering; [15] and the same may be said of the law of first shearings.[16] These minor commandments, tender [17] as lilies, when Israel put them into practice, lead them to the life of the world to come.

What is the hedge which Moses made about his words? [18] Lo, it says, *And the Lord said unto Moses: Go unto the people and sanctify them today and tomorrow* (Exod. 19:10). Moses the righteous did not wish to speak to Israel the way the Holy One, blessed be He, had spoken to him. Instead, this is what he said to them: *Be ready against the third day; come not near a woman* (Exod. 19·15). And of his own accord Moses added one day for their sake. For thus reasoned Moses: If a man cohabits with his wife and on the third day semen issues from her, they will be unclean; in that event Israel will receive the words of the Torah from Mount Sinai in impurity. I shall therefore add a day for their sake, so that no man shall cohabit with his wife, on the third day no semen will issue from her, and they will be clean. And thus Israel will receive the words of the Torah from Mount Sinai in purity.

This is but one of the things which Moses did of his own accord. He reasoned by inference [19] and his judgment coincided with God's: He kept away from his wife, and his judgment coincided with God's. He kept away from the tent of meeting, and his judgment coincided with God's. He broke the tables of the Commandments, and his judgment coincided with God's.

He kept away from his wife, and his judgment coincided with God's. What is that? He said to himself: If as regards Israel—who were sanctified for the occasion only and invited only to receive the Ten Commandments from Mount Sinai—the Holy One, blessed be He, instructed me, *Go unto the people and sanctify them today and tomorrow* (Exod. 19:10); all the more as regards myself, that am appointed for this each and every day and every single hour, and know not when He will speak to me, whether by day or by night, that I keep away from my wife! And his judgment coincided with God's.

Rabbi Judah ben Bathyra says: Moses kept away from his wife only because he was so told by the mouth of the Almighty, as it is said, *With him do I speak mouth to mouth* (Num. 12:8): mouth to mouth I told him "Keep away from thy wife," and he stayed away.

Some say: Moses did not keep away from his wife until he was so told by the mouth of the Almighty; for it is said, *Go say to them: Return ye to your tents* (Deut. 5:27), and it is written, *But as for thee, stand thou here by Me* (Deut. 5:28). He went back [20] but kept away from his wife. And his judgment coincided with God's.[21]

He kept away from the tent of meeting. What is that? He said to himself: If as regards my brother Aaron—who was anointed with the anointing oil and clothed in many priestly garments which he wears in a state of holiness only—the Holy One, blessed be He, said, *Speak unto Aaron thy brother, that he come not at all times into the holy place* (Lev. 16:2); all the more as regards myself, that am [not] [22] appointed for this, that I keep away from the tent of meeting! He kept away from the tent of meeting, and his judgment coincided with God's.

He broke the tables of the Commandments. What is that? It
was said: When Moses went up on high to receive the tables of
the Commandments, which had been inscribed and put away
since the six days of Creation—as it is said, *And the tables were the
work* [23] *of God, and the writing was the writing of God, graven
upon the tables* (Exod. 32:16): read not *graven* (*ḥaruṯ*) but *freedom* (*ḥeruṯ*), for whosoever studies Torah is a free man—at that
time the ministering angels conspired against Moses and exclaimed, "Master of the Universe, *What is man, that Thou art
mindful of him? and the son of man, that Thou thinkest of him?
Yet Thou hast made him but little lower than the angels, and hast
crowned him with glory and honor. Thou hast made him to have
dominion over the works* [24] *of Thy hands; Thou hast put all
things under his feet; sheep and oxen, all of them, yea, and the
beasts of the fields; the fowl of the air, and the fish of the sea,*"
etc. (Ps. 8:5–9). They kept murmuring against Moses, saying
"What is this offspring of woman who has come up on high?" As
it is said, *Thou hast ascended on high, thou hast led captivity
captive; thou hast taken gifts* (Ps. 68:19).

But he took the tables of the Commandments and descended,
and was exceedingly glad. When he beheld that offense which
they committed in the making of the golden calf,[25] he said to
himself, "How can I give them the tables of the Commandments?
I shall be obligating them to major commandments and con-
demning them to death at the hands of Heaven; for thus is it
written in the Commandments, *Thou shalt have no other gods
before Me*" (Exod. 20:3).

He then started back, but the seventy Elders saw him and ran
after him. He held fast to one end of the tables and they held fast
to the other end of the tables; but the strength of Moses prevailed
over theirs, as it is said, *And in all the mighty hand, and in all the
great terror, which Moses wrought in the sight of all Israel*
(Deut. 34:12).

He looked at the tables and saw that the writing had disappeared from them. How can I give Israel tables which have
naught to them, he thought; better that I take hold and break

them. As it is said, *And I took hold of the two tables, and cast them out of my two hands, and broke them* (Deut. 9:17).

Rabbi Yose the Galilean says: I shall tell thee a parable; to what may this be likened? To a king of flesh and blood who said to his steward, "Go and betroth unto me a beautiful and pious [26] maiden, of seemly conduct." That steward went and betrothed her. After he had betrothed her, he went and discovered that she played the harlot with another man. Forthwith, of his own accord, he made the following inference; [27] said he, "If I now go ahead and give her the marriage deed,[28] she will be liable to the penalty of death, and thus we shall have separated her from my master forever." [29]

So too did Moses the righteous make an inference of his own accord. He said: "How shall I give these tables to Israel? I shall be obligating them to major commandments and make them liable to the penalty of death, for thus is it written in the tables,[30] *He that sacrificeth unto the gods, save unto the Lord only, shall be utterly destroyed* (Exod. 22:19). Rather, I shall take hold of them and break them, and bring Israel back [31] to good conduct."

[*And I broke them before your eyes* (Deut. 9:17)] [32] lest Israel say, "Where are the first tables which thou wert to bring down? The whole story is naught but fiction!"

Rabbi Judah ben Bathyra says: Moses broke the tables only because he was so told by the mouth of the Almighty,[33] as it is said, *With him do I speak mouth to mouth* (Num. 12:8): mouth to mouth I said to him, "Break the tables."

And some say: Moses broke the tables only because he was so told by the mouth of the Almighty, as it is said, (*And the two tables of the Covenant were in my two hands.*) *And I saw, and behold, ye had sinned against the Lord your God* (Deut. 9:15 f.): [34] it says *And I saw* only because he saw that the writing had disappeared from them.

Others say: Moses broke the tables only because he was so told by the mouth of the Almighty, as it is said, *And there they are, as He commanded me* (Deut. 10:5): it says *He commanded me* only because he was commanded to break them.

Rabbi Eleazar ben Azariah says: Moses broke the tables only because he was so told by the mouth of the Almighty, as it is said, *Which Moses wrought in the sight of all Israel* (Deut. 34:12): even as in that instance [35] he acted by command, so here [36] he acted by command.

Rabbi 'Aḳiba says: Moses broke the tables only because he was so told by the mouth of the Almighty, as it is said, *And I took hold of the two tables . . . and I broke them* (Deut. 9:17). (Now,) what does a man take hold of? What he can . . .[37]

Rabbi Me'ir says: Moses broke the tables only because he was so told by the mouth of the Almighty, as it is said, *Which thou didst break* (Deut. 10:2), (that is to say,) "More power to thee for having broken them!" [38]

Hezekiah king of Judah did four things (of his own accord) and his judgment coincided with God's. He suppressed the book of healings,[39] and his judgment coincided with God's.

He broke the brazen serpent in pieces and his judgment coincided with God's, as it is said, *And he broke in pieces the brazen serpent . . . for unto those days the children of Israel did offer to it; and it was called Nehushtan* (II Kings 18:4).

He removed the high places and the altars and his judgment coincided with God's, as it is said, *Hezekiah hath taken away His high places and His altars, and commanded Judah and Jerusalem, saying, Ye shall worship before one altar, and upon it shall ye offer* (II Chron. 32:12).

He stopped the waters of Gihon and his judgment coincided with God's,[40] as it is said, *Hezekiah stopped the upper spring of the waters of Gihon, and brought them straight down on the west side of the city of David. And Hezekiah prospered in all his works* (II Chron. 32:30).

What is the hedge which Job made about his words? [41] Lo, it says, *A wholehearted and an upright man, one that feareth God, and shunneth evil* (Job 1:8). This teaches that Job kept himself far from things which lead to transgression, from what is hideous and whatever seems hideous.[42] And why does the verse add,[43] *A wholehearted and an upright man?* This teaches that Job was born circumcised.[44]

Adam, too, was born circumcised, for it is said, *And God created man in His own image* [45] (Gen. 11:27).

Seth, too, was born circumcised, for it is said, *And (Adam) begot a son in his own likeness, after his image* (Gen. 5:3).

Noah, too, was born circumcised, for it is said, *Noah was in his generations a man righteous and perfect* (Gen. 6:9).

Shem, too, was born circumcised, for it is said, *And Melchizedek king of Salem* [46] (Gen. 14:18).

Jacob, too, was born circumcised, for it is said, *And Jacob was a perfect man, dwelling in tents* (Gen. 25:27).

Joseph, too, was born circumcised, for it is said, *These are the generations of Jacob, Joseph* (Gen. 37:2). For properly it should say, "These are the generations of Jacob, Reuben." [47] Why then does the verse say *Joseph?* Only (to teach us that) even as Jacob was born circumcised, so also was Joseph born circumcised.

And Moses, too, was born circumcised, for it is said, *And when she saw him that he was a goodly child* (Exod. 2:2). Now, what did his mother see in him that made him more comely and magnificent than all other human beings? Only that he was born circumcised.

The wicked Balaam, too, was born circumcised, for it is said, *The saying of him who heareth the words of God* [48] (Num. 24:4).

Samuel, too, was born circumcised, for it is said, *And the child Samuel grew on, and increased in favor* [49] (I Sam. 2:26).

David, too, was born circumcised, for it is said, *Michtam* [50] *of David. Keep me, O God; for I have taken refuge in Thee* (Ps. 16:1).

Jeremiah, too, was born circumcised, for it is said, *Before I formed thee in the belly I knew thee, and before thou camest forth out of the womb I sanctified thee* (Jer. 1:5).

Zerubbabel, too, was born circumcised, for it is said, *In that day . . . will I take thee, O Zerubbabel, My servant, the son of Shealtiel, saith the Lord, and will make thee as a signet* [51] (Hag. 2:23).

Lo, it says, *I made a covenant with mine eyes; how then should I look upon a maid* (Job 31: 1). This teaches that Job was particularly strict with himself and would not look even upon a maiden. Now, is there not an inference to be drawn here? If even in regard to a maiden—whom if he so desired he might wed himself, or give to his son to wed, or to his brother, or to a relation—Job was particularly strict with himself and would not look upon her; all the more in regard to another man's wife! And why was Job so strict with himself that he would not look even upon a maiden? For Job said, If I should look upon her today and on the morrow another man comes and weds her, it will turn out that I have been looking upon another man's wife.

What was the hedge which the Prophets made about their words? [52] Lo, it says, *The Lord will go forth as a mighty man, He will stir up jealousy like a man of war; He will cry, yea, He will shout aloud* (Isa. 42:13): (yet God is) not merely like one mighty man but [53] like all the mighty men in the world.

So, too, *The lion hath roared, who will not fear? The Lord God hath spoken, who can but prophesy* (Am. 3:8): (yet God is) not merely like one lion but like all the lions in the world.

So, too, *And behold, the glory of the Lord [54] God of Israel came from the way of the east; and His voice was like the sound of many waters; and the earth did shine with His glory* (Ezek. 43:2).—

The sound of many waters refers to the angel Gabriel.

And the earth did shine with His glory refers to the presence of the Shekinah.—

Now is there not an inference to be drawn here? If Gabriel, who is but one of thousands upon thousands and myriads upon myriads that stand before Him, has a voice which travels from one end of the world to the other, how much more so the King of kings of kings, the Holy One, blessed be He, who created the whole universe, who created the beings on high and the beings below! But the eye is shown what it can see and the ear is permitted to hear what it can hear.[55]

What is the hedge which the Holy Writings made about their words? [56] Lo, it says, *Remove thy way far from her, and come not nigh the door of her house* (Prov. 5:8).

Remove thy way far from her refers to sectarianism.[57] When a man is told, "Go not among [58] the sectarians and enter not into their midst,[59] lest thou stumble through them," he might retort, "I have confidence in myself that, although I enter into their midst,[59] I shall not stumble through them"; (or) perhaps [60] thou mightest say, "I will listen to their talk and then retire." Therefore the verse says, *None that go unto her return, neither do they attain unto the paths of life* (Prov. 2:19).

It is written, *She hath prepared her meat, she hath mingled her wine: she hath also furnished her table* (Prov. 9:2). Such are the wicked.[61] For when a man enters into their circle, they feed him and give him drink and clothe him and shelter him and give him much money. As soon as he becomes one of them, they each claim their own and take it away from him. And of them it is said, *Till an arrow strike through the liver; as a bird hasteneth to the snare—and knoweth not that it is at the cost of his life* (Prov. 7:23).

Another interpretation. *Remove thy way far from her* refers to a harlot. For a man is told, "Walk not in this market place and enter not this lane, for a comely and far-famed harlot is there." And if he says, I have confidence in myself that, although I go there, I shall not stumble because of her, he is told, Although thou hast confidence in thyself, walk not there lest thou stumble through her. For lo, the Sages have said that a man should not get into the habit of passing by a harlot's door, for it is said, *For she hath cast down many wounded; yea, a mighty host are all her slain* (Prov. 7:26).

What is the hedge which the Sages made about their words? [62] In that the Sages say: The evening *Shema* [63] may be recited until midnight (only). Rabban Gamaliel says: Until the cock crows.

Wherein is the hedge?

When a man returns from his work, let him not say, I will eat a bit and drink a bit and nap awhile and afterward I shall recite the Shema; for he will sleep through the night and not recite the Shema. Instead, when a man returns from his work in the evening, let him go to the synagogue or to the study house. If he is accustomed to study Scripture, let him study Scripture; if he is accustomed to study Mishnah, let him study Mishnah; and if not, let him (at least) recite the Shema and pray. And whoever transgresses the words of the Sages is guilty of a mortal offense.

Rabban [Simeon] ben Gamaliel says: Sometimes a man may recite the Shema twice in one night, once immediately before the morning star rises and once immediately after the morning star rises, and thus fulfill his obligation for the day and for the night. (Thereupon,) the Sages arose and made a tall hedge about their words.[64]

CHAPTER 3

AND RAISE MANY DISCIPLES.[1] For the School of Shammai says: One ought to teach only him who is talented [2] and meek and of distinguished ancestry and rich. But the School of Hillel says: One ought to teach every man, for there were many sinners in Israel who were drawn to the study of Torah, and from them descended righteous, pious, and worthy folk.[3]

Rabbi ʻAḳiba says: Whoever takes a *pĕruṭah* [4] from charity when he does not need it shall not depart from this world before he falls in need of his fellow men.[5]

He used to say: He that binds rags on his eyes or his loins and cries, "Help the blind,[6] help the afflicted" [7] shall in the end be speaking the truth.

He used to say: He that tramples his bread in the dust or in frenzy scatters his coin shall not depart from the world before he falls in need of his fellow men.

He used to say: He that in frenzy tears his clothes, or in frenzy

smashes his furniture, will in the end worship idols. For such is
the art of the evil impulse: [8] today it says to him, "Tear thy
clothes," and on the morrow it says to him, "Worship idols." And
he goes and worships idols.[9]

He used to say: He who has his eye on his wife in the hope
that she die so that he may get the inheritance, or that she die so
that he may wed her sister, and whoever has his eye on his brother
in the hope that he die so that he may wed his wife, will in the end
be buried in their lifetime.[10] Of him the verse says, *He that dig-
geth a pit shall fall into it; and whoso breaketh through a fence,
a serpent shall bite him* (Eccl. 10:8).

There was once a certain man who transgressed the words of
Rabbi 'Akiba [11] and uncovered a woman's head in the market
place. So she came before Rabbi 'Akiba, and he sentenced him to
pay her four hundred *zuz*.[12] Said the man to him, "Master, let me
have some time." 'Akiba granted it.

When the man came out, his friend said to him: "I shall give
thee advice and thou shalt not have to give her even as much as a
pĕruṭah."

"Let me have it," he said to his friend.

"Go," said the friend to him, "take about an *'issar's* [13] worth of
oil and break the jar at the woman's door." (This the man did.)

What did that woman do? She came out of her house, uncovered her head in the market place, and began scooping up the
oil in her hand and putting it on her head.

Now, the man had stationed witnesses to observe her. So he
came before Rabbi 'Akiba and said to him: "To this slut I am to
give four hundred zuz! Why, over an 'issar's worth of oil she did
not spare her self-respect but went out of her house and uncovered
her head in the market place and began scooping up the oil in
her hand and putting it on her head!"

"Thou hast said naught," Rabbi 'Akiba answered him, "for he
that injures himself, albeit he is not permitted to do so, is not
culpable; but if others injure him, they are culpable. She who
abused herself is not culpable; but thou who didst abuse her, go
and give her four hundred zuz!"

Rabbi Dostai, son of Rabbi Yannai, says: If thou wast early and didst sow in the first rainfall, go again and sow in the second rainfall; for if a hail comes down on the world and the former sowing is blighted, the latter will survive. *For thou knowest not which will prosper, the one or the other;* or perhaps both shall survive in thy hand and they *shall both* alike *turn out well* (cf. Eccl. 11:6b). As it is said, *In the morning sow thy seed, and in the evening withhold not thy hand* (Eccl. 11:6a). If thou wast early and didst sow in the first and second rainfall, go again and sow in the third rainfall; for if a blast comes upon the world and the first sowings are blasted, the last will survive. *For thou knowest not which will prosper, the one or the other;* or perhaps *both shall alike turn out well.* As it is said, *In the morning sow thy seed,* etc.[14]

Rabbi Ishmael says: If thou hast studied Torah in thy youth, say not "I shall not study in my old age." Instead, study Torah (at all times), *for thou knowest not which* (study) *will prosper.* If thou hast studied Torah in riches, do not sit idle in poverty. If thou hast studied Torah with a full stomach, do not sit idle when hungry. If thou hast studied Torah in leisure, do not sit idle under pressure. For better for man is one thing in distress than a hundred in ease, as it is said, *In the morning sow thy seed, and in the evening withhold not thy hand.*

Rabbi 'Akiba says: If thou hast studied Torah in thy youth, study Torah in thine old age. Say not, "I shall not study Torah in my old age"; *for thou knowest not which* (study) *will prosper,* if both will survive in thy hand or *both shall* alike *turn out well.* [If thou hast raised disciples in thy youth, raise disciples in thine old age also,] [15] as it is said, *In the morning sow thy seed* (etc.).

Rabbi Me'ir says: If thou hast studied with one master, say not, "Enough for me." On the contrary, go to another sage and study Torah. Yet go not to anyone, but first to him that is close to thee, as it is said, *Drink waters out of thine own cistern, and running waters out of thine own well* (Prov. 5:15).

A man [16] is duty bound to attend upon *four* scholars, such as Rabbi Eliezer, Rabbi Joshua, Rabbi Ṭarfon,[17] and Rabbi 'Akiba, as it is said, *Happy is the man that hearkeneth to me, watching daily at my gates, waiting at the posts of my doors* (Prov. 8: 34): read not *my gates* (dalṭotai) but *my four* [18] *gates* (dalet dalṭotai).

For thou knowest not if both will survive in thy hand, if *both shall alike turn out well*. As it is said, *In the morning sow thy seed* (etc.).

Rabbi Joshua says: [19] Wed a wife in thy youth and wed a wife in thine old age. Beget children in thy youth and beget children in thine old age. Say not, "I shall not wed a wife (in my old age)." On the contrary, wed a wife and beget sons and daughters, and add fruitfulness and increase to the world. *For thou knowest not* if both will survive in thy hand, if *both alike shall turn out well*. As it is said, *In the morning sow thy seed,* etc.

He used to say: If thou hast given a pĕruṭah to a poor man in the morning and another poor man came and stood before thee in the evening, give to him too; for thou knowest not if both acts will survive in thy hand, if *both shall alike turn out well*. As it is said, *In the morning sow thy seed,* etc.[20]

There was once a saint who gave a *denar* [21] to some poor man during a famine. When his wife reprimanded him, he went to spend the night in the cemetery.

He heard two spirits chatting with each other. Said one to the other, "Come, friend, and let us go to and fro in the world, and see what calamity is to come upon the world."

"Friend," the second spirit said, "I cannot get out for I am buried in a matting of reeds.[22] But go thou and what thou overhearest tell me."

The first spirit went off and then came back. Said her companion to her: "Hast thou heard anything from beyond the veil, what calamity is to come upon the world?"

"I heard," she replied, "that whoever sows in the first rainfall, his sowings a hail shall strike."

The man went and sowed in the second rainfall. Everyone's sowing the hail struck down, and his was not struck.

The following year he went to spend the night in the cemetery and heard (the) two spirits chatting with each other. And one said to the other, "Come, let us go to and fro in the world and see what calamity is to come upon the world."

"Friend," the other said to her, "have I not told thee thus, I cannot get out for I am buried in a matting of reeds? But go thou and what thou overhearest tell me."

She went off and then came back. "Hast thou heard anything from beyond the veil?" her companion asked her.

"I heard," she replied, "that whoever sows in the second rainfall, his sowings a blast shall strike."

The man went and sowed in the first rainfall. A blast came upon the world; everyone's sowings were blasted, and his were not blasted.

"Why is it," said his wife to him, "that in the calamity which came upon the world, everyone's sowing was struck and blasted, and thine was neither struck nor blasted?" He told her the whole story.

Some time after, a quarrel broke out between the wife of that saint and the mother of that maiden. Said the wife to the mother, "Come and I will show thee thy daughter buried in a matting of reeds!"

The following year he went to spend the night in the cemetery and heard those two spirits chatting with each other. Said the first to the second, "Come, friend, and let us go to and fro in the world and hear what is being said beyond the veil."

"Friend," her companion said, "leave me alone. Words between thee and me have already been overheard amongst the living." 23

There was once a saint who was habitually charitable. One time he set out in a boat; a wind rose and sank his boat in the sea. Rabbi 'Aḳiba witnessed this and came before the court to testify that his wife might remarry. Before he could take the stand, the man came back and stood before him.

"Art thou not he who went down in the sea?" Rabbi 'Aḳiba said to him.

"Yes," he replied.

"And who raised thee up out of the sea?"

"The charity which I practiced," he answered; "it raised me out of the sea."

"How dost thou know this?" Rabbi 'Aḳiba inquired.

He said to him: "When I sank to the depths of the sea, I heard the sound of a great noise of the waves of the sea, one wave saying to the other and the other to another 'Hurry! and let us raise this man out of the sea, for he practiced charity all his days.'"

Then Rabbi Aḳiba spoke up and declared: "Blessed be God, the God of Israel, who hath chosen the words of the Torah and the words of the Sages, for the words of the Torah and the words of the Sages are established forever and unto all eternity. For it is said, *Cast thy bread upon the waters, for thou shalt find it after many days* (Eccl. 11:1); moreover it is written, *Charity delivereth from death*" (Prov. 10:2).

The following occurred to Benjamin the Righteous, who was in charge of the community charity chest. A woman came before him and said: "Master, take care of me."

"By the Temple service!"[24] he said to her, "there is nothing in the charity chest."

"Master," she said to him, "if thou dost not take care of me, thou wilt be the death of a widow and her seven[25] sons."

He thereupon gave her money from his own funds.

Some time after, Benjamin the Righteous fell sick and lay in bed in pain. Said the ministering angels to the Holy One, blessed be He: "Master of the Universe, Thou hast said 'One who saves a single soul in Israel[26] is as though he had saved a whole world.' How much more so Benjamin the Righteous who saved a widow and her seven sons! Yet he is sorely sick upon his bed."

Forthwith they beseeched mercy for him, and his (death) sentence was torn up. And twenty-two years[27] were added to his life.[28]

CHAPTER 4

SIMEON THE RIGHTEOUS WAS AMONG THE LAST OF THE MEN OF THE
GREAT ASSEMBLY. HE USED TO SAY: ON THREE THINGS THE WORLD
STANDS—ON THE TORAH, ON THE TEMPLE SERVICE, AND ON ACTS OF
LOVING-KINDNESS.[1]

O N THE TORAH:[2] how so? Lo, it says, *For I desire mercy and
not sacrifice, and the knowledge of God rather than
burnt offerings* (Hos. 6:6). Hence[3] we see that the
burnt offering is the most beloved of sacrifices, for the burnt
offering is entirely consumed by the flames, as it is said, *And the
priest shall make the whole smoke on the altar* (Lev. 1:9), and
elsewhere it says, *And Samuel took a sucking lamb, and offered
it for a whole burnt offering unto the Lord*[4] (I Sam. 7:9). But
the study of Torah is more beloved by God than burnt offerings.
For if a man studies Torah he comes to know the will of God,
as it is said, *Then shalt thou understand the fear of the Lord,
and find the will of God* (Prov. 2:5). Hence, when a sage sits
and expounds to the congregation, Scripture accounts it to him as
though he had offered up fat and blood on the altar.

If two scholars sit and study Torah and before them passes a
bridal procession or the bier of a dead man: if there are enough
in the procession they ought not to neglect their study, but if not
let them get up and cheer and hail[5] the bride,[6] or accompany the
dead.[7]

Once as Rabbi Judah bar Il'ai sat teaching his disciples, a bride
passed by. So he took myrtle twigs[8] in his hand and cheered[9] her
until the bride passed out of his sight.

Another time as Rabbi Judah bar Il'ai sat teaching his disciples,
a bride passed by. "What was that?" he asked them.

"A bride passing by," they replied.

"My sons," he said to them, "get up and attend upon the bride.

For thus we find concerning the Holy One, blessed be He, that he attended upon a bride, as it is said, *And the Lord God built the rib* (Gen. 2:22). If He attended upon a bride, how much more so we!"

And where do we find that the Holy One, blessed be He, attended upon a bride? For it is said, *And the Lord God built* [10] *the rib.* Now, in the sea towns they call plaiting *binyaṭa.* Hence we learn that the Holy One, blessed be He, fixed Eve's hair and outfitted her as a bride and brought her to Adam, as it is said, *And He brought her unto the man* (*ibid.*). The first time the Holy One, blessed be He, acted as best man for Adam; henceforth one must get a best man for himself. [11]

It [12] is said, *This is now* [13] *bone of my bones, and flesh of my flesh* (Gen. 2:23). The first time Eve was brought forth from Adam; henceforth one shall betroth his fellow's daughter. [14]

ON THE TEMPLE SERVICE: [15] how so? So long as the Temple service is maintained, the world is a blessing to its inhabitants and the rains come down in season, as it is said, *To love the Lord your God, and to serve Him with all your heart and with all your·soul, that I will give the rain of your land in its season, the former rain and the latter rain ... and I will give grass in thy fields for thy cattle* (Deut. 11:13-15). But when the Temple service is not maintained, the world is not a blessing to its inhabitants and the rains do not come down in season, as it is said, *Take heed to yourselves, lest your heart be deceived ... and He shut up the heaven, so that there shall be no rain* (Deut. 11:16-17).

And so, too, it says, *I pray you, consider from this day and forward—before a stone was laid upon a stone in the temple of the Lord, through all that time, when one came to a heap of twenty measures, there were but ten; when one came to the wine vat to draw out fifty press-measures, there were but twenty* (Hag. 2:15-16).

Why is it not said of the wine vat, "Twenty measures, there were but ten," as it is said of the wheat, *Twenty measures* (etc.)? Because the (yield of the) wine vat is a better sign (of the year's fortune) than wheat. This is to teach thee that whenever wine suffers it is a bad sign for the remainder of the year.[16]

Said Israel to the Holy One, blessed be He: "Master of the Universe, why didst Thou do this to us?"

The Holy Spirit replied: *"Ye looked for much, and, lo, it came to little . . . because of My house that lieth waste, while ye run every man for his own house* (Hag. 1:9). But if you will busy yourselves with the service of the Temple, I shall bless you as in the beginning; as it is said, *Consider, I pray you . . . from the four and twentieth day of the ninth month, even from the day that the foundation of the Lord's temple was laid. . . . Is the seed yet in the barn? Yea, the vine, and the fig tree, and the pomegranate, and the olive tree hath not brought forth—from this day will I bless you"* (Hag. 2:18–19).

Thus thou dost learn that there is no service more beloved of the Holy One, blessed be He, than the Temple service.

ON ACTS OF LOVING-KINDNESS: how so? Lo, it says, *For I desire mercy and not sacrifice* (Hos. 6:6). From the very first the world was created only with mercy, as it is said, *For I have said, The world is built with mercy; in the very heavens Thou dost establish Thy faithfulness* (Ps. 89:3).

Once [17] as Rabban Johanan ben Zakkai was coming forth from Jerusalem, Rabbi Joshua followed after him and beheld the Temple in ruins.

"Woe unto us!" Rabbi Joshua cried, "that this, the place where the iniquities of Israel were atoned for, is laid waste!"

"My son," Rabban Johanan said to him, "be not grieved; we have another atonement as effective as this. And what is it? It is acts of loving-kindness, as it is said, *For I desire mercy and not sacrifice"* (Hos. 6:6).[18]

For thus we find concerning Daniel, that greatly beloved man,[19] that he was engaged in acts of loving-kindness [all his days. For it is said of him, *Thy God whom thou servest continually, He will deliver thee* (Dan. 6:17).] [20]

Now, what were the acts of loving-kindness [21] in which Daniel was engaged? Canst thou say that he offered burnt offerings and sacrifices in Babylon? Verily it had been said, *Take heed to thyself that thou offer not thy burnt offerings in every place that thou seest; but in the place which the Lord shall choose in one of thy tribes, there shalt thou offer thy burnt offerings* (Deut. 12: 13–14). What then were the acts of loving-kindness in which he was engaged? He used to outfit the bride and make her rejoice, accompany the dead, give a pĕruṭah to the poor, and pray three times a day—and his prayer was received with favor; as it is said, *And when Daniel knew that the writing was signed, he went into his house—now his windows were open in his upper chamber toward Jerusalem—and he kneeled upon his knees three times a day, and prayed, and gave thanks before his God, as he did aforetime* (Dan. 6: 11).

Now,[22] when Vespasian came to destroy Jerusalem he said to the inhabitants: "Fools, why do you seek to destroy this city and why do you seek to burn the Temple? For what do I ask of you but that you send me one bow or one arrow,[23] and I shall go off from you?"

They said to him: "Even as we went forth against the first two who were here before thee and slew them,[24] so shall we go forth against thee and slay thee."

When Rabban Johanan ben Zakkai heard this, he sent for the men of Jerusalem and said to them: "My children, why do you destroy this city and why do you seek to burn the Temple? For what is it that he asks of you? Verily he asks naught of you save one bow or one arrow, and he will go off from you."

They said to him: "Even as we went forth against the two before him and slew them, so shall we go forth against him and slay him."

Vespasian had men stationed inside the walls of Jerusalem. Every word which they overheard they would write down, attach (the message) to an arrow, and shoot it over the wall, saying that Rabban Johanan ben Zakkai was one of the Emperor's friends.

Now, after Rabban Johanan ben Zakkai had spoken to them

one day, two and three days, and they still would not attend to him, he sent for his disciples, for Rabbi Eliezer and Rabbi Joshua.

"My sons," he said to them, "arise and take me out of here. Make a coffin for me that I might lie in it." [25]

Rabbi Eliezer took hold of the head end of it, Rabbi Joshua took hold of the foot; and they began carrying him as [26] the sun set, until they reached the gates of Jerusalem.

"Who is this?" the gatekeepers demanded.

"It's a dead man," they replied. "Do you not know that the dead may not be held overnight in Jerusalem?" [27]

"If it's a dead man," the gatekeepers said to them, "take him out."

So they took him out and continued carrying him [28] until they reached Vespasian. They opened the coffin and Rabban Johanan stood up before him.

"Art thou Rabban Johanan ben Zakkai?" Vespasian inquired; "tell me, what may I give thee?"

"I ask naught of thee," Rabban Johanan replied, "save Jamnia, where I might go and teach my disciples and there establish a prayer [house] [29] and perform all the commandments."

"Go," Vespasian said to him, "and whatever thou wishest to do, do."

Said Rabban Johanan to him: "By thy leave, may I say something to thee?"

"Speak," Vespasian said to him.

Said Rabban Johanan to him: "Lo, thou art about to be appointed king."

"How dost thou know this?" Vespasian asked.

Rabban Johanan replied: "This has been handed down to us, that the Temple will not be surrendered to a commoner, but to a king; as it is said, *And he shall cut down the thickets of the forest with iron, and Lebanon* [30] *shall fall by a mighty one*" (Isa. 10:34).

It was said: No more than a day, or two or three days, passed before messengers reached him from his city [31] (announcing) that the emperor was dead and that he had been elected to succeed as king.[32]

A catapult [33] was brought to him, drawn up [34] against the wall of Jerusalem. Boards of cedar were brought to him which he set into the catapult, and with these he struck against the wall until he made a breach in it. A swine's head was brought and set into the catapult, and this he hurled toward the (sacrificial) limbs which were on the altar.[35]

It was then that Jerusalem was captured.

Meanwhile Rabban Johanan ben Zakkai sat and waited trembling, the way Eli had sat and waited; as it is said, *Lo, Eli sat upon his seat by the wayside watching; for his heart trembled for the ark of God* (I Sam. 4: 13). When Rabban Johanan ben Zakkai heard that Jerusalem was destroyed and the Temple was up in flames, he tore his clothing, and his disciples tore their clothing, and they wept, crying aloud and mourning.

It says, *Open thy doors, O Lebanon, that the fire may devour thy cedars* (Zech. 11: 1). This refers to the high priests who were in the Temple, who took their keys [36] in their hands and threw them up to the sky, saying to the Holy One, blessed be He: "Master of the Universe, here are Thy keys which Thou didst hand over to us, for we have not been trustworthy custodians to do the King's work and to eat of the King's table."

Abraham, Isaac, and Jacob and the twelve tribes wept, crying aloud and mourning.

And it says, *Wail, O cypress tree, for the cedar is fallen, because the glorious ones are spoiled; wail, O ye oaks of Bashan, for the strong forest is come down* (Zech. 11: 2).

Wail, O cypress tree, for the cedar is fallen refers to the Temple.

Because the glorious ones are spoiled refers to Abraham, Isaac, and Jacob, and the twelve tribes.

Wail, O ye oaks of Bashan refers to Moses, Aaron, and Miriam.

For the strong forest has come down refers to the Temple.[37]

Hark, the wailing of the shepherds, for their glory is spoiled (Zech. 11: 3) refers to David and Solomon, his son.

Hark, the roaring of young lions, for the thickets of the Jordan are spoiled (*ibid.*) refers to Elijah and Elisha.

In three things did the Holy One, blessed be He, distinguish men from each other, to wit, in voice, in taste,[38] and in appearance.

In voice: what is that? This teaches that the Holy One, blessed be He, distinguished men's voices from each other. For if the Holy One, blessed be He, had not distinguished men's voices from each other, there would have been much unchastity in the world —when a man would go out of his house, another would come and seize his wife in his own home. Therefore the Holy One, blessed be He, distinguished men's voices from each other: the voice of one is not like the voice of another.

In taste: what is that? This teaches that the Holy One, blessed be He, distinguished men's tastes from each other. For if the Holy One, blessed be He, had not distinguished men's tastes from each other, they would have envied one another. Therefore the Holy One, blessed be He, distinguished men's tastes from each other: the taste of one is not like another's, and the other's taste is not like the first's.

In appearance: what is that? This teaches that the Holy One, blessed be He, distinguished men's appearances from each other. For if the Holy One, blessed be He, had not distinguished appearances from each other, the women of Israel could not recognize their husbands and men could not recognize their wives. Therefore the Holy One, blessed be He, distinguished appearances from each other.[39]

CHAPTER 5

ANTIGONUS OF SOKO TOOK OVER FROM SIMEON THE RIGHTEOUS. HE
USED TO SAY: BE NOT LIKE SLAVES THAT SERVE THEIR MASTER FOR THE
SAKE OF COMPENSATION; [1] BE RATHER LIKE SLAVES WHO SERVE THEIR
MASTER WITH NO THOUGHT OF COMPENSATION. AND LET THE FEAR
OF HEAVEN BE UPON YOU, so that your reward may be doubled in
the age to come.[2]

ANTIGONUS of Soko had two disciples who used to study his
words. They taught them to their disciples, and their
disciples to their disciples. These proceeded to examine the
words closely and demanded: "Why did our ancestors see fit to
say this thing? Is it possible that a laborer should do his work all
day and not take his reward in the evening? If our ancestors, for-
sooth, had known that there is another world and that there will
be a resurrection of the dead, they would not have spoken in this
manner."

So they arose and withdrew from the Torah [3] and split into two
sects, the Sadducees and the Boethusians: Sadducees named after
Zadok, Boethusians, after Boethus.[4] And they used [5] silver vessels
and gold vessels all their lives—not because they were ostentatious; [6] but the Sadducees said, "It is a tradition amongst the
Pharisees [7] to afflict themselves in this world; yet in the world to
come they will have nothing." [8]

CHAPTER 6

YOSE BEN JOEZER SAYS: LET THY HOUSE BE A MEETING PLACE FOR
THE SAGES, AND SIT IN THE VERY DUST AT THEIR FEET, AND THIRSTILY
DRINK IN THEIR WORDS.[1]

LET THY HOUSE BE A MEETING PLACE FOR THE SAGES: how so? This
teaches that a man's house ought to be a center [2] for the
Sages, disciples, and disciples of the disciples—as it is when
one says to his fellow, "I shall await thee at such and such a
place." [3]

Another interpretation. LET THY HOUSE BE A MEETING PLACE FOR
THE SAGES: how so? When a scholar comes to thy house with the
request, "Teach me," if it is within thy power to teach, teach him;
otherwise let him go at once.

And [4] let him not sit in thy presence on the couch or stool or
bench. Instead let him sit before thee on the ground. And every
single word which comes forth from thy mouth let him take in
with awe, fear, dread, and trembling—the way our fathers received (the Torah) from Mount Sinai: with awe, fear, dread, and
trembling; so let him too take in every single word which comes
forth from thy mouth with awe and fear, dread and trembling.[5]

AND SIT IN THE VERY DUST AT THEIR FEET: how so? When a scholar
comes to the city, say not "I have no need of him." On the contrary,
go to him. And do not sit with him on the couch or stool or bench.
Instead sit in his presence on the ground. And every word which
comes forth from his mouth take in with awe, fear, dread, and
trembling, the way thy fathers received (the Torah) from Mount
Sinai, with awe, fear, dread, and trembling.[6]

Another interpretation. SIT IN THE VERY DUST AT THEIR FEET
refers to Rabbi Eliezer. AND THIRSTILY DRINK IN THEIR WORDS
refers to Rabbi 'Akiba.

What were the beginnings of Rabbi 'Aḳiba? [7]

It is said: When he was forty years of age he had not yet studied a thing. One time he stood by the mouth of a well. "Who hollowed out this stone?" he wondered.

He was told: "It is the water which falls upon it every day, continually." It was said to him: "'Aḳiba, hast thou not heard,[8] *The waters wear away the stones?*" (Job 14: 19).[9]

Thereupon Rabbi 'Aḳiba drew the inference with regard to himself: If what is soft wears down the hard, all the more shall the words of the Torah, which are as hard as iron, hollow out my heart, which is flesh and blood! Forthwith he turned to the study of Torah.

He went together with his son and they appeared before an elementary teacher. Said Rabbi 'Aḳiba to him: "Master, teach me Torah."

Rabbi 'Aḳiba took hold of one end of the tablet and his son the other end of the tablet. The teacher wrote down *'aleph beṭ* [10] for him and he learned it; *'aleph taw*,[10] and he learned it; the book of Leviticus,[11] and he learned it. He went on studying until he learned the whole Torah.

Then he went and appeared before Rabbi Eliezer and Rabbi Joshua. "My masters," he said to them, "reveal the sense of Mishnah to me."

When they told him one halakha [12] he went off to be by himself. "This 'aleph," he wondered, "why was it written? That beṭ, why was it written? [13] This thing, why was it said?" He came back and asked them—and reduced them to silence.

Rabbi Simeon ben Eleazar says: I shall tell thee a parable; to what may this be likened? To a stonecutter who was hacking away in the mountains. One time he took up his pickaxe and went and sat on the mountain and began to chip tiny pebbles from it. Now some men came by and asked him, "What art thou doing?"

"I am uprooting the mountain," he replied, "and shall cast it into the Jordan."

"Thou canst not uproot the whole mountain," they said to him. But he continued hacking away until he hit upon a big rock. He crawled under it, broke it loose and uprooted it, and cast it into the Jordan; and he said to it: "Not here is thy place but there."

This is what Rabbi 'Aḳiba did with (the instruction of) Rabbi Eliezer and Rabbi Joshua.

Rabbi Ṭarfon said to him: " 'Aḳiba, of thee the verse says, *He bindeth the streams that they trickle not; and the thing that is hid bringeth he forth to light* (Job 28:11): things concealed from men (thou) Rabbi 'Aḳiba didst bring forth to light."

Each day Rabbi 'Aḳiba would gather a bundle of straw; [14] part he would sell to provide for his food and part for his clothing. His neighbors rose up in protest and said to him, "'Aḳiba, thou art slaying us with the smoke! [15] Sell the straw to us and with the money buy oil, and study by the light of a lamp."

"I fill many needs with it," he answered them; "first, I study by its light; then again, I keep warm by its heat; and finally, I sleep on it."

In the future, at Judgment, Rabbi 'Aḳiba will put all the poor in a guilty light. For if they are asked, "Why did you not study Torah?" and they say, "Because we were poor," they shall be told: "Indeed, was not Rabbi 'Aḳiba even poorer and in more wretched circumstances!" And if they say, "Because of our children," they shall be asked, "And did not Rabbi 'Aḳiba have sons and daughters?" But they are told: "Because Rachel, his wife, had merit." [16]

At the age of forty he went to study Torah; at the end of thirteen years he taught Torah to multitudes.

It is said: Before he departed from the world he owned tables of silver and gold, and mounted his couch on ladders of gold. His wife used to go about in golden sandals [17] and in a golden tiara.[18]

"Master," his disciples said to him, "thou hast put us to shame by what thou hast done for her."

He said to them: "Many were the trials she endured for my sake, that I might study Torah." [19]

What were the beginnings of Rabbi Eliezer ben Hyrcanus? [20]

He was twenty-two years old and had not yet studied Torah. One time he resolved: "I will go and study Torah with Rabban Johanan ben Zakkai." Said his father Hyrcanus to him: "Not a taste of food shalt thou get before thou hast plowed the entire furrow."

He rose early in the morning and plowed the entire furrow (and then departed for Jerusalem).

It is told: That day was the eve of the Sabbath, and he went for the Sabbath meal to his father-in-law's. And some say: He tasted nothing from six hours before the eve of the Sabbath until six hours after the departure of the Sabbath.

As he was walking along the road he saw a stone; he picked it up and put it in his mouth. And some say: It was cattle dung. He went to spend the night at a hostel.[21]

Then he went and appeared before Rabban Johanan ben Zakkai in Jerusalem—until a bad breath rose from his mouth. Said Rabban Johanan ben Zakkai to him: "Eliezer, my son, hast thou eaten at all today?"

Silence.

Rabban Johanan ben Zakkai asked him again.

Again silence.

Rabban Johanan ben Zakkai sent for the owners of his hostel and asked them: "Did Eliezer have anything to eat in your place?"

"We thought," they replied, "he was very likely eating with thee, master."

He said to them: "And I thought he was very likely eating with you! You and I, between us, left Rabbi Eliezer to perish!"

(Thereupon) Rabban Johanan said to him: "Even as a bad breath rose from thy mouth, so shall fame of thee travel for thy mastery of the Torah."

When Hyrcanus his father heard of him, that he was studying Torah with Rabban Johanan ben Zakkai, he declared: "I shall go and ban my son Eliezer from my possessions."

It is told: That day Rabban Johanan ben Zakkai sat expounding in Jerusalem and all the great ones of Israel sat before him. When he heard that Hyrcanus was coming, he appointed guards and said to them, "If Hyrcanus comes, do not let him sit down."

Hyrcanus arrived and they would not let him sit down. But he pushed on ahead [22] until he reached the place near Ben Ṣiṣiṭ Hakkeseṭ, Naḳdimon ben Gorion, and Ben Kalba Śabua'. He sat among them trembling.

It is told: On that day Rabban Johanan ben Zakkai fixed his gaze upon Rabbi Eliezer and said to him: "Deliver the exposition." [23]

"I am unable to speak," [24] Rabbi Eliezer pleaded.

Rabban Johanan pressed him to do it and the disciples pressed him to do it. So he arose and delivered a discourse upon things which no ear had ever before heard. As the words came from his mouth Rabban Johanan ben Zakkai rose to his feet and kissed him upon his head and exclaimed, "Rabbi Eliezer, master, thou hast taught me the truth!"

Before the time had come to recess, Hyrcanus, his father, rose to his feet and declared: "My masters, I came here only in order to ban my son Eliezer from my possessions. Now, all my possessions shall be given to Eliezer my son, and all his brothers are herewith disinherited and have naught of them." [25]

Now why was Ṣiṣiṭ Hakkeseṭ so called? Because he used to recline on a silver couch [26] at the head of all the great ones of Israel.

It is told of the daughter of Naḳdimon ben Gorion that her couch was overlaid with a spread worth twelve thousand golden denar, that she would spend a Tyrian gold denar every single Sabbath eve for spice puddings, and that she was awaiting a levirate marriage.[27]

Now why was Naḳdimon ben Gorion so called? Because the sun shone through [28] for his sake.

One time Israel went up on pilgrimage to Jerusalem and had no water to drink. Naḳdimon went to a certain hegemon and said to him: "Lend me twelve wells of water from now until such and such a day. If I do not return to thee twelve wells of water, I shall give thee twelve talents of silver." And he set a date.

When the time approached, the hegemon sent to him, saying: "Send me either water for twelve wells or twelve talents of silver."

Said Naḳdimon to him: "There's still time today."

That hegemon jeered at him and exclaimed: "All year long no rains came down, and shall the rains come down now!"

So that hegemon went to the bathhouse cheerfully and Naḳdimon ben Gorion went to the study house. He wrapped himself in his cloak and stood in prayer and said before Him: "Master of the Universe, to Thee it is manifest and known that not for my glory did I do this, nor for the glory of my father's house did I do this; only for Thy glory I did it, so that there might be water for the pilgrims."

Immediately the skies knotted up with clouds and rains came down, until twelve wells were filled with water—and there was more still.

So he sent to the hegemon: "Send me the money for my surplus water which is in thy possession."

Said the hegemon to him: "The sun has already set and the water fell in my domain."

Naḳdimon went back into the study house, wrapped himself in his cloak, and stood in prayer. He said before Him: "Master of the Universe, perform yet another miracle for me like the first one."

Immediately the wind blew, the clouds were scattered, and the sun shone through.

As he came out (of the study house) they met each other; and the hegemon said to him, "I know that the Holy One, blessed be He, shook the world for thy sake only."

Now why was Kalba Śabua' so called? Because whoever entered his house hungry as a dog came out of it with a full stomach.[29]

Now when the Emperor Vespasian came to destroy Jerusalem, the Zealots [30] sought to burn all that wealth (of Kalba Śabua'''s)

in fire. Kalba Ṣaḇuaʿ said to them: "Why are you destroying this
city and why do you seek to burn all that wealth in fire? Give me
time to go and see what I have in the house."

He went and found that he had food for twenty-two years,[31]
enough for a feast for each and every one in Jerusalem. Thereupon he gave orders that food be heaped up and sorted out and
sifted and kneaded and baked and prepared for twenty-two years
for each and every one in Jerusalem. But they paid no attention
to him.[32]

What did the men of Jerusalem do?[33] They would bring
loaves[34] and brick them into walls[35] and plaster them over with
clay.[36]

The men of Jerusalem did yet another thing: they would boil
straw and eat it.[37]

And every one in Israel stationed at the walls of Jerusalem would
exclaim: "Someone give me five dates and I will go down and
capture five heads!" When given five dates, he would go down and
capture five heads of Vespasian's men.

As Vespasian looked at their excrement and saw that there was
in it no sign of corn, he said to his troops: "If these who eat
nothing but straw kill a number of you[38] in this fashion, how they
would kill you if they ate everything you eat and drink!"

CHAPTER 7

JOSEPH BEN JOHANAN OF JERUSALEM SAYS: LET THY HOUSE BE
OPENED WIDE, AND LET THE POOR BE MEMBERS OF THY HOUSEHOLD,
AND TALK NOT OVERMUCH WITH WOMEN.[1]

LET THY HOUSE BE OPENED WIDE:[2] how so? This teaches that a
man's house should have a spacious entrance on the north,
south, east, and west, like Job's, who made four doors to his
house. And why did Job make four doors to his house? So that
the poor would not be troubled to go all around the house: one
coming from the north could enter in his stride, one coming from

the south could enter in his stride, and so in all directions. For that reason Job made four doors to his house.

AND LET THE POOR BE MEMBERS OF THY HOUSEHOLD. Not actually members of thy household.[3] But let the poor talk about what they had to eat and drink in thy house the way the poor used to talk about what they had to eat and drink in Job's house. When they met, one would say to the other:

"Where art thou coming from?"

"From Job's house. And where art *thou* going?"

"To Job's house."

Now when that great calamity came upon Job, he said unto the Holy One, blessed be He: "Master of the Universe, did I not feed the hungry and give the thirsty to drink; as it is said, *Or have I eaten my morsel myself alone and the fatherless hath not eaten thereof* (Job 31:17)? And did I not clothe the naked, as it is said, *And if he were not warmed with the fleece of my sheep*" (Job 31:20)?

Nevertheless the Holy One, blessed be He, said to Job: "Job, thou hast not yet reached half the measure of Abraham. Thou sittest and tarriest within thy house and the wayfarers come in to thee. To him who is accustomed to eat wheat bread, thou givest wheat bread to eat; to him who is accustomed to eat meat, thou givest meat to eat; to him who is accustomed to drink wine, thou givest wine to drink. But Abraham did not act in this way. Instead he would go forth and make the rounds everywhere, and when he found wayfarers he brought them in to his house. To him who was unaccustomed to eat wheat bread, he gave wheat bread to eat; to him who was unaccustomed to eat meat, he gave meat to eat; to him who was unaccustomed to drink wine, he gave wine to drink. Moreover he arose and built stately mansions on the highways and left there food and drink, and every passerby ate and drank and blessed Heaven. That is why delight of spirit was vouchsafed to him. And whatever one might ask for was to be found in Abraham's house, as it is said, *And Abraham planted a tamarisk tree* [4] *in Beer-Sheba*" (Gen. 21:33).

Teach the members of thy household humility.[5] For when one is humble and the members of his household are humble, if a poor man comes and stands in the doorway of the master of the house and inquires of them, "Is your father within?" they answer, "Ay, come in, enter." Even before he has entered, a table is set for him. When he enters and eats and drinks and offers a blessing up to Heaven, great delight of spirit is vouchsafed to the master of the house.[6]

But when one is not humble and the members of his household are short tempered, if a poor man comes and stands in the doorway and inquires of them, "Is your father within?" they answer, "No!" and rebuke him and drive him off in anger.

Another interpretation. Teach the members of thy household humility: what is that? When a man is humble and the members of his household are humble, if he goes overseas and prays,

> I give thanks unto Thee,
> O Lord my God,
> that my wife does not quarrel with others,
> and my children do not quarrel with others,

there is no fear in his heart and his mind is at ease even to the moment he returns.

But when a man is not humble and the members of his household are short tempered, if he goes overseas and prays,

> May it be Thy will,
> O Lord my God,
> that my wife enter into no quarrel with others,
> and my children enter into no quarrel with others,

there is fear in his heart and his mind is not at ease until he returns.

AND TALK NOT OVERMUCH WITH WOMEN—EVEN WITH THINE OWN WIFE,[7] AND NEEDLESS TO SAY WITH THY FELLOW'S WIFE! [8] FOR SO LONG AS A MAN TALKS OVERMUCH WITH WOMEN HE BRINGS EVIL UPON HIMSELF, NEGLECTS THE STUDY OF TORAH, AND IN THE END GEHENNA IS HIS PORTION.[9]

Another interpretation. TALK NOT OVERMUCH WITH WOMEN; [10]

what is that? If a man came to the study house and was not treated with honor, or if he fell out with his fellow, he is not to go and tell his wife, "Thus and so did I fall out with my fellow; he said this to me and I said that to him." For (in so doing) he disgraces himself, disgraces his wife, and disgraces his fellow. And his wife who used to treat him with honor now stands and scoffs at him. Then his fellow hears of it and cries: "Woe unto me! words between himself and me he went and told his wife!" And thus such a person disgraces himself, disgraces his wife, disgraces his fellow.

CHAPTER 8

JOSHUA BEN PERAḤYAH AND NITTAI THE ARBELITE TOOK OVER FROM THEM.[1] JOSHUA BEN PERAḤYAH SAYS: PROVIDE THYSELF WITH A TEACHER, AND GET THEE A COMPANION, AND JUDGE EVERYONE WITH THE SCALE WEIGHTED IN HIS FAVOR.[2]

PROVIDE THYSELF WITH A TEACHER:[3] how so? This teaches that one should provide himself with a single[4] teacher and study with him Scripture and Mishnah—Midrash, Halakha, and Agada.[5] Then the interpretation which the teacher neglected to tell him in the study of Scripture he will eventually tell him in the study of Mishnah; the interpretation which he neglected to tell him in the study of Mishnah he will eventually tell him in the study of Midrash;[6] the interpretation which he neglected to tell him in the study of Midrash he will eventually tell him in the study of Halakha; the interpretation which he neglected to tell him in the study of Halakha he will eventually tell him in the study of Agada. Thus that man remains in one place and is filled with good and blessing.

Rabbi Me'ir used to say: He that studies Torah with a single teacher, to whom may he be likened? To one who had a single field, part of which he sowed with wheat and part with barley, and planted part with olives and part with oak trees. Now that man is full of good and blessing. But when one studies with two or three teachers he is like him who has many fields: one he sows with wheat and one he sows with barley, and plants one with olives and one with oak trees. Now this man's (attention) is divided among many pieces of land, without good or blessing.[7]

AND GET THEE A COMPANION:[8] how so? This teaches that a man should get a companion for himself, to eat with him, drink with him, study Scripture with him, study Mishnah with him, sleep with him, and reveal to him all his secrets, the secrets of the Torah [9] and the secrets of worldly things.[10]

When two sit studying Torah and one of them makes a mistake [in] a matter of Halakha or of a chapter heading—or says of the unclean that it is clean or of the clean that it is unclean, or of the forbidden that it is permitted or of the permitted that it is forbidden—his companion will correct him. And where do we hear that when his companion corrects him and studies with him they are well rewarded for their labor? It is said, *Two are better than one; because they have a good reward for their labor* (Eccl. 4:9).

When [11] three sit studying Torah the Holy One, blessed be He, accounts it to them as though they made up one band [12] in His sight, as it is said, *It is He that buildeth His upper chambers in the heaven, and hath founded His band upon the earth; He that calleth for the waters of the sea, and poureth them out upon the face of the earth; the Lord is His name* (Am. 9:6). Thus thou dost learn that three who sit studying Torah are accounted as though they made up one band in the sight of the Holy One, blessed be He.

When two sit studying Torah their reward is stored up [13] on high, as it is said, *Then they that feared the Lord spoke one with another; and the Lord hearkened . . . and a book of remembrance was written before Him, for them that feared the Lord, and that thought upon His name* (Mal. 3:16).

—These are *They that feared the Lord:* those who are decisive [14] and say, "Let us go and release the prisoners and ransom the captives"; then the Holy One, blessed be He, provides them with the means to go and act immediately.

And these are *They that thought upon His name*: those who keep deliberating in their hearts and say, "Let us go and release the prisoners and ransom the captives"; [15] and the Holy One, blessed be He, does not provide them with the means. Then an angel comes and strikes them down.—

When one sits by himself studying Torah, his reward is stored up [13] on high, as it is said, *Though he sit alone and keep silence, surely He hath laid up (reward) for him* (Lam. 3:28).

A parable is told: to what may this be likened? To one who had a young son whom he left at home when he went out to the market place. The child then proceeded to take down a scroll, laid it in his lap, and sat studying it. When his father returned from the market place, he exclaimed: "See what my little son, whom I left alone when I went out to the market place, has done! By himself he proceeded [16] to take down the scroll, laid it in his lap and sat studying it." Thus thou dost learn that even when one sits by himself studying Torah, his reward is stored up [13] on high.

AND JUDGE EVERYONE WITH THE SCALE WEIGHTED IN HIS FAVOR.

There [17] was once a young girl who had been taken captive, and two saintly folk went after her to ransom her. One of them entered the harlots' apartment.[18] When he came out he asked his companion:

"What didst thou suspect me of?"

The other replied: "Of finding out perhaps for how much money she is being held." [19]

Said the first: "By the Temple service, so it was!" And he added: "Even as thou didst judge me with the scale weighted in my favor, so may the Holy One, blessed be He, judge thee with the scale weighted in thy favor."

Again it once happened that a young girl was taken captive. Two saintly folk went after her to ransom her, and one of them was seized on a charge of brigandage and imprisoned. Every single day his wife would bring him bread and water. One day he said to her: "Go to so and so and tell him that I am being held in prison because of unchastity,[20] while he sits and amuses himself at home and pays no attention to (the fate of) the girl."

Said his wife to him: "Is it not enough for thee that thou art held in prison, but thou must [21] busy thyself with idle matters?" [22] She did not go; instead she busied herself with idle matters.

"I beg of you," he said to her, "go and tell him." So she went and told him.

What did that man do? He went and brought silver and gold and other men with him and they freed both the saint and the girl.

When he was freed the saint said to them: "Let this girl sleep with me on a bed in her clothes."

In the morning he said to them: "Let me immerse myself."

They had him immerse himself.

["Let her immerse herself," he said.

They had her immerse herself.] [23]

Then he asked them: "When I asked to be immersed what did you suspect me of?"

"We thought," they replied, "all those days while thou wast held in prison thou wast hungry and thirsty; and now when thou didst come out into the open air, thy flesh grew hot all over and perhaps thou didst suffer pollution." [24]

"What of the immersion of the girl," he asked them; "what did you suspect her of?"

They replied: "Seeing that all those days when she dwelt among the heathen she ate and drank of their food, thou didst now order, 'Let her immerse herself,' so that she should become clean." [25]

"By the Temple service," he exclaimed, "so it was! And even as you judged me with the scale weighted in my favor, so may God judge you with the scale weighted in your favor."

Even as the righteous of old were saintly, so were their beasts saintly.

It is said: The camels of Abraham, our father, would not enter into a house in which there was an idol, as it is said, *For I have cleared the house, and made room for the camels* (Gen. 24:31).

For I have cleared the [26] *house* of teraphim.

And why does the verse say, *And made room for the camels?* This teaches that they would not enter into the house of Laban, the Aramean, until all the idols were removed from their sight.

Once the ass of Rabbi Ḥanina ben Dosa was stolen by brigands. They tied the ass up in a yard, and put before it straw and barley and water. But it would not eat or drink.

They said: "Why should we let it die and befoul our yard?"

So forthwith they opened the gate before it, and drove it out.

It walked along braying [27] until it reached the house of Rabbi Ḥanina ben Dosa. When it reached his house, his son heard its voice. "Father," he said, "this sounds like our beast." Said Rabbi Ḥanina to him: "My son, open the door for it, for it has almost died of hunger." He arose and opened the door, and put before it straw, barley, and water, and it ate and drank.

Therefore it was said: Even as the righteous of old were saintly, so were their beasts saintly, like their masters.[28]

CHAPTER 9

NITTAI THE ARBELITE SAYS: KEEP FAR AWAY FROM AN EVIL NEIGHBOR, DO NOT ASSOCIATE WITH THE WICKED, AND DO NOT LOSE HOPE OF THE FINAL RECKONING.[1]

KEEP FAR AWAY FROM AN EVIL NEIGHBOR—whether it be your neighbor indoors or your neighbor outdoors [2] or your neighbor out in the field. This teaches that plagues come only because of the iniquity of the wicked: the iniquities of the wicked cause the wall of the righteous to be torn down.[3] How so? If there is a wall separating the wicked from the righteous, and a plague appears in the house of the wicked on the wall separating him from the righteous, the wall of the righteous has to be torn down [4] because of the iniquity [5] of the wicked.

Rabbi Ishmael, son of Rabbi Johanan ben Baroḳa says: Woe to the wicked and woe to his neighbor! The iniquities of the wicked cause the wall of the righteous to be torn down.

With ten trials our ancestors tried the Holy One, blessed be He,[6] but they were punished for slanderous speech only. And these are the trials: [two] [7] at the Red Sea, one when the manna began to fall,[8] one when the manna ceased to fall,[9] one when the first quail were seen,[10] one when the last quail were seen,[11] one at Marah,[12] one at Rephidim,[13] one at Horeb,[14] and one when the spies (returned).[15] This trial of the spies was the gravest of them all, as it is said, *And they have put Me to proof these ten times, and have not hearkened to My voice* (Num. 14:22); so too, *Even those men that did bring up an evil report of the land, died by the plague before the Lord* [16] (Num. 14:37).

Now is there not an inference to be drawn here? If the Holy One, blessed be He, resented the spies' insult to the land—which has neither mouth for speech, nor face, nor feeling of shame—how much more will the Holy One, blessed be He, resent the insult when one says things against his fellow and puts him to shame! [17]

Rabbi Simeon says: Upon them that speak slander plagues come. For thus we find concerning Aaron and Miriam, that they engaged in slandering Moses and punishment came upon them; as it is said, *And Miriam and Aaron spoke against Moses* (Num. 12:1).

Why does the verse mention Miriam before Aaron? This teaches that Zipporah went and told Miriam; Miriam went and told Aaron; then both of them stood and spoke against that righteous man.[18] Because they both stood and spoke against that righteous man, punishment came upon them; as it is said, *And the anger of the Lord was kindled against them; and He departed* (Num. 12:9).[19]

Why does the verse say, *And He departed?* This teaches that the punishment removed from Aaron and clove to Miriam: for Aaron was no tale bearer; Miriam however, who was the tale bearer, was thereupon punished more severely.

Miriam said: "The Word was upon me, but I did not keep away from my husband."

Aaron said: "The Word was upon me,[20] but I did not keep away from my wife. And the Word was also upon our fathers of old, but they did not keep away from their wives. But he, because of his presumptuous spirit, kept away from his wife!"

Now they did not pass judgment on him to his face, but out of his sight. Nor did they pass judgment on him with certainty, but doubtfully: was he of presumptuous spirit or was he not of presumptuous spirit? Is there not, then, an inference to be drawn here? If Miriam—who spoke against her brother only, and did not speak to Moses' face—was punished, how much greater will be the punishment of the ordinary person who says things to his fellow's face and puts him to shame! [21]

At that time Aaron said to Moses: "Moses, my brother, dost thou think that this leprosy is being visited upon Miriam (alone)? It is visited indeed upon the flesh of our father Amram! [22] I shall tell thee a parable: to what may this be likened? To one who held a glowing coal in his hand; although he keeps juggling it, his flesh is nevertheless seared"—as it is said, *Let her not, I pray, be as one dead* (Num. 12:12).[23]

It was at that time that Aaron began to conciliate Moses. He said to him: "Moses, my brother, have we ever done evil to anyone in the world?"

"No," he answered.

"If we have done no evil to others in the world," said Aaron, "how could we think of doing evil to thee that art our brother? But what am I to do? It was an error on our part: we neglected the covenant between us and thee—as it is said, *And they remembered not the brotherly covenant* [24] (Am. 1:9). Because of the covenant drawn up between us, which we neglected, shall we lose our sister?"

Thereupon Moses drew a small circle and stood within it,[25] and beseeched mercy in her behalf, saying, "I shall not stir from here until Miriam my sister is healed." As it is said, *Heal her now, O God, I beseech Thee* (Num. 12:13).

It was then that the Holy One, blessed be He, said to Moses: "If a king had rebuked her, if her father had rebuked her, would she not be in shame seven days? How much the more when I, the King of kings of kings, (rebuke her)! By all rights she should be in shame fourteen days! But for thy sake (seven days) shall be pardoned her." As it is said, *And the Lord said to Moses, If her father had but spit in her face,* etc. (Num. 12:14).[26]

Now the man Moses was very meek, more so than all men upon the face of the earth (Num. 12:3).

Perhaps he was meek in the sense that he was not of magnificent appearance? No. The verse says, *And he spread the tent of the tabernacle* (Exod. 40:19): even as the tabernacle measured ten cubits, so Moses measured ten cubits in height.

Was he perhaps *more meek* than [27] the ministering angels? No. The verse says *More so than all men:* more than men, it is said, but not more than the ministering angels.

Was he perhaps *more meek* than [27] the generations of old? No. The verse says, *upon the face of the earth:* more than his generation, it is said, but not more than the generations of old.

Three kinds of furunculars were created in the world: the victim of moist boils, of dry boils, and he that has a polypus. And the soul of Moses was more humble than them all.

Rabbi Simeon ben Eleazar says: So, too,[28] on them that speak slander plagues come. For thus we find concerning Gehazi that he told a lying tale [29] about his master and leprosy clove to him until the day of his death, as it is said, *The leprosy therefore of Naaman shall cleave unto thee . . . and he went out from his presence a leper as white as snow* (II Kings 5:27).

He used to say: Upon the arrogant of spirit plagues come. For thus we find concerning Uzziah, as it is said, *But when he was strong, his heart was lifted up so that he did corruptly, and he trespassed* [30] *against the Lord his God; for he went into the*

*temple of the Lord to burn incense upon the altar of incense. And
Azariah the priest went in after him, and with him fourscore
priests of the Lord, that were valiant men; and they withstood
Uzziah the king, and said unto him: It pertaineth not unto thee,
Uzziah, to burn incense unto the Lord, but to the priests, the sons
of Aaron, that are consecrated, it pertaineth to burn incense;* [31]
*go out of the sanctuary; for thou hast trespassed; neither shall it
be for thy honor from the Lord God. Then Uzziah was wroth;
and he had a censer in his hand to burn incense; and while he
was wroth with the priests, the leprosy broke forth in his forehead* (II Chron. 26: 16–19).

At that time the sanctuary split in two parts, leaving a cleft of
twelve miles; [32] and the priests thrust him out quickly, *Yea, himself made haste also to go out, because the Lord had smitten him.
And he* [33] *was a leper unto the day of his death, and dwelt in a
house set apart, being a leper; for he was cut off from the house of
the Lord; and Jotham his son was over the king's house, judging
the people of the land* (II Chron. 26: 20–21).

DO NOT ASSOCIATE WITH THE WICKED. This teaches that one should
associate neither with an evil man nor with a wicked man. For
thus we find concerning Jehoshaphat, that he associated with Ahab
and went up with him to Ramoth Gilead, and wrath came down
upon him from before the Lord; as it is said, *Shouldst thou help
the wicked, and love them that hate the Lord? for this thing
wrath is upon thee from before the Lord* (II Chron. 19: 2).

At another time he associated with Ahaziah and they made ships
in Ezion-Geber, and the Lord shattered his works, as it is said,
*Because thou hast joined thyself with Ahaziah, the Lord hath
made a breach in thy works. And the ships were broken* (II Chron.
20: 37).

And so, too, we find concerning Amnon, that he associated with
Jonadab and Jonadab gave him evil counsel, as it is said, *But
Amnon had a friend, whose name was Jonadab, the son of
Shimeah,*[34] *David's brother; and Jonadab was a very subtle man*
(II Sam. 13: 3)—*subtle* in evil.[35]

Another interpretation. DO NOT ASSOCIATE WITH THE WICKED, even for the study of Torah.[36]

AND DO NOT LOSE HOPE OF THE FINAL RECKONING: what is that? This teaches that a man's heart should be in a state of fear at all times and he should say, "Woe unto me, perhaps calamity will come upon me today, perhaps tomorrow!" He will thus be in a state of fear at all times. For thus is it said of Job: *The thing which I did fear is come upon me* (Job 3:25).[37]

Another interpretation. DO NOT LOSE HOPE OF THE FINAL RECKONING: what is that? When a man sees his affairs prosper, let him not say: Because I have merited it, God has given me food and drink in this world and the stock is laid up for me for the world to come. Instead let him say: "Woe unto me! Perhaps no more than one good deed was found before Him in my behalf, and He has given me food and drink in this world so that He might destroy me in the world to come."[38]

CHAPTER 10

JUDAH BEN ṬABBAI AND SIMEON BEN SHEṬAḤ TOOK OVER FROM THEM.[1] JUDAH BEN ṬABBAI SAYS: DO NOT PLAY THE PART OF CHIEF JUSTICE;[2] AND WHEN THERE ARE LITIGANTS STANDING BEFORE THEE LOOK UPON THEM AS LIKELY TO BE GUILTY; BUT WHEN THEY DEPART FROM THY PRESENCE LOOK UPON THEM AS LIKELY TO BE INNOCENT, AS SOON AS THEY HAVE ACCEPTED THE SENTENCE.[3]

DO NOT PLAY THE PART OF CHIEF JUSTICE: what is that? This teaches that if thou hast come to the study house and heard an interpretation[4] or a statement of Halakha, do not be in haste to dispute it. Instead, sit still and ask for what reason it was said, in what connection was the judgment or the Halakha which has been discussed.[5]

And[6] when two litigants come before thee for judgment, one poor and one rich, say not: How shall I acquit the poor and condemn the rich? or, How shall I acquit the rich and condemn the poor? For if I condemn the poor one, he will be my enemy; and if I acquit the poor one, the rich one will be my enemy. And say not: How shall I take the money from the one and give it to the other? Yea, the Torah hath said, *Ye shall not respect persons in judgment* (Deut. 1:17).[7]

Rabbi Me'ir used to say: Why does the verse say, *Ye shall hear the small and the great alike (ibid.)*? So that one of the litigants shall not be kept standing and the other sit, one be allowed to speak his fill while to the other thou sayest, "Cut thy words short!"

Rabbi Judah said: I have heard that if the judges wish to have both alike sitting, they may be seated. What is forbidden is that one be standing and the other sitting.

Let a minor lawsuit be to thee like a major lawsuit, a lawsuit over a pĕruṭah like a lawsuit over a hundred *mina*.

He [8] used to say: Whenever someone said to me before I entered into high office, "Enter it," I had one wish: to hound him to death! [9] Now that I have come into it, whenever someone tells me to quit it, I have one wish: to upset a kettle of boiling water on him! [10] For to high office it is hard to rise; and even as it is hard to rise up to it, so is it difficult to come down from it.[11] For thus we find concerning Saul: When he was told, "Rise to kingship," he hid, as it is said, *And the Lord answered, Behold, he hath hid himself among the baggage* (I Sam. 10:22); but when he was told, "Get down from there," he hunted after David to kill him.[12]

SIMEON BEN SHEṬAḤ SAYS: AGAIN AND AGAIN EXAMINE THE WIT-NESSES; [13] in the course of examining them be guarded in thy speech, lest from thy words they that hear hear and add to thy words falsehood. . . .[14]

CHAPTER 11

SHEMAIAH AND ABṬALYON TOOK OVER FROM THEM.[1] SHEMAIAH
SAYS: LOVE WORK, HATE LORDSHIP, AND SEEK NO INTIMACY WITH THE
RULING POWERS.[2]

LOVE WORK: what is that? This teaches that a man should love
work and that no man should hate work. For even as the
Torah was given as a covenant, so was work given as a
covenant; as it is said, *Six days shalt thou labor, and do all thy
work; but the seventh day is a sabbath unto the Lord thy God*[3]
(Exod. 20:9 f.).

Rabbi 'Akiba says: There are times when a man does work and
thereby escapes death, and there are times when a man does no
work and in consequence is sentenced to death by Heaven. How
so? If a man sat idle all week and did no work, on the Sabbath
eve he would have nothing to eat; if he happened to have consecrated funds at home and took some to buy food, he is mortally
guilty in the sight of Heaven. But if he were a laborer engaged in
the building of the Temple, even if he had been given consecrated
funds for his wages and took some to buy food, he would escape
death.[4]

Rabbi Dostai says: How may it happen that if one did no work
on the six days, he would work even on the seventh? Suppose that
he sits idle all the days of the week and does no work and on the
Sabbath eve has nothing to eat. He might then go and fall in
with a troop of bandits. Then he would be seized and taken in
chains and put to work on the Sabbath! All this because he would
not work on the six days (of the week)![5]

Rabbi Simeon ben Eleazar says: Even Adam tasted nothing before he worked, as it is said, *And He put him into the Garden of
Eden to dress it and to keep it;* (only then,) *Of every tree of the
garden thou mayest freely eat* (Gen. 2:15 f.).[6]

Rabbi Ṭarfon says: The Holy One, blessed be He, likewise did
not cause His Shekinah to rest upon Israel before they did work, as

it is said, *And let them make Me a sanctuary, then shall I dwell among them* (Exod. 25:8).[7]

Rabbi Judah ben Bathyra says: If a man has no work to do, what should he do? If he has a run-down yard or run-down field let him go and occupy himself with it, for it is said, *Six days shalt thou labor, and do all* [8] *thy work* (Exod. 20:9). Now, why does the verse say, *And do all thy work?* To include him who has run-down yards and fields—let him go and occupy himself with them! [9]

Rabbi Yose says: A man dies through idleness only, as it is said, *And he expired, and was gathered unto his people* [10] (Gen. 49:33). If [11] he were standing on the rooftop or at the seashore and fell and died, his death would be the result of idleness only.

Indeed? If he were overcome and fell alongside his furrow and died, would his death be the result of idleness only?

. . . We [12] hear therefore of the men (having worked). But what of the women? It is said, *Let neither man nor woman make any more work for the offering of the sanctuary* (Exod. 36:6). And what of the little ones? It is said, *So everyone* [13] *was restrained from bringing (ibid.).*

Said Rabbi Nathan: So long as Moses was engaged in the work of the Tabernacle he did not wish to take counsel with the rulers of Israel, and the rulers of Israel sat in silence, thinking, "Now Moses will need us." When they heard it proclaimed in the camp, saying, *For the stuff they had was sufficient* (Exod. 36:7), they cried: "Woe unto us that we had no part in the work of the Tabernacle!" So they arose and added a large gift of their own accord, as it is said, *And the rulers brought the onyx stones* (Exod. 35:27).[14]

HATE LORDSHIP: [15] what is that? This teaches that no man should put a crown on his head of his own accord; instead let others put it on him, as it is said, *Let another man praise thee, and not thine own mouth; a stranger, and not thine own lips* (Prov. 27:2).

Said Rabbi 'Aḳiba: Whoever exalts himself above the words of the Torah, to what may he be likened? To a carcass abandoned on the highway—every passerby puts his hand to his nose, turns away from it, and walks off; as it is said, *If thou hast done foolishly in lifting up thyself, or if thou hast planned devices, lay thy hand upon thy mouth* (Prov. 30:32).

Said Ben 'Azzai to him: "Interpret it in its context! If one wastes away over the words of the Torah, eats dried-out dates and wears soiled clothing and sits faithfully at the door of the Sages, every passerby says, 'Probably that's a fool!' But in the end thou wilt find the whole Torah at his command."

Rabbi Yose says: Get down [16] to come up and up to come down: Whoever exalts himself above the words of the Torah is in the end degraded; and whoever degrades himself for the sake of the words of the Torah is in the end exalted.[17]

AND SEEK NO INTIMACY WITH THE RULING POWERS: what is that? This teaches that one's name should not come to the attention of the ruling powers. For once his name comes to the attention of the ruling powers, they cast their eye upon him and slay him and take away all his property from him. How so? One's fellow sits in the market place and says: "May the Holy One, blessed be He, continue to be gracious to so-and-so. Today there came forth from his house a hundred oxen, a hundred sheep, and a hundred goats!" An official overhears him and goes and informs the hegemon. The hegemon forthwith has his house surrounded and takes away all his wealth from him. Of such friends the verse says, *He that blesseth his friend with a loud voice . . . it shall be counted a curse to him* (Prov. 27:14).

Another interpretation. SEEK NO INTIMACY WITH THE RULING POWERS.[18] One's fellow sits in the market place and says: "May the Holy One, blessed be He, continue to be gracious to so-and-so. Today he brought into his house so many *ḳor* [19] of wheat, so many *ḳor* of barley!" Brigands overhear him, come and surround his house, and take away all his wealth from him. On the following morning the man has nothing! Of such friends the verse says, *He that blesseth his friend with a loud voice,* etc.

Another interpretation. SEEK NO INTIMACY WITH THE RULING POWERS: what is that? This teaches that one should not think of saying "I am prince of the city," or "I am viceroy" [20]—for these rob Israel.

Another interpretation: One should not think of resorting to the ruling powers: albeit at first they open a door for him and escort him,[21] in the end it is fatal for him.

ABṬALYON SAYS: SAGES, WATCH YOUR WORDS LEST YE DECIDE SOMETHING NOT IN ACCORD WITH THE TEACHING OF THE TORAH, AND INCUR THE PENALTY OF EXILE AND BE CARRIED OFF TO A PLACE OF EVIL WATERS; AND YOUR DISCIPLES ALSO WHO COME AFTER YOU DECIDE IN YOUR NAME SOMETHING NOT IN ACCORD WITH THE TEACHING OF THE TORAH, AND THEY INCUR THE PENALTY OF EXILE AND BE CARRIED OFF TO A PLACE OF EVIL WATERS.[22]

What are the EVIL WATERS? Say thou: *And they mingled themselves with the nations, and learned their works* (Ps. 106: 35).[23]

Another interpretation: EVIL WATERS means just that.[24]

And some say: Lest they be carried off for heavy labor.[25]

CHAPTER 12

HILLEL AND SHAMMAI TOOK OVER FROM THEM.[1] HILLEL SAYS: BE OF THE DISCIPLES OF AARON, LOVING PEACE AND PURSUING PEACE, LOVING MANKIND AND DRAWING THEM TO THE TORAH.

HE USED TO SAY: A NAME MADE GREAT IS A NAME DESTROYED. AND HE THAT DOES NOT INCREASE, CEASES. AND HE THAT DOES NOT LEARN DESERVES TO DIE. AND HE THAT PUTS THE CROWN TO HIS OWN USE SHALL PERISH.

HE USED TO SAY: IF NOT I FOR MYSELF, WHO THEN? AND BEING FOR MYSELF, WHAT AM I? IF NOT NOW, WHEN?[2]

LOVING PEACE:[3] how so? This teaches that one should love peace in Israel between man and man the way Aaron loved peace in Israel between man and man, as it is said, *The law of truth was in his mouth, and unrighteousness was not found in his lips; he walked with Me in peace and uprightness, and did turn away many from iniquity* (Mal. 2:6).

Rabbi Me'ir says: Why does the verse say, *And did turn away many from iniquity?* For [4] when Aaron would walk along the road and meet an evil or wicked man, he would greet him. On the morrow if that man sought to commit a transgression, he would think: "Woe unto me! how shall I lift my eyes afterward and look upon Aaron? I should be ashamed before him, for he greeted me." And thus that man would refrain from transgression.

So, too, when two men had quarreled with each other, Aaron would go and sit down with one of them and say to him: "My son, mark what thy fellow is saying! He beats his breast and tears his clothing,[5] saying, 'Woe unto me! how shall I lift my eyes and look upon my fellow! I am ashamed before him, for I it is who treated him foully.'"

He would sit with him until he had removed all rancor from his heart, and then Aaron would go and sit with the other one and say to him: "My son, mark what thy fellow is saying! He beats his breast and tears his clothing,[5] saying, 'Woe unto me! how shall I lift my eyes and look upon my fellow! I am ashamed before him, for I it is who treated him foully.'"

He would sit with him until he had removed all rancor from his heart. And when the two men met each other, they would embrace and kiss each other. That is why (of Aaron's death) it is said, *They wept for Aaron thirty days, even all the house of Israel* (Num. 20:29).

Another interpretation Why did (all) Israel weep for Aaron thirty days [while for Moses only the men wept?] Because [Moses] rendered judgment strictly according to the truth; [but Aaron] [6] never said to a man, "Thou hast acted offensively," or to a woman, "Thou hast acted offensively." That is why it is said, *And all the house of Israel wept for him.* But of Moses, who reproved them with strong words, it is said, *And the men of Israel wept for Moses* (Deut. 34:8).

Moreover, how many thousands there were in Israel named Aaron! For had it not been for Aaron these children would not have come into the world.[7]

And some say: This is why it is said, *They wept for Aaron*

thirty days, even all the house of Israel—for who could see Moses,
our master, standing and weeping and himself not weep!

And some say: Who could see Eleazar and Phineas, the two
distinguished priests,[8] standing and weeping and himself not
weep!

At that time Moses begged for a death like Aaron's death: for he
saw Aaron's bier laid out with great honor,[9] and bands and bands
of ministering angels mourning him. Now was it in the presence
of anyone that he made the request? Nay, when he was by himself he made the request, but the Holy One, blessed be He, heard
his whispering. And how do we know that Moses begged for a
death like Aaron's death and that God heard his whispering? For
it is said, *Die in the mount whither thou goest up, and be gathered
unto thy people; as Aaron thy brother died in Mount Hor* (Deut.
32:50). Thus thou dost learn that Moses begged for a death like
Aaron's death.

At that time [10] He said to the angel of death: "Go, bring to
Me the soul of Moses."

The angel of death went and stood before him. "Moses," he
demanded, "give me thy soul."

Moses rebuked him and retorted: "Where I sit thou hast no
permission to stand! And thou sayest 'Give me thy soul'!" He
rebuked him and drove him off angrily.

Finally the Holy One, blessed be He, said to Moses: "Moses,
thou hast had enough of this world, for lo, the world to come
awaits thee: for thy place hath been ready for thee since the six
days of Creation"—as it is said, *And the Lord said, Behold a
place by Me, and thou shalt stand upon the rock* (Exod. 33:21).

Then the Holy One, blessed be He, took the soul of Moses and
put it in safekeeping under the throne of glory. And when He
took it, He took it only by means of a kiss, as it is said, *By the
mouth of the Lord* (Deut. 34:5).

Nor is the soul of Moses alone in safekeeping under the throne
of glory; rather the souls of all the righteous are in safekeeping
under the throne of glory, as it is said, *Yet the soul of my lord*

shall be bound in the bundle of life with the Lord thy God (I Sam. 25:29). Is the same perhaps true for the wicked? The verse says, *And the souls of thine enemies, them shall he sling out, as from the hollow*[11] *of a sling* (*ibid.*), for[12] they are tossed from place to place and know not on what to rest.[13] So too the souls of the wicked go roving[14] and roaming all over the universe not knowing on what to rest.

Again: the Holy One, blessed be He, said to the angel of death: "Go and bring to Me the soul of Moses."

He went to the dwelling place of Moses, searched for him, but could not find him. He went to the Great Sea and asked: "Has Moses come here?"

The Sea answered: "Since Israel passed through me I have seen nothing of him."

He went to the mountains and hills and asked them: "Has Moses come here?"

They answered: "Since Israel received the Torah at Mount Sinai we have seen no more of him."

He went to Sheol and Destruction and asked them: "Has Moses come here?"

They answered: "His name we have heard but himself we have not seen."

He went to the ministering angels and asked them: "Has Moses come here?"

They answered: *"God understandeth his way and He knoweth his place.*[15] God hath put him in safekeeping for life in the world to come and no creature knoweth (his whereabouts)"—as it is said, *But wisdom,*[16] *where shall it be found? and where is the place of understanding? Man knoweth not the price thereof; neither is it found in the land of the living. The deep saith: It is not in me; and the sea saith: It is not with me. . . . Destruction and Death say: We have heard a rumor thereof with our ears* (Job 28:13–15, 22).

Joshua also was sitting and worrying about Moses, until the Holy One, blessed be He, said to him: "Joshua, why art thou worried about Moses? *Moses My servant is dead"* (Josh. 1:2).[17]

PURSUING PEACE: how so? This teaches that one should pursue peace in Israel between man and man the way Aaron used to pursue peace in Israel between man and man. For it is said, *Depart from evil, and do good; seek peace, and pursue it* (Ps. 34: 15).

Rabbi Simeon ben Eleazar says: [18] If a man sits in his own place and is inactive, how can he pursue peace in Israel between man and man? Let him therefore go forth from his place and move around in the world and pursue peace in Israel, as it is said, *Seek peace and pursue it.* Now what is that? Seek it in thine own place, pursue it to another place.

So too the Holy One, blessed be He, made peace on high. And what is the peace which the Holy One, blessed be He, made on high? He did not name ten (angels) Gabriel, ten Michael, ten Uriel, ten Raphael, the way men name ten individuals Reuben, ten Simeon, ten Levi, ten Judah.[19] For had He acted the way men act, when He called for one of them, they would all have come before Him envious of each other. Instead He named one Gabriel, one Michael: when He calls for one of them, that one comes and stands before Him and He sends him whithersoever He pleases.

And how do we know that they revere one another and honor one another and are more humble than men? [20] For when they open their mouths and recite the Song,[21] one says to the other: "Begin thou, for thou art greater than I"; and the other says to the first: "Begin thou, for thou art greater than I." Not the way men do, where one says to the other: "I am greater than thou," and the other says to the first: "I am greater than thou."

And some say: Group by group the angels (recite), one group saying to the other: "Begin thou, for thou art greater than I"; for it is said, *And one* [22] *called unto another, and said* (Isa. 6: 3).[23]

LOVING MANKIND: how so? This teaches that one should love mankind and not hate mankind. For thus we find regarding the men of the generation of dispersion—because they loved one another [24] the Holy One, blessed be He, had no desire to wipe them out of the world; instead, He scattered them to the four corners of the earth. But as for the men of Sodom, because they hated one another the Holy One, blessed be He, wiped them out of this world and the world to come, as it is said, *Now the Men of Sodom were wicked and sinners against the Lord exceedingly* (Gen. 13:13).

Wicked toward one another.

Sinners refers to unchastity.

Against the Lord refers to the profaning of the Name.

Exceedingly, in that by their sins they had in mind (to rebel against God).[25]

Thus thou dost learn: Because they hated each other the Holy One, blessed be He, wiped them out of this world and the world to come.

AND DRAWING THEM TO THE TORAH: what is that? This teaches that one should bend men to [26] and lead them under the wings of the Shekinah the way Abraham our father used to bend men to and lead them under the wings of the Shekinah. And not Abraham alone did this, but Sarah as well; for it is said, *And Abram [27] took Sarai his wife, and Lot his brother's son, and all their substance that they had gathered, and the souls that they had made in Haran* (Gen. 12:5). Now, not all the inhabitants of the world together can create even a single gnat! How then does the verse say, *And the souls that they had made in Haran?* This teaches that the Holy One, blessed be He, accounted it to Abraham and Sarah as though they had made them.[28]

Even as no man shares in the reward of his fellow in this world,[29] so he does not share in the reward of his fellow in the world to come, as it is said, *And behold the tears of such as are oppressed, and they have no comforter; and on the side of their oppressors there is power, and they have no comforter* (Eccl. 4:1).

Why was *they have no comforter* said twice? (The first time) it refers to those people [30] who eat and drink and prosper in sons and daughters in this world, but in the world to come have nothing. (The second) *and they have no comforter* (refers to the following: In this world) if something is stolen from a person or if some relation of his dies, his sons and brothers come to comfort him: perhaps it will be so in the world to come as well? The verse says, *Yea, he hath neither son nor brother* (Eccl. 4: 8).

So, too, if one commits a transgression and begets a bastard son, they say to him: "Wretch! thou hast injured thyself, thou hast injured him." [31] For if that bastard wished to study Torah with those disciples who sit and study in Jerusalem, and if the bastard went along with them until they reached Ashdod, there he would have to stop. "Woe unto me!" he would cry, "had I not been a bastard child I might now sit and study together with the disciples with whom I studied till now. But because I am a bastard I cannot sit and study together with the disciples, for a bastard may not enter Jerusalem under any circumstance!" As it is said, *And a bastard will dwell in Ashdod, and I will cut off the pride of the Philistines* (Zech. 9:6).[32]

He used to say: IF NOT I FOR MYSELF, WHO THEN? If I do not lay up merit in my lifetime,[33] who will lay up merit for me?

AND BEING FOR MYSELF, WHAT AM I? If I do not lay up merit in my own behalf, who will lay up merit for me in my behalf? [34]

IF NOT NOW, WHEN? If I do not lay up merit in my lifetime, who will lay up merit for me after I am dead?

And so, too, it says, *For a living dog is better than a dead lion* (Eccl. 9: 4).

For a living dog is better refers to the wicked one who is alive in this world.

Than a dead lion—(better) even than Abraham, Isaac, and Jacob: for they dwell in the dust.[35]

Another interpretation. *For a living dog is better* refers to the wicked who is alive in this world: [36] if he repents, the Holy One, blessed be He, receives him; but the righteous, once he dies, can no longer lay up additional merit.

He [37] used to say: If thou wilt come to My house, I shall come to thy house; to the place My heart loves, My feet lead Me.

If thou wilt come to My house, I shall come to thy house: what is that? It refers to those men who early in the morning and in the evening are off to the synagogues and study houses: them the Holy One, blessed be He, blesses with [38] the world to come, even as it is said, *In every place where I cause My name to be mentioned I will come unto thee and bless thee* (Exod. 20:21).

To the place My heart loves, My feet lead Me: what is that? It is a reference to those men who leave their silver and gold and go up on pilgrimage to greet the presence of the Shekinah in the Temple: the Holy One, blessed be He, watches over them while they are in their camps, as it is said, *Neither shall any man covet thy land, when thou goest up to appear before the Lord thy God* (Exod. 34:24).

He used to say: If I'm here, all's here; if I'm not here, who's here? [39] SEARCH [40] IT, SEARCH IT AGAIN, FOR EVERYTHING'S IN IT. AND IN WHATEVER THERE IS, ACCORDING TO THE PAINSTAKING, THE REWARD. [41]

Once [42] Hillel the Elder was walking along the road and met men carrying wheat. "At how much a *se'ah?*" [43] he asked them.

"Two denar," they replied.

Then he met others; he asked them: "At how much a se'ah?"

"Three denar," they said.

"But the former said two!" he protested.

"Stupid Babylonian!" they retorted, "knowest thou not that 'according to the painstaking is the reward'!"

"Wretched fools!" he answered, "is this the way you retort to my question?"

What did Hillel the Elder do with them? He brought them to a correct understanding. [44]

MOREOVER HE ONCE SAW A SKULL FLOATING ON THE FACE OF THE WATERS. HE SAID TO IT: FOR DROWNING OTHERS THOU WAST DROWNED; AND THEY THAT DROWNED THEE SHALL BE DROWNED. [45]

Moreover in the Babylonian tongue [46] he said four things: A NAME MADE GREAT IS A NAME DESTROYED. AND HE THAT DOES NOT ATTEND UPON THE SAGES DESERVES TO DIE. AND HE THAT DOES NOT

INCREASE, LOSES. AND HE THAT PUTS THE CROWN TO HIS OWN USE SHALL
UTTERLY PERISH.

A NAME MADE GREAT IS A NAME DESTROYED: how so? This teaches
that one's name should not come to the attention of the government. For once a man's name comes to the attention of the
government, the end is that it casts its eye upon him, slays him,
and takes away all his wealth from him.[47]

AND HE THAT DOES NOT ATTEND UPON THE SAGES DESERVES TO DIE:
what is that? The story is told:

There was once a certain man of Bet Ramah [48] who cultivated
a saintly manner. Rabban Johanan ben Zakkai sent a disciple to
examine him. The disciple went and found him taking oil and
putting it on a pot-range, and taking it from the pot-range and
pouring it into a porridge of beans.

"What art thou doing?" the disciple asked him.

"I am an important [49] priest," he replied, "and I eat heave
offering [50] in a state of purity."

The disciple asked: "Is this range unclean or clean?"

Said the priest: "Have we then anything in the Torah about a
range being unclean? On the contrary, the Torah speaks only of
an oven being unclean, as it is said, *Whatsoever is in* [51] *it shall
be unclean*" (Lev. 11:33).

Said the disciple to him: "Even as the Torah speaks of an oven
being unclean, so the Torah speaks of a range being unclean, as it
is said, *Whether oven or range for pots, it shall be broken in
pieces, they are unclean*" (Lev. 11:35). The disciple continued: "If
this is how thou hast been conducting thyself, thou hast never in
thy life eaten clean heave offerings!" [52]

AND HE THAT DOES NOT INCREASE, LOSES: how so? This teaches
that if a man studies one or two or three tractates and does not
add to them, he forgets the first ones in the end.[53]

AND HE THAT PUTS THE CROWN TO HIS OWN USE SHALL UTTERLY
PERISH: what is that: Whoever makes use of the tetragrammaton
has no share in the world to come.[54]

CHAPTER 13

MAKE THY STUDY OF TORAH A FIXED PRACTICE: how so? This teaches that if one has heard something from the mouth of a sage in the study house, he is not to treat it casually but to treat it attentively.[2] And what a man learns, let him practice himself and then teach others that they may practice it, as it is said, *That ye may learn them, then observe to do them* (Deut. 5:1). And so too of Ezra it says, *For he had set his heart to seek the law of the Lord, and to do it,* and afterward, *And to teach in Israel statutes and ordinances* (Ezra 7:10).[3]

SAY LITTLE AND DO MUCH:[4] what is that? This teaches that the righteous say little and do much, but the wicked say much and do not do even a little.

And how do we know that the righteous say little and do much? For thus we find concerning Abraham, our father, who said to the angels: "You shall eat bread with me today"—as it is said, *And I will fetch a morsel of bread, and stay ye your heart* (Gen. 18:5). But in the end see what Abraham did for the ministering angels: for he went and prepared for them three oxen and nine measures of fine meal. And how do we know that he prepared for them nine measures of fine meal? For it is said, *And Abraham hastened into the tent unto Sarah, and said: Make ready quickly three measures of fine meal* (Gen. 18:6): *Three* literally. *Meal* makes six. *Fine* makes nine.

And how do we know that he prepared three oxen for them? For it is said, *And Abraham ran unto the herd and fetched a calf tender and good* (Gen. 18:7): *The herd*—one. *A calf*—two. *Tender*—three. And some say: *Good*—four.[5]

And he gave it unto the servant; and he hastened to dress it (*ibid.*) : he gave it to Ishmael his son to train him in the practice of pious works.

So too the Holy One, blessed be He, said little and did much, as it is said, *And the Lord said unto Abram: Know of a surety that thy seed shall be a stranger in a land that is not theirs, and shall serve them, and they shall afflict them four hundred years; and also that nation, whom they shall serve, will I punish; and afterward shall they come out with great substance* (Gen. 15: 13 f.) : He promised him no more than (punishment) by means of His *D* and *N* [6] name; but in the end, when the Holy One, blessed be He, requited Israel's enemies, He did so in fact by means of His seventy-two letter name,[7] as it is said, *Or hath God assayed to go and take Him a nation from the midst of another nation, by trials, by signs, and by wonders . . . and by great terrors* (Deut. 4: 34).[8]

Thus thou dost learn that when He requites the enemies of Israel, He does so indeed by means of His seventy-two letter name.

And how do we know that the wicked say much and do not do even a little? For thus we find concerning Ephron, who said to Abraham: *A piece of land worth four hundred shekels of silver, what is that betwixt me and thee* (Gen. 23: 15). But in the end when he weighed the silver to him, *And Abraham hearkened unto Ephron; and Abraham weighed to Ephron,* etc. (Gen. 23: 16).

AND RECEIVE ALL MEN WITH A CHEERFUL COUNTENANCE: [9] what is that? This teaches that if one gives his fellow all the good gifts in the world with a downcast face, Scripture accounts it to him as though he had given him naught. But if he receives his fellow with a cheerful countenance, even though he gives him naught, Scripture accounts it to him as though he had given him all the good gifts in the world.

CHAPTER 14

RABBAN JOHANAN BEN ZAKKAI TOOK OVER FROM HILLEL AND SHAMMAI.[1]

Eighty[2] disciples Hillel the Elder had. Thirty of them were worthy to have the Shekinah rest upon them as upon Moses, our master, but their generation was unworthy of it.[3] Thirty of them were worthy to intercalate the year,[4] and twenty were middling. The greatest of them all was Jonathan ben Uzziel; the least of them all was Rabban Johanan ben Zakkai.[5]

They tell of Rabban Johanan ben Zakkai that he did not neglect Scripture or Mishnah, Gemara, Halakha, Agada, or Supplements,[6] the subtleties of Scripture or the subtleties of the Scribes,[7] or any of the Sages' rules of interpretation [8]—not a single thing in the Torah did he neglect to study, confirming the statement, *That I may cause those that love me to inherit substance, and that I may fill their treasuries* (Prov. 8:21).

HE USED TO SAY: IF THOU HAST WROUGHT MUCH IN THY STUDY OF TORAH, TAKE NO CREDIT FOR THYSELF, FOR TO THIS END WAST THOU CREATED:[9] for men were created only on condition that they study Torah.

FIVE DISCIPLES DID RABBAN JOHANAN BEN ZAKKAI HAVE, for each of whom he had a name.

ELIEZER BEN HYRCANUS he called "PLASTERED CISTERN WHICH LOSES NOT A DROP, pitch-coated flask which keeps its wine."

JOSHUA BEN HANANIAH he called "Threefold cord not quickly broken." [10]

YOSE THE PRIEST he called "The generation's SAINT."

SIMEON BEN NATHANEL he called "Oasis [11] in the desert which holds onto its water." [12]

And ELEAZAR BEN 'ARAK he called "Overflowing stream and EVERFLOWING STREAM whose waters ever flow and overflow"—confirming the statement, *Let thy springs be dispersed abroad, and courses of water in the streets* (Prov. 5:16). Happy [13] the disciple whose master praises him and testifies to his gifts!

HE USED TO SAY: IF ALL THE SAGES OF ISRAEL WERE IN ONE SCALE OF THE BALANCE AND RABBI ELIEZER BEN HYRCANUS WERE IN THE OTHER SCALE, HE WOULD OUTWEIGH THEM ALL.

ABBA SAUL SAYS IN HIS NAME: IF ALL THE SAGES OF ISRAEL WERE IN ONE SCALE OF THE BALANCE, AND EVEN IF RABBI ELIEZER BEN HYRCANUS WERE WITH THEM, AND RABBI ELEAZAR BEN ʿARAḴ WERE IN THE OTHER SCALE, HE WOULD OUTWEIGH THEM ALL.[14]

RABBAN JOHANAN SAID TO THEM: "GO OUT AND SEE WHICH IS THE GOOD WAY TO WHICH A MAN SHOULD CLEAVE so that through it he might enter the world to come."

RABBI ELIEZER came in and said: "A LIBERAL EYE."

RABBI JOSHUA came in and said: "A GOOD COMPANION."

RABBI YOSE came in and said: "A GOOD NEIGHBOR, a good impulse, and a good wife."

RABBI SIMEON (came in and) said: "FORESIGHT."

RABBI ELEAZAR came in and said: "WHOLEHEARTEDNESS [15] toward Heaven [and wholeheartedness toward the commandments] [16] and wholeheartedness toward mankind."

SAID RABBAN JOHANAN TO THEM: "I PREFER THE WORDS OF RABBI ELEAZAR BEN ʿARAḴ TO YOUR WORDS, FOR IN HIS WORDS YOUR WORDS ARE INCLUDED." [17]

HE SAID TO THEM: "GO OUT AND SEE WHICH IS THE EVIL WAY WHICH A MAN SHOULD SHUN, so that he might enter the world to come."

RABBI ELIEZER came in and said: "A GRUDGING EYE."

RABBI JOSHUA came in and said: "AN EVIL COMPANION."

RABBI YOSE came in and said: "AN EVIL NEIGHBOR, an evil impulse, and an evil wife."

RABBI SIMEON came in and said: "BORROWING AND NOT REPAYING; FOR HE THAT BORROWS FROM MAN IS AS ONE WHO BORROWS FROM GOD, AS IT IS SAID, THE WICKED BORROWETH, AND PAYETH NOT; BUT THE RIGHTEOUS DEALETH GRACIOUSLY, AND GIVETH" (Ps. 37:21).

RABBI ELEAZAR came in and said: "MEAN HEARTEDNESS toward Heaven and mean heartedness toward the commandments and mean heartedness toward mankind."

AND RABBAN JOHANAN SAID TO THEM: "ᵀ PREFER THE WORDS OF

RABBI ELEAZAR TO YOUR WORDS, FOR IN HIS WORDS YOUR WORDS ARE INCLUDED." [18]

When Rabban Johanan ben Zakkai's son died, his disciples came in to comfort him. Rabbi Eliezer entered, sat down before him, and said to him: "Master, by thy leave, may I say something to thee?"

"Speak," he replied.

Rabbi Eliezer said: "Adam had a son who died, yet he allowed himself to be comforted concerning him. And how do we know that he allowed himself to be comforted concerning him? For it is said, *And Adam knew his wife again* (Gen. 4:25). Thou, too, be thou comforted."

Said Rabban Johanan to him: "Is it not enough that I grieve over my own, that thou remindest me of the grief of Adam?"

Rabbi Joshua entered and said to him: "By thy leave, may I say something to thee?"

"Speak," he replied.

Rabbi Joshua said: "Job had sons and daughters, all of whom died in one day, and he allowed himself to be comforted concerning them. Thou too, be thou comforted. And how do we know that Job was comforted? For it is said, *The Lord gave, and the Lord hath taken away; blessed be the name of the Lord*" (Job 1:21).

Said Rabban Johanan to him: "Is it not enough that I grieve over my own, that thou remindest me of the grief of Job?"

Rabbi Yose entered and sat down before him; he said to him: "Master, by thy leave, may I say something to thee?"

"Speak," he replied.

Rabbi Yose said: "Aaron had two grown sons, both of whom died in one day, yet he allowed himself to be comforted for them, as it is said, *And Aaron held his peace* (Lev. 10:3)—silence is no other than consolation. Thou too, therefore, be thou comforted."

Said Rabban Johanan to him: "Is it not enough that I grieve over my own, that thou remindest me of the grief of Aaron?"

Rabbi Simeon entered and said to him: "Master, by thy leave, may I say something to thee?"

"Speak," he replied.

Rabbi Simeon said: "King David had a son who died, yet he allowed himself to be comforted. Thou too, therefore, be thou comforted. And how do we know that David was comforted? For it is said, *And David comforted Bath-Sheba his wife, and went in unto her, and lay with her; and she bore a son, and called his name Solomon* (II Sam. 12:24). Thou too, master, be thou comforted."

Said Rabban Johanan to him: "Is it not enough that I grieve over my own, that thou remindest me of the grief of King David?"

Rabbi Eleazar ben 'Arak entered. As soon as Rabban Johanan saw him, he said to his servant: "Take my clothing and follow me to the bathhouse,[19] for he is a great man and I shall be unable to resist him."

Rabbi Eleazar entered, sat down before him, and said to him: "I shall tell thee a parable: to what may this be likened? To a man with whom the king deposited some object. Every single day the man would weep and cry out, saying: 'Woe unto me! when shall I be quit of this trust in peace?' Thou too, master, thou hadst a son: he studied the Torah, the Prophets, the Holy Writings, he studied Mishnah, Halakha, Agada,[20] and he departed from the world without sin. And thou shouldst be comforted when thou hast returned thy trust unimpaired." [21]

Said Rabban Johanan to him: "Rabbi [22] Eleazar, my son, thou hast comforted me the way men should give comfort!"

When they left his presence, Rabbi Eleazar said: "I shall go to Emmaus,[23] a beautiful place with beautiful and delightful waters."

But they said: "We shall go to Jamnia,[24] where there are scholars in abundance who love the Torah."

Because he went to Emmaus—a beautiful place with beautiful and delightful waters—his name was made least in the Torah.[25] Because they went to Jamnia—where there are scholars in abundance who love the Torah—their names were magnified in the Torah.

CHAPTER 15

AND EACH OF THEM [1] SAID THREE THINGS.

RABBI ELIEZER SAYS: LET THE HONOR OF THY FELLOW BE AS DEAR TO THEE AS THINE OWN. BE NOT EASILY ANGERED. REPENT ONE DAY BEFORE THY DEATH.[2]

LET THE HONOR OF THY FELLOW BE AS DEAR TO THEE AS THINE OWN: how so? This teaches that even as one looks out for his own honor, so should he look out for his fellow's honor. And even as no man wishes that his own honor be held in ill repute, so should he wish that the honor of his fellow shall not be held in ill repute.[3]

Another interpretation. LET THE HONOR OF THY FELLOW BE AS DEAR TO THEE AS THINE OWN: For example, (even) when a man has had a million and then all his wealth is taken away, let him not discredit himself [4] over so much as a pĕruṭah's worth.[5]

BE NOT EASILY ANGERED: what is that? This teaches that one should be patient like Hillel the Elder and not short tempered like Shammai the Elder.

What was this patience of Hillel the Elder? The story is told: [6]

Once two men decided to make a wager of four hundred zuz with each other. They said: "Whoever can put Hillel into a rage gets the four hundred zuz."

One of them went (to attempt it). Now that day was a Sabbath eve, toward dusk, and Hillel was washing his head. The man came and knocked on his door. "Where's Hillel? Where's Hillel?" he cried.

Hillel got into a cloak and came out to meet him. "My son," he said, "what is it?" [7]

The man replied: "I need to ask about a certain matter." [8]

"Ask," Hillel said.

The man asked: "Why are the eyes of the Tadmorites bleary?"

"Because," said Hillel, "they make their homes on the desert sands which the winds come and blow into their eyes. That is why their eyes are bleary."

The man went off, waited a while, and returned and knocked on his door. "Where's Hillel?" he cried, "where's Hillel?"

Hillel got into a cloak and came out. "My son," he said, "what is it?"

The man replied: "I need to ask about a certain matter."

"Ask," Hillel said.

The man asked: "Why are the Africans' feet flat?"

"Because they dwell by watery marshes," said Hillel, "and all the time they walk in water. That is why their feet are flat."

The man went off, waited a while, and returned and knocked on the door. "Where's Hillel?" he cried, "where's Hillel?"

Hillel got into a cloak and came out. "What is it thou wishest to ask?" he inquired.

"I need to ask about some matter," the man said.

"Ask," Hillel said to him. In his cloak he sat down before him and said: "What is it?"

Said the man: "Is this how princes [9] reply! May there be no more like thee in Israel!"

"God forbid!" Hillel said, "tame thy spirit! What dost thou wish?"

The man asked: "Why are the heads of Babylonians long?"

"My son," Hillel answered, "thou hast raised an important question. Since there are no skillful midwives there, when the infant is born, slaves and maidservants tend it on their laps. That is why the heads of Babylonians are long. Here,[10] however, there are skillful midwives, and when the infant is born it is taken care of in a cradle and its head is rubbed. That is why the heads of Palestinians are round."

"Thou hast put me out of four hundred zuz!" the man exclaimed.

Said Hillel to him: "Better that thou lose four hundred zuz because of Hillel than that Hillel lose his temper."

What was this impatience of Shammai the Elder? [11] The story is told:

A certain· man once stood before Shammai and said to him: "Master, how many Torahs have you?"

"Two," Shammai replied, "one written and one oral."

Said the man: "The written one I am prepared to accept, the oral one I am not prepared to accept."

Shammai rebuked him and dismissed him in a huff.

He came before Hillel and said to him: "Master, how many Torahs were given?"

"Two," Hillel replied, "one written and one oral."

Said the man: "The written one I am prepared to accept, the oral one I am not prepared to accept."

"My son," Hillel said to him, "sit down."

He wrote out the alphabet for him (and pointing to one of the letters) asked him: "What is this?"

"It is *'aleph*," the man replied.

Said Hillel: "This is not *'aleph* but *beṯ*. What is that?" he continued.

The man answered: "It is *beṯ*."

"This is not *beṯ*," said Hillel, "but *gimmel*." [12]

(In the end) [13] Hillel said to him: "How dost thou know that this is *'aleph* and this *beṯ* and this *gimmel*? Only because so our ancestors of old handed it down to us that this is *'aleph* and this *beṯ* and this *gimmel*. Even as thou hast taken this in good faith, so take the other in good faith."

A certain heathen [14] once passed behind a synagogue and heard a child reciting: *And these are the garments which they shall make: a breastplate, and an ephod, and a robe* (Exod. 28:4). He came before Shammai and asked him: "Master, all this honor, whom is it for?"

Shammai said to him: "For the High Priest, who stands and serves at the altar."

Said the heathen: "Convert me on condition that thou appoint me High Priest, so I might serve at the altar."

"Is there no priest in Israel," Shammai exclaimed, "and have we no High Priests to stand and serve in high priesthood at the altar, that a paltry proselyte who has come with naught but his staff and bag should go and serve in high priesthood!" He rebuked him and dismissed him in a huff.

The heathen then came to Hillel and said to him: "Master, convert me on condition that thou appoint me High Priest, so that I might stand and serve at the altar."

"Sit down," Hillel said to him, "and I will tell thee something. If one wishes to greet a king of flesh and blood, is it not right that he learn how to make his entrances and exits?"

"Indeed," the heathen replied.

"Thou wishest to greet the King of kings of kings, the Holy One, blessed be He: is it not all the more right that thou learn how to enter into the Holy of Holies, how to fix the lights, how to approach the altar, how to set the table, how to prepare the row of wood?"

Said the heathen: "Do what seems best in thine eyes."

First Hillel wrote out the alphabet for him and taught it to him. Then he taught him the book of Leviticus.[15] And the heathen went on studying until he got to the verse, *And the common man that draweth nigh shall be put to death* (Num. 1:51). Forthwith, of his own accord, he reasoned by inference as follows: "If Israel, who were called children of God and of whom the Shekinah said, *And ye shall be unto Me a kingdom of priests, and a holy nation* (Exod. 19:6), were nevertheless warned by Scripture, *And the common man that draweth nigh shall be put to death,* all the more I, a paltry proselyte, come with naught but my bag!" Thereupon that proselyte was reconciled of his own accord.

He came to Hillel the Elder and said to him: "May all the blessings of the Torah rest upon thy head! For hadst thou been like Shammai the Elder I might never have entered the community of Israel. The impatience of Shammai the Elder well nigh caused me to perish [16] in this world and the world to come. Thy patience has brought me to the life of this world and the one to come."

It is said: To that proselyte were born two sons; one he named Hillel and the other he named Gamaliel;[17] and they used to be called "proselytes of Hillel."

REPENT ONE DAY BEFORE THY DEATH.[18] Rabbi Eliezer was asked by his disciples: "Does, then, a man know on what day he will die, that he should know when to repent?"

"All the more," he replied; "let him repent today lest he die on the morrow; let him repent on the morrow lest he die the day after: and thus all his days will be spent in repentance."

Rabbi Yose bar Judah says in the name of Rabbi Judah son of Rabbi Il'ai who said it in the name of Rabbi Il'ai his father who said it in the name of Rabbi Eliezer the Great:[19] REPENT ONE DAY BEFORE THY DEATH. KEEP WARM AT THE FIRE OF THE SAGES. BEWARE OF THEIR GLOWING COAL LEST THOU BE SCORCHED: FOR THEIR BITE IS THE BITE OF A JACKAL AND THEIR STING THE STING OF A SCORPION— MOREOVER ALL THEIR WORDS ARE LIKE COALS OF FIRE.[20]

CHAPTER 16

RABBI JOSHUA SAYS: A GRUDGING EYE, EVIL IMPULSE, AND HATRED OF MANKIND PUT A MAN OUT OF THE WORLD.[1]

A GRUDGING EYE: what is that? This teaches that even as a man looks out for his own home, so should he look out for the home of his fellow. And even as no man wishes that his own wife and children be held in ill repute, so should no man wish that his fellow's wife and his fellow's children be held in ill repute.[2]

Another interpretation. A GRUDGING EYE: what is that? That one should not begrudge another his learning.

There was once a certain man who begrudged his companion his learning. His life was cut short and he passed away.

THE EVIL IMPULSE: what is that? It is said:

By thirteen years is the evil impulse older than the good impulse. In the mother's womb the evil impulse begins to develop and is born with a person. If he begins to profane the Sabbath, it does not prevent him; if he commits murder, it does not prevent him; if he goes off to another heinous transgression,[3] it does not prevent him.

Thirteen years later the good impulse is born. When he profanes the Sabbath, it reprimands him: "Wretch! lo it says, *Every one that profaneth it shall surely be put to death*" (Exod. 31:14). If he goes to commit murder, it reprimands him: "Wretch! lo it says, *Whoso sheddeth man's blood, by man shall his blood be shed*" (Gen. 9:6). If he goes off to another heinous transgression, it reprimands him: "Wretch! lo it says, *Both the adulterer and the adulteress shall surely be put to death*" (Lev. 20:10).

When a man bestirs himself and goes off to some unchastity, all his limbs obey him, for the evil impulse is king over his two hundred and forty-eight limbs. When he goes off to some good deed, all his limbs begin to drag. For the evil impulse within man is monarch over his two hundred and forty-eight limbs, while the good impulse is like a captive in prison, as it is said, *For out of prison he came forth to be king* (Eccl. 4:14), that is to say, the good impulse.

And some say: The verse in Ecclesiastes refers to Joseph the righteous.[4] When that wicked woman[5] came along she kept outraging him by her words. She said to him: "I shall shut thee up in prison!"

He answered: *"The Lord looseth the prisoners"* (Ps. 146:7).

She said to him: "I shall put out thine eyes!"

He answered: *"The Lord openeth the eyes of the blind"* (Ps. 146:8).

"I shall make thee to stoop!" she said.

"The Lord raiseth up them that are bowed down" (*ibid.*), he retorted.

"I shall fill thee with wickedness!" she said.

"The Lord loveth the righteous" [6] (*ibid.*), he retorted.

She said to him: "I shall make thee a pagan!" [7]

He answered: *"The Lord preserveth the strangers"* (Ps. 146:9). Finally he said: *"How then can I do this great wickedness?"* (Gen. 39:9).

And do not be astonished at Joseph the righteous, for lo, there was (the case of) Rabbi Zadok, the leader of his generation. When he was taken captive to Rome, a certain matron acquired him and sent a beautiful maidservant to him. As soon as he saw her, he turned his eyes to the wall so as not to look upon her. And all night he sat studying. In the morning the maidservant went and complained to her mistress. "I would rather die," she cried, "than be given to this man." The mistress sent for him and asked him: "Why didst thou not do with this woman as men generally do?"

"Now what could I do?" he pleaded; "I am of a family of high priests,[8] I come from a distinguished family. I thought: If I come to her I shall bring bastards into Israel!" [9]

When she heard what he said, she gave orders that he be sent off in great honor.

And do not be astonished at Rabbi Zadok, for lo, there was (the case of) Rabbi 'Aḳiba, greater than he. When he went to Rome, he was slandered [10] before a certain hegemon. He sent two beautiful women to him. They were bathed and anointed and outfitted like brides. And all night they kept thrusting themselves at him, this one saying "Turn to me," and that one saying "Turn to me." But he sat there [11] in disgust and would not turn to them. In the morning they went off and complained to the hegemon and said to him: "We would rather die than be given to this man!"

The hegemon sent for him and asked: "Now why didst thou not do with these women as men generally do with women? Are they not beautiful? Are they not human beings like thyself? Did not He who created thee create them?" [12]

"What could I do?" Rabbi 'Aḳiba answered; "I was overcome by their breath because of the forbidden meats [13] they ate!"

And do not be astonished at Rabbi 'Aḳiba, for lo, there was (the case of) Rabbi Eliezer the Great,[14] greater than he. Now he raised his sister's daughter for thirteen years, and she slept with him in

the same bed until the signs of her puberty appeared. Then he said
to her: "Go now and be wedded to a man."

Said she: "Is not thy handmaid a servant to wash the feet of
thy disciples?" [15]

"My child," he declared, "I am already an old man. Go now
and be wedded to a young man thine own age."

"Have I not already told thee," she insisted, "is not thy handmaid a servant to wash the feet of thy disciples?"

When he heard what she said, asking her permission [16] he betrothed her and came to her.[17]

Rabbi Reuben ben Aṣtroboli says: How can a man escape from
the evil impulse within him? For the first seminal drop a man
puts into a woman is the evil impulse! [18] And the evil impulse lies
verily at the opening of the heart, as it is said, *Sin coucheth at the
door* [19] (Gen. 4:7). In [20] the case of a human being, while the infant is still in his cradle, the evil impulse says to him: "There's a
man who wants to kill thee!", and the infant gets an urge to
pull him by his hair.[21] When an infant still in his cradle puts his
hand on a serpent or scorpion and is stung, it is brought on only
by the evil impulse within him. When he puts his hand on glowing coals and is scorched, it is brought on only by the evil impulse within him. For it is the evil impulse which drives him
headlong.[22] But come and look at a kid or lamb—as soon as it
sees a well it starts back! For there is no evil impulse in beasts.

Rabbi Simeon ben Eleazar says: Let me tell thee by way of
parable to what this may be compared. The evil impulse is like
iron which one holds in a flame. So long as it is in the flame one
can make of it any implement he pleases. So too the evil impulse:
its only remedy is in the words of the Torah, for they are like
fire, as it is said, *If thine enemy be hungry, give him bread to
eat, and if he be thirsty, give him water to drink: for thou wilt
heap coals of fire upon his head, and the Lord will reward thee*
(Prov. 25:21 f.)—read not *will reward thee* (*yĕšallem laḵ*) but
will put him at peace with thee (*yašlimennu laḵ*).

Rabbi Judah the Prince says: I shall tell thee a parable; to what
may this be likened? With the evil impulse it is as when two men

enter an inn and one of them is seized as a brigand. When asked, "Who is with thee?" he could say, "No one is with me." Instead he decides: "Since I am to be slain, let my companion be slain along with me." So, too, the evil impulse says: "Since all hope for me is lost in the world to come, I shall destroy the whole body." [23]

Said Rabbi Simeon ben Yoḥai: How do we know that Israel shall never see the inside of Gehenna? A parable is told as to what this may be likened: To a king of flesh and blood who had an inferior field. Some men came along and rented it at ten kor of wheat per year. They fertilized it, tilled it, watered it, cleared it —and harvested from it no more than one kor of wheat for the year.

"What is this?" the king demanded.

"Our lord, the king!" they cried, "thou knowest that from the field which thou didst give us, thou didst harvest naught at first. And now that we have fertilized it and cleared it and watered it, we harvested from it at least one kor of wheat!"

So shall Israel plead before the Holy One, blessed be He: Master of the Universe, Thou knowest [24] that the evil impulse stirs us up—as it is said, *For He knoweth our impulse* (Ps. 103:14).[25]

AND HATRED OF MANKIND: what is that? This teaches that no man should think of saying, "Love the Sages but hate the disciples"; or "Love the disciples but hate the *'am ha-'areṣ*." [26] On the contrary, love all these. But hate the sectarians,[27] apostates, and informers; and so said David: *Do I not hate them, O Lord, that hate Thee? And do I not strive with those that rise up against Thee? I hate them with utmost hatred; I count them mine enemies* (Ps. 139:21 f.).

But does it not say, *But thou shalt love thy neighbor as thyself: I am the Lord* (Lev. 19:18): and why is that? [28] Because I [the Lord] [29] have created him.[30]

Indeed! if he acts as thy people do, thou shalt love him; but if not, thou shalt not love him.[31]

Rabbi Simeon ben Eleazar says: Under solemn oath [32] was this statement pronounced,[33] *But thou shalt love thy neighbor as thyself:* (for) I the Lord have created him (cf. Isa. 45:8)—if thou lovest him, I am faithful to reward thee in goodly measure; but if not, I am the judge to punish.[34]

CHAPTER 17

RABBI YOSE SAYS: LET THY FELLOW'S PROPERTY BE AS DEAR TO THEE AS THINE OWN. MAKE THYSELF FIT FOR THE STUDY OF TORAH, FOR IT WILL NOT BE THINE BY INHERITANCE. LET ALL THY ACTIONS BE FOR THE SAKE OF HEAVEN.[1]

LET THY FELLOW'S PROPERTY BE AS DEAR TO THEE AS THINE OWN:] how so? This teaches that even as one has regard for his own property, so should he have regard for his fellow's property; and even as no man wishes that his own property be held in ill repute, so should he wish that his fellow's property shall not be held in ill repute.[2]

Another interpretation. LET THY FELLOW'S PROPERTY BE AS DEAR TO THEE AS THINE OWN: how so? When a scholar comes to thee saying, "Teach me," if it is in thy power to teach, teach him. Otherwise, send him away at once and do not take his money from him, as it is said, *Say not unto thy neighbor, Go, and come again, and tomorrow I will give; when thou hast it by thee* (Prov. 3:28).[3]

MAKE THYSELF FIT FOR THE STUDY OF TORAH, FOR IT WILL NOT BE THINE BY INHERITANCE: what is that? When Moses, our master, perceived that in his sons was no Torah, that they might be able to succeed him as leaders, he stood up in his cloak to pray. "Master of the Universe," he said, "let me know who shall come in and who shall go out at the head of all this people"—as it is said, *And Moses spoke unto the Lord, saying: Let the Lord, the God of the spirits of all flesh, set a man over the congregation, who may go out before them, and who may come in before them* [4] (Num. 27:15 ff.).

Said the Holy One, blessed be He, to Moses: *"Moses, take thee Joshua"* (Num. 27:18).

The Holy One, blessed be He, said to Moses: "Go and act as

the interpreter for him and let him address in thy presence the great ones of Israel." [5]

In that hour Moses said to Joshua: "Joshua, this people which I am handing over to thee, not goats but kids I hand over to thee, not sheep but lambs I hand over to thee, for they have not yet had much practice in the commandments and they are not yet become goats and sheep." As it is said, *If thou know not, O thou fairest among women, go thy way forth by the footsteps of the flock and feed thy kids beside the shepherds' tents* (Cant. 1:8).

One time as Rabban Johanan ben Zakkai was walking in the market place he saw a girl picking up barley grains from under the feet of Arab cattle. "My child," he asked her, "who art thou?" She did not answer.

Again he asked her: "My child, who art thou?" But she would not answer. Finally she said to him: "Wait one moment." She covered herself with her hair [6] and sat down before him. "Master," she said, "I am the daughter of Naḳdimon ben Gorion."

"My child," he asked, "the wealth of thy father's house, where is it?"

"Master," she replied, "is this not how the proverb goes in Jerusalem: 'Your wealth will keep if you don't keep it.' "—And some say: ('Your wealth will keep) if you give alms.' [7]—

"And your father-in-law's," he asked, "where is that wealth?"

"Master," she said, "the one went down and dragged the other down with it." [8]

Thereupon Rabban Johanan ben Zakkai said to his disciples: "All my life I've read this verse, *If thou know not, O thou fairest among women, go thy way forth by the footsteps of the flock,* and not understood what it meant, and now I come along and learn what the meaning is: That Israel has been surrendered to the meanest of peoples, and not merely to a mean people but to their cattle dung!"

Moreover, she said to him: "Master, dost thou remember when thou didst sign my marriage deed?" [9]

"Indeed!" he answered. "By the Temple service!" he exclaimed to his disciples, "I signed this girl's marriage deed and it read, 'A million gold denar in Tyrian denar.' In the prosperous days of the household of this girl's father, they did not go from their home to the Temple unless woolen carpets were laid for them to walk on!"

A young girl was once taken captive along with her ten maidservants, and a certain Greek bought her. And she was brought up as part of his household. One day as he gave her pitcher to her and said, "Go out and bring me water," one of her maidservants arose and took it from her. "What is this?" he demanded.

"By the life of thy head, master!" she declared, "I was one of five hundred maidservants of this girl's mother!"

When he heard these words he set the girl free along with her ten maidservants.

Another story. A young girl was once taken captive and a certain Greek bought her. And she was brought up as part of his household. There appeared to him the spirit [10] of dreams and said: "Send this girl away from thy house."

Said his wife to him: "Do not send her away."

Once again appeared the spirit of dreams and said: "If thou dost not send her away I shall kill thee."

He thereupon sent her away.

But he followed behind her. "I will go," he said to himself, "and see what will be the end of this girl."

As she was walking along the highway she grew thirsty; so she stepped down to drink water from a spring. As soon as she put her hand on the wall a serpent attacked her and bit her, and she died. And she lay floating on the face of the water. He came down and lifted her up and brought her back to be buried. And he came and said to his wife: "This people which thou seest, none but their Father in heaven is angry with them."

AND LET ALL THY ACTIONS BE FOR THE SAKE OF HEAVEN—for the sake of Torah,[11] as it is said, *In all thy ways acknowledge Him and He will direct thy paths* (Prov. 3:6).

RABBI SIMEON SAYS: BE PROMPT IN RECITING THE SHEMA AND THE PRAYER.[12] WHEN THOU PRAYEST, DO NOT MAKE THY PRAYER A CHATTER-ING, BUT A SUPPLICATION BEFORE THE HOLY ONE, BLESSED BE HE, FOR IT IS SAID, FOR HE IS A GOD COMPASSIONATE AND GRACIOUS, LONG SUFFER-ING, AND ABUNDANT IN MERCY, AND REPENTETH HIM OF THE EVIL (Joel 2: 13).[13] AND BE NOT WICKED IN THINE OWN SIGHT.[14]

RABBI ELEAZAR [15] SAYS: BE DILIGENT IN THE STUDY OF TORAH, AND KNOW HOW TO ANSWER AN EPICUROS.[16] LET NOT ONE WORD OF THE TORAH ESCAPE THEE. KNOW IN WHOSE PRESENCE THOU ART TOILING, AND WHO IS AUTHOR OF THE COVENANT WITH THEE.[17]

CHAPTER 18

IN like manner [1] Rabbi Judah the Prince used to list the excellences of the Sages: of Rabbi Ṭarfon, Rabbi ʿAḳiba, Rabbi Eleazar ben Azariah, Rabbi Johanan ben Nuri, and Rabbi Yose the Galilean.

Rabbi Ṭarfon he called "A heap of stones" or, some say, "A heap of nuts"—when a person removes one from the pile, they all go tumbling over each other. This is what Rabbi Ṭarfon was like. When a scholar came to him and said, "Teach me," Rabbi Ṭarfon would cite for him Scripture and Mishnah, Midrash, Halakha, and Agada. When the scholar parted from him, he went away filled with blessing and good.

Rabbi ʿAḳiba he called "A well-stocked storehouse." To what might Rabbi ʿAḳiba be likened? To a laborer who took his basket and went forth. When he found wheat, he put some in the basket; when he found barley, he put that in; spelt, he put that in; lentils, he put them in. Upon returning home he sorted out the wheat by itself, the barley by itself, the beans by themselves, the lentils by themselves. This is how Rabbi ʿAḳiba acted, and he arranged the whole Torah in rings.[2]

Rabbi Eleazar ben Azariah he called "A spice-peddler's basket." For to what might Rabbi Eleazar be likened? To a spice peddler who takes up his basket and comes into a city; when the people of the city come up and ask him, "Hast thou good oil with thee? hast thou ointment with thee? hast thou balsam with thee?" they find he has everything with him. Such was Rabbi Eleazar ben Azariah when scholars came to him. If questioned on Scripture, he answered; on Mishnah, he answered; on Midrash, he answered; on Halakha, he answered; on Agada, he answered. When the scholar parted from him, he was filled with good and blessing.

(Once,) [3] in Rabbi Joshua's old age, his disciples came to visit him. "My sons," he said to them, "what new interpretation have you had in the study house?"

"We are thy disciples," they replied, "and it is thy waters we drink."

"Heaven forbid!" he exclaimed, "there is no generation bereft of Sages. Whose [4] Sabbath was it?"

"It was the Sabbath of Rabbi Eleazar ben Azariah," they answered.

"And on what (text) was the agadic discourse today?" he asked.

"It was," they replied, "on the section, *Assemble the people, the men and the women, and the little ones*" (Deut. 31:12).

"And how did he interpret it?" he asked them.

They said to him: "This is how he interpreted it: As to *the men,* they come to study; as to *the women,* they come to listen. Why do *the little ones* come? So that a goodly reward might be given to those who bring them."

Said Rabbi Joshua to them: "A precious pearl was in your hands and you were about to deprive me of it! Had you gone to hear no more than that, it would have been enough."

They said to him: "He also offered an interpretation of *The words of the wise are as goads, and as nails well fastened are those that sit together in groups; they are given from one shepherd* (Eccl. 12:11):

"Even as a goad directs the beast along the furrows, so the words of the Torah direct man along the paths of life. Perhaps even as the goad is withdrawn, so also the words of the Torah may be withdrawn? [5] The verse says, *And as nails well fastened:* even as the well fastened is not removable, so are the words of the Torah not removable.

"Those that sit together in groups are the scholars who come into (the academy) and sit down in groups: some forbid and others permit, some declare a thing unclean and others declare it clean, some pronounce a thing unfit and others pronounce it fit. Lest anyone say to thee, (In that event) I shall sit back and not study, Scripture declares, *They are given from one shepherd:* one God created them, one leader [6] gave them, the Master of all things uttered them! Thou too, therefore, make thine ear like a hopper and take in the words of them that forbid and the words of them that permit, the words of them that declare unclean and the words of them that declare clean, the words of them that pronounce unfit and the words of them that pronounce fit."

Rabbi [7] Johanan ben Nuri, Rabbi Judah called "A basket of *hălakot.*"

And Rabbi Yose the Galilean, "A discriminating gatherer (of traditions) free from arrogance"—for he held fast to the quality of the Sages (impressed upon all) at Mount Sinai, and he used to praise all the Sages of Israel for the same quality.[8]

Isi ben Judah (too) used to coin phrases to describe the Sages: Rabbi Me'ir, "A sage and a scribe"; [9]

Rabbi Judah, "Profound when he wishes to be so";

Rabbi Eliezer ben Jacob, "Little but spotless"; [10]

Rabbi Yose, "Carries his learning with him";

Rabbi Johanan ben Nuri, "A basket of hălakot";

Rabbi Yose the Galilean, "A very discriminating gatherer free from arrogance";

Rabbi Simeon ben Gamaliel, "A shopful of precious purple";

Rabbi Simeon (ben Yoḥai), "Studies much and forgets little."

Once [11] Rabbi Simeon came upon Isi ben Judah. "Why dost thou cause my words to be despised [12] by the Sages?" Rabbi Simeon demanded.

"What have I said of thee," Isi rejoined, "but that thou studiest

much, forgetest little, and what thou dost forget is no more than
the bran of thy learning!"

CHAPTER 19

'AḴAB̲YA [BEN] MAHĀLALEL SAYS: HE WHO TAKES TO HEART FOUR
THINGS WILL SIN NO MORE: WHENCE HE IS COME, WHITHER HE IS
GOING, WHAT HE IS DESTINED TO BE, AND WHO IS HIS JUDGE.
WHENCE HE IS [COME]: FROM A PLACE OF DARKNESS.
WHITHER HE IS GOING: TO A PLACE OF DARKNESS AND GLOOM.
WHAT HE IS DESTINED TO BE: DUST, WORM, AND MAGGOT.
AND WHO IS HIS JUDGE: THE KING OF KINGS OF KINGS, THE HOLY ONE,
BLESSED BE HE.[1]

RABBI SIMEON SAYS: HE COMES FROM A PLACE OF DARK-
NESS AND RETURNS TO A PLACE OF DARKNESS:[2] He comes from
a putrid drop,[3] from a place which no eye can see. AND
WHAT IS HE DESTINED TO BE? DUST, WORM, AND MAGGOT; as it is said,
Surely man is a worm! and the son of man is a maggot! (Job 25:6).

Rabbi Eliezer ben Jacob says: *Man is a worm* while he lives.
And the son of man is a maggot when he is dead.

What is the "worm while he lives?" It is vermin.

"And the son of man is a maggot when he is dead?" That is,
he breeds worms when he is dead.[4]

Rabbi Simeon ben Eleazar says: I shall tell thee a parable; to
what may this be likened? To a king who built a large palace and
decorated it,[5] but a tannery pipe led through it and emptied at
its doorway. Says every passerby: "How magnificently beautiful
this palace would be were it not for the tannery pipe coming
through it!"

So too is man. If now, with a foul stream issuing from his
bowels, he exalts himself over other creatures, how much the more
would he exalt himself over other creatures if a stream of precious
oil, balsam, or ointment issued from him!

When Rabbi Eliezer fell sick his disciples came to visit him, and they sat down before him. "O master," they urged, "teach us (at least) one thing (more)." [6]

He said to them: "Let me teach you this: Go forth and watch over each other's honor. When you pray remember before whom you stand praying, for thereby you shall merit the life of the world to come."

Said Rabbi Eleazar ben Azariah: Five things we learned from Rabbi Eliezer (on his deathbed) and these gave us more delight (then) than they had given us during his lifetime. These concern: a round cushion, a ball, a shoe last, an amulet, or a phylactery, which was torn.[7] (We asked: "When these objects contract uncleanness) what is the status (of that which is within them)? Is it indeed as thou didst teach us?" [8]

"It is unclean," [9] he replied. "And be careful with such objects and immerse them in an immersion pool as they are—for these are established laws [10] which were transmitted to Moses at Sinai."

CHAPTER 20

RABBI Hananiah,[1] prefect of the priests, says: He who takes to heart the words of the Torah is relieved of [2] many preoccupations—preoccupations with hunger, foolish preoccupations, unchaste preoccupations, preoccupations with the evil impulse, preoccupations with an evil wife,[3] idle preoccupations, and preoccupations with the yoke of flesh and blood. For thus is it written in the Book of Psalms by David, king of Israel: *The precepts of the Lord are right, rejoicing the heart; the commandment of the Lord is pure, enlightening the eyes* (Ps. 19:9). But he who does not take to heart the words of the Torah is given over to many preoccupations—preoccupations with hunger, foolish preoccupations, unchaste preoccupations, preoccupations with the evil impulse, preoccupations with an evil wife, idle preoccupations, preoccupations with the yoke of flesh and blood. For thus is it written in Deuteronomy by Moses our master: *And they shall*

*be upon thee for a sign and for a wonder, and upon thy seed for
ever; because thou didst not serve the Lord thy God with joyful-
ness, and with gladness of heart, by reason of the abundance of
all things: therefore shalt thou serve thine enemy whom the Lord
shall send against thee, in hunger, and in thirst, and in nakedness, and in want of all things* (Deut. 28: 46 ff.).

In hunger: For example, at a time when one craves food and
cannot find even coarse bread, the heathen nations demand from
him white bread and choice meat.

And in thirst: For example, at a time when one longs for drink
and cannot find even a drop of vinegar or a drop of bitters, the
heathen nations demand from him the finest wine in the world.

And in nakedness: For example, at a time when one is in need [4]
of clothing and cannot find even a wool shirt or flaxen one, the
heathen nations demand from him silks and the best *kallak* in the
world.[5]

And in want of all things: (That is,) in want of light, of knife,
of table.[6]

Another interpretation of *In want of all things:* (In want) of
vinegar and salt. This is the meaning of the curse that men utter:
"Mayest thou have neither vinegar nor salt in thy house!"

Lo,[7] it says, *Look not upon me, that I am swarthy, that the sun
hath tanned me; my mother's sons were incensed against me, they
made me keeper of the vineyards; but mine own vineyard have
I not kept* (Cant. 1:6).

*Look not upon me, that I am swarthy, that the sun hath tanned
me; my mother's sons were incensed against me*—this refers to
the assemblies of Judah who shook off the yoke of the Holy One,
blessed be He, and made a creature of flesh and blood king over
themselves.[8]

Another interpretation. *My mother's sons were incensed against
me* refers to [Dathan and Abiram,] [9] (who informed against)
Moses when he slew the Egyptian. For it is said, *And it came to
pass in those* [10] *days, when Moses was grown up, that he went
out unto his brethren, and looked on their burdens. . . . And he*

looked this way and that way, and when he saw that there was no man, he smote the Egyptian, and hid him in the sand (Exod. 2: 11 f.).—

Why does the verse say, *That there was no man?* This teaches that Moses summoned a court of ministering angels and asked them: "Shall I kill this Egyptian?" "Kill him!" they answered. Was it then a sword he killed him with? Not at all! He slew him by means of the Word, as it is said, *Wilt thou kill me by means of the Word, as thou didst kill the Egyptian* (Exod. 2: 14)? This teaches that he killed him by pronouncing God's name.[11]—

Another interpretation of *My mother's sons were incensed against me, they made me keeper of the vineyards; but mine own vineyard have I not kept.* The verse refers to Moses at the time he fled to Midian.

For it is said, *Now when Pharaoh heard this thing, he sought to slay Moses. But Moses fled from the face of Pharaoh, and dwelt in the land of Midian; and he sat down by a well. Now the priest of Midian had seven daughters . . . and the shepherds came and drove them away; but Moses stood up and helped them, and watered their flock* (Exod. 2: 15 ff.). (Which is to say,) Moses came along and set himself up as their judge. "It is worldwide practice," he said to them, "for men to draw up water and for women to water the beasts. Here women draw the water and men water the beasts! Justice is perverted in this place! [12] . . ."

—And some say: So long as Moses remained standing at the mouth of the well, the waters continued to flow and rise up toward him; when he stepped back, the waters receded.—

It was then he exclaimed: "Woe unto me that I had to leave my people and came to dwell with the Gentiles!" [13]

Another interpretation of *My mother's sons were incensed against me.* The verse refers to Israel at the time they made the golden calf. For at first they had declared, *All that the Lord hath spoken will we do, and obey* (Exod. 24: 7); later they cried, *This is thy God, O Israel* (Exod. 32: 4).

Another interpretation. *My mother's sons were incensed against me* refers to the spies who spread an evil report of the land and brought death upon Israel,[14] (as it is said,) *Your carcasses shall fall in this wilderness* (Num. 14:29).

They made me keeper of the vineyards, but mine own vineyard have I not kept. Said the Holy One, blessed be He: "Who has caused me to show favor to the Gentiles? Only Israel!" For so long as the Gentiles enjoy tranquility, the people of Israel are afflicted, cast off, driven about.

Another interpretation of *They made me keeper of the vineyards, but mine own vineyard have I not kept.* The verse refers to Israel at the time they were exiled to Babylon. Up rose the prophets in their midst and urged them: "Set aside heave offerings and tithes!"

They answered: "This very exile from our land has been visited upon us only because we did not set aside heave offerings and tithes. And now you tell us to set aside heave offerings and tithes!"

It is of this the verse speaks: *They made me keeper of the vineyards, but mine own vineyard have I not kept.*[15]

CHAPTER 21

RABBI DOSA BEN HARKINAS SAYS: MORNING SLEEP, MIDDAY WINE, CHILDREN'S PRATTLE, AND SITTING IN THE GATHERING PLACES OF THE 'AM HA-'AREṢ PUT A MAN OUT OF THE WORLD.[1]

MORNING SLEEP: what is that? This teaches that a man should not plan to sleep until the time of reciting the Shema has passed. For when a man sleeps until the time for reciting the Shema has passed, he thereby neglects the study of Torah,[2] as it is said, *The sluggard saith: There is a lion in the way; yea, a lion is in the streets. The door is turning upon its hinges, and the sluggard is still upon his bed* (Prov. 26:13 f.).

MIDDAY WINE: what is that? This teaches that a man should not plan to drink wine at midday. For when a man drinks wine at midday he thereby neglects the study of Torah,[3] as it is said, *Woe to thee, O land, when thy king is a boy, and thy princes feast in the morning* (Eccl. 10:16)! It says also, *Happy art thou, O land, when thy king is a free man, and thy princes eat in due season, in strength, and not in drunkenness* (Eccl. 10:17)!—

Now, when is that time to be?[4] Say thou, In the age to come, as it is said, *I the Lord will hasten it in its time* (Isa. 60:22). It also says, *After a lapse of time like this shall it be said of Jacob and of Israel: O, what God hath wrought* (Num. 23:23). This is what the Holy One, blessed be He, said to the wicked Balaam: "After a lapse of time like this, but not now:[5] not while thou art standing in their midst, but at the time when I shall redeem Israel (will their king be free and prophecy be restored)."—

CHILDREN'S PRATTLE: what is that? This teaches that a man should not plan to stay at home and study. For when a man stays home to study, he chatters away with his children and with the folk in his household, and thus neglects the study of Torah. And[6] it is said, *This book of the Torah shall not depart out of thy mouth, but thou shalt meditate therein day and night* (Josh. 1:8).

AND SITTING IN THE GATHERING PLACES OF THE 'AM HA-'AREṢ: what is that? This teaches that a man should not plan to sit down with those that loiter at street corners in the market place. For when a man sits down with those that loiter at street corners in the market place, he neglects the study of Torah. And it is said, *Happy is the man that hath not walked in the counsel of the wicked, nor stood in the way of sinners. . . . But his delight is in the Torah of the Lord* (Ps. 1:1 f.).

Rabbi Me'ir says: What does the verse mean by *Nor sat in the seat of the scornful* (*ibid.*)? It is a reference to the theaters and circuses of the heathen, for in these, lives are condemned to death; and it is said, *I hate the gathering of evil doers, and will not sit with the wicked*[7] (Ps. 26:5).

Now, *evil doers* are none but the wicked, as it is said, *For the evil doers shall be cut off. . . . And*[8] *yet a little while, and the wicked is no more* (Ps. 37:9 f.).

Now what will be their punishment in the age to come? As it is said: *For behold the day cometh, it burneth as a furnace, and all*

the proud and all that work wickedness shall be stubble (Mal.
3:19). And the *proud* are none but the scornful, as it is said,
A proud and haughty man, scorner is his name (Prov. 21:24).

Once as Rabbi 'Akiba sat teaching his disciples and remembered
what he had done in his youth,[9] he exclaimed:

> I give thanks unto Thee,
> O Lord my God,
> that Thou hast set my portion
> amongst those that sit in the study house,
> and didst not set my portion
> amongst those that loiter at street corners in the market place.[10]

CHAPTER 22

RABBI ḤANINA BEN DOSA SAYS: HE WHOSE FEAR OF SIN TAKES
PRECEDENCE OVER HIS WISDOM, HIS WISDOM SHALL ENDURE; BUT HE
WHOSE WISDOM TAKES PRECEDENCE OVER HIS FEAR OF SIN, HIS WISDOM
SHALL NOT ENDURE:[1] as it is said, *The fear of the Lord is the be-
ginning of wisdom* (Ps. 111:10).

HE USED TO SAY: HE WHOSE WORKS EXCEED HIS WISDOM, HIS WISDOM
SHALL ENDURE; BUT HE WHOSE WISDOM EXCEEDS HIS WORKS, HIS WIS-
DOM SHALL NOT ENDURE:[2] as it is said, *We will do and study (there-
after)* (Exod. 24:7).

RABBAN Johanan ben Zakkai was asked: "If one is wise
and fears sin, what is he like?"
He replied: "Lo, that's a craftsman with the tools of
his craft in his hand."

"If one is wise but does not fear sin, what is he like?"

"Lo, that's a craftsman without the tools of his craft in his hand,"
he replied.

"If one fears sin but is not wise, what is he like?"

He replied: "He is no craftsman, but the tools of the craft are in
his hand."

RABBI ELEAZAR BEN AZARIAH SAYS: WHERE THERE IS NO TORAH, THERE'S NO RIGHT CONDUCT; WHERE THERE IS NO RIGHT CONDUCT, THERE'S NO TORAH. WHERE THERE IS NO WISDOM, THERE'S NO FEAR (OF GOD); WHERE THERE IS NO FEAR (OF GOD), THERE'S NO WISDOM.[2]

HE USED TO SAY: ONE IN WHOM THERE ARE GOOD WORKS, WHO HAS STUDIED MUCH TORAH, TO WHAT MAY HE BE LIKENED? TO A TREE WHICH STANDS BY THE WATERS, WHOSE BRANCHES ARE FEW BUT WHOSE ROOTS ARE NUMEROUS: EVEN IF THE FOUR WINDS OF THE WORLD COME ALONG, THEY CANNOT STIR IT FROM ITS PLACE, AS IT IS SAID, AND HE SHALL BE LIKE A TREE PLANTED BY STREAMS OF WATER, ETC. (Ps. 1:3). ONE IN WHOM THERE ARE NO GOOD WORKS, THOUGH HE STUDIED MUCH TORAH, TO WHAT MAY HE BE LIKENED? TO A TREE WHICH STANDS IN THE DESERT, WHOSE BRANCHES ARE NUMEROUS BUT WHOSE ROOTS ARE FEW: EVEN IF (ONLY ONE) WIND BLOWS AGAINST IT, IT UPROOTS IT AND SWEEPS IT DOWN, AS IT IS SAID, FOR HE SHALL BE LIKE A TAMA-RISK IN THE DESERT, AND SHALL NOT SEE WHEN GOOD COMETH (Jer. 17:6).[2]

RABBAN GAMALIEL SAYS: PROVIDE THYSELF WITH A TEACHER, AND GET THEE A COMPANION, AND ESCHEW DOUBTFUL MATTERS, AND TITHE NOT OVERMUCH BY GUESSWORK.[3]

SIMEON HIS SON SAYS: ALL MY LIFE I GREW UP AMONG THE SAGES AND HAVE FOUND NOTHING BETTER FOR ANYBODY THAN SILENCE. IF FOR THE WISE SILENCE IS BECOMING, HOW MUCH MORE FOR THE FOOLISH! WISDOM DOES NOT LEAD TO WORDS; NOR IS IT WORDS THAT LEAD TO WIS-DOM—ONLY WORKS. HE WHO IS VERBOSE BRINGS ON SIN, AS IT IS SAID, IN THE MULTITUDE OF WORDS THERE WANTETH NOT TRANSGRESSION (Prov. 10:19); AND IT SAYS, EVEN AS A FOOL, WHEN HE HOLDETH HIS PEACE, IS COUNTED WISE (Prov. 17:28).[4]

CHAPTER 23

BEN ZOMA SAYS:

WHO IS IT THAT IS WISE? HE THAT LEARNS FROM ALL MEN, AS IT IS
SAID, FROM ALL MY TEACHERS HAVE I GOT UNDERSTANDING (Ps.
119:99).

WHO IS IT THAT IS MOST HUMBLE? ONE WHO IS AS HUMBLE AS
MOSES OUR MASTER, AS IT IS SAID, NOW THE MAN MOSES WAS VERY
MEEK (Num. 12:3).

WHO IS IT THAT IS MOST RICH? ONE WHO IS CONTENT WITH HIS
PORTION, AS IT IS SAID, WHEN THOU EATEST THE LABOR OF THY HANDS,
HAPPY SHALT THOU BE, AND IT SHALL BE WELL WITH THEE (Ps. 128:2).

WHO IS IT THAT IS MOST MIGHTY? ONE WHO SUBDUES HIS EVIL IM-
PULSE, AS IT IS SAID, HE THAT IS SLOW TO ANGER IS BETTER THAN THE
MIGHTY; AND HE THAT RULETH HIS SPIRIT THAN HE THAT TAKETH A
CITY (Prov. 16:32).[1]

AND to him who subdues his evil impulse, it is accounted as
though he had conquered a city full of mighty men, as it is
said, *A wise man scaleth the city of the mighty, and
bringeth down the stronghold wherein it trusteth* (Prov. 21:22).
And *the mighty* are none other than the strong in Torah, as it is
said, *Ye mighty in strength, that fulfill His word, hearkening unto
the voice of His word* (Ps. 103:20).

And some say: This verse refers to the ministering angels, for
it is said, *Ye angels of His, ye mighty in strength* (*ibid.*).

And some say: (Mighty is he) who makes of his enemy a friend.

RABBI NEHORA'I SAYS: BETAKE THYSELF TO A PLACE OF TORAH AND
SAY NOT THAT IT WILL COME AFTER THEE, THAT THY COMPANIONS
WILL MAKE IT SECURE IN THY HAND; AND LEAN NOT UPON THINE OWN
UNDERSTANDING.[2]

HE USED TO SAY: DESPISE NO MAN AND CONSIDER NOTHING IM-
POSSIBLE,[3] as it is said, *Whoso despiseth the word shall suffer
thereby; but he that feareth the commandment shall be rewarded*
(Prov. 13:13).

He used to say: He that studies Torah as a child, to what may he be likened? To a heifer subdued while yet young, as it is said, *And Ephraim is a heifer well broken, that loveth to thresh* (Hos. 10: 11). But he that studies Torah in his old age is like a beast not subdued until its old age, as it is said, *For Israel is stubborn as a rebelling old beast* (Hos. 4: 16).[4]

He used to say: He that studies Torah as a child is like a woman who kneads in hot water, but he that studies Torah in his old age is like a woman who kneads in cold water.

Rabbi Eliezer ben Jacob says: HE THAT STUDIES TORAH AS A CHILD IS LIKE WRITING WRITTEN ON FRESH PAPER; HE THAT STUDIES TORAH IN HIS OLD AGE IS LIKE WRITING WRITTEN ON OLD PAPER.[5]

Rabban Gamaliel [6] adds to this: He that studies Torah as a child is like a young man who weds a maiden: [7] for she is suited to him and he is suited to her, and she is drawn to him and he is drawn to her.[8] He that studies Torah in his old age, to what may he be likened? To an old man who weds a maiden: she may be suited to him but he is unsuited to her, she may be drawn to him but he withdraws from her. For it is said, *As arrows in the hand of a mighty man, so are the children of one's youth* (Ps. 127: 4); and following this (v. 5) it is written, *Happy is the man that hath his quiver full of them; they shall not be put to shame, when they speak with their enemies in the gate.*[9]

He that studies and forgets is like a woman who gives birth to children and buries them, as it is said, *Yea, though they bring up their children, yet will I bereave them, that there be not a man left* (Hos. 9: 12): read not *I will bereave them* (wĕ-šikkaltim), but *I will cause them to forget* (wĕ-šikkaḥtim).

Rabbi Simeon ben Eleazar says: He that studies Torah as a child is like a physician who, when a wound is brought before him, has a scalpel to cut it and drugs to heal it; he that studies Torah in his old age is like a physician who, when a wound is brought before him, has a scalpel to cut it but has no drugs to heal it.[10]

Moreover,[11] let the words of the Torah be distinctly marked one from the other, and let them be distinctly marked one beside the other; [12] as it is said, *Bind them upon thy fingers, write them upon the table of thy heart* (Prov. 7:3), and it says, *Bind them continually upon thy heart, tie them about thy neck* (Prov. 6:21).

CHAPTER 24

ELISHA ben Abuyah says: [1] One in whom there are good works, who has studied much Torah, to what may he be likened? To a person who builds first with stones and afterward with bricks: even when much water comes and collects by their side, it does not dislodge them. But one in whom there are no good works, though he studied Torah, to what may he be likened? To a person who builds first with bricks and afterward with stones: even when a little water gathers, it overthrows them immediately.

He used to say: One in whom there are good works, who has studied much Torah, to what may he be likened? To lime poured over stones: even when any number of rains fall on it, they cannot push it out of place. One in whom there are no good works, though he studied much Torah, is like lime poured over bricks: even when a little rain falls on it, it softens immediately and is washed away.[2]

He used to say: One in whom there are good works, who has studied much Torah, to what may he be likened? To a cup that has a base. But one in whom there are no good works, though he studied much Torah, to what may he be likened? To a cup that has no base: as soon as the cup is filled it overturns, and whatever was in it spills.

He used to say: One in whom there are good works, who has studied much Torah, to what may he be likened? To a horse that has a bridle. But one in whom there are no good works, though he has studied much Torah, to what may he be likened? To a horse that has no bridle: when one mounts it, it throws him off headlong.[3]

He used to say: When one studies Torah as a child, the words of the Torah are absorbed by his blood and come out of his mouth distinctly.[4] But if one studies Torah in his old age, the words of the Torah are not absorbed by his blood and do not come out of his mouth distinctly. And thus the maxim goes: "If in thy youth thou didst not desire them, how shalt thou acquire them in thine old age?"[5]

He used to say: Like gold vessels, the words of the Torah are hard to acquire, and like glass vessels they are easy to wreck,[6] as it is said, *Gold and glass cannot equal it, neither shall the exchange thereof be vessels of fine gold* (Job 28:17): Scripture compares gold [7] to glass—even [8] as gold vessels can be mended after they have been broken, and glass vessels cannot be mended when they are broken unless they are restored to their original state.[9]

And how interpret *Neither shall the exchange thereof be vessels of fine gold?* This says: If one toils over the words of the Torah and carries them out, his face shines like fine gold; but if one toils over them and does not carry them out, his face darkens like glass.

He used to say: One may learn Torah for ten years and forget it (all) after two years. How so? For example: If for six months one neglects to review, he then says of the unclean "It is clean" and of the clean "It is unclean." If for twelve months he does not review, he then confuses the Sages with one another.[10] If for eighteen months he does not review, he forgets the chapter headings. If for twenty-four months he does not review, he forgets the treatise headings. And after saying of the unclean, "It is clean," and of the clean, "It is unclean," after confusing the Sages with one another, after forgetting the chapter headings and treatise headings, he sits and keeps quiet in the end. And of him said Solomon, *I went by the field of the slothful, and by the vineyard of the man void of understanding; and lo, it was all grown over with thistles; the face thereof was covered with nettles, and the stone wall thereof was broken down* (Prov. 24:30 f.): for once the wall [11] of the vineyard falls, the whole vineyard is destroyed.

He used to say: If one makes his fellow carry out some commandment, Scripture accounts it to him as though he had done it himself, (as [12] it is said, *Only take heed to thyself and keep thy*

soul diligently, lest thou forget the things which thine eyes saw
. . . but teach them to thy sons, and thy sons' sons (Deut. 4:9).)

A parable is told; to what may this be likened? To the following: A king of flesh and blood snared a bird and gave it to
one of his servants. He said to him: "Take care of this bird. Now, if
thou art careful with it, well and good; otherwise I shall have thy
life for it." This is what the Holy One, blessed be He, said to
Israel: "The words of the Torah which I have given to you, if
you keep them, well and good; otherwise I shall have your life
for it" [13]—as it is said, *Only take heed to thyself, and keep thy*
soul diligently, lest thou forget the things which thine eyes saw
. . . but teach them to thy sons; and it says, *For it is no vain thing*
for you; because it is your life (Deut. 32:47).

CHAPTER 25

BEN 'Azzai says:
If one's mind is serene because of his learning, it is a
good sign for him; but if his mind is distressed because of
his learning, it is a bad sign for him.

If one's mind is serene because of his impulse, it is a good sign
for him; but if his mind is distressed because of his impulse, it is
a bad sign for him.[1]

If the Sages are pleased with one in the hour of his death, it is
a good sign for him; if the Sages are displeased with him, it is a
bad sign for him.

If one's face is turned upward (at death), it is a good sign for
him; but if his face is cast downward, it is a bad sign for him.

If (at death) one fixes his gaze on men, it is a good sign for
him; if he fixes his gaze on the wall, it is a bad sign for him.

If (at death) one's face is bright, it is a good sign for him; if
one's face is overcast, it is a bad sign for him.

In his last hours Rabban Johanan ben Zakkai kept weeping
out loud. "O master,"[2] his disciples exclaimed, "O tall pillar,

light of the world,[3] mighty hammer, why art thou weeping?"

Said he to them: "Do I then go to appear before a king of flesh and blood—whose anger, if he should be angry with me, is but of this world; and whose chastising, if he should chastise me, is but of this world; and whose slaying, if he should slay me, is but of this world; whom I can moreover appease with words or bribe with money? Verily, I go rather to appear before the King of kings of kings, the Holy One, blessed be He—whose anger, if He should be angry with me, is of this world and the world to come; whom I cannot appease with words or bribe with money! [4] Moreover I have before me two roads, one to Paradise and one to Gehenna, and I know not whether He will sentence me to Gehenna or admit me into Paradise; and of this [5] the verse says, *Before Him shall be sentenced all those that go down to the dust, even he that cannot keep his soul alive*" (Ps. 22:30).

Of Moses it says,[6] (. . .) *And I will take away My hand, and thou shalt see My back, but My face shall not be seen* (Exod. 33:23). And it says, *And He spread it before me, and it was written on its face and on its back* (Ezek. 2:10).

Face refers to this world.

Back refers to the world to come.[7]

Another interpretation:

Face refers to the suffering of the righteous in this world and the tranquility of the wicked in this world.

Back [7] refers to the rewarding of the righteous in the age to come and the punishment of the wicked in Gehenna.

And there was written therein lamentations, and jubilant sound, and woe (ibid.).

Lamentations refers to the punishment of the wicked in this world, as it is said, *This is the lamentation wherewith they shall lament; the daughters of the nations shall lament therewith* (Ezek. 32:16).

And jubilant sound refers to the rewarding of the righteous in the age to come, as it is said, *With an instrument of ten strings, and with the psaltery; with a jubilant sound upon the harp* (Ps. 92:4).[8]

And woe refers to the punishment of the wicked in the world to come, as it is said, *Calamity shall come upon calamity, and rumor shall be upon rumor* (Ezek. 7:26).

He [9] said: "Clear the house of uncleanness and prepare a throne for Hezekiah, king of Judah." [10]

He [11] used to say:

If one dies with a clear mind, it is a good sign for him; if deranged, it is a bad sign for him.

If one dies while speaking, it is a good sign for him; if in silence, it is a bad sign for him.

If one dies while words of the Torah are spoken, it is a good sign for him; if in the course of a business matter,[12] it is a bad sign for him.

If one dies in the course of carrying out some religious commandment, it is a good sign for him; if while engaged in some idle matter, it is a bad sign for him.

If one dies in the midst of joy, it is a good sign for him; if in the midst of sadness, it is a bad sign for him.

If one dies while laughing, it is a good sign for him; if while weeping, it is a bad sign for him.

If one dies on the Sabbath eve, it is a good sign for him; if at the departure of the Sabbath, it is a bad sign for him.

If one dies on the eve of the Day of Atonement, it is a bad sign for him; if at the departure of the Day of Atonement, it is a good sign for him.

Of Rabbi Eliezer's (last) illness it is told:

That day was a Sabbath eve, and Rabbi 'Aḳiba and his colleagues arrived to visit him. He was sleeping in his room, sitting back on a canopied couch; so they sat down in his hall. Hyrcanus his son entered (his father's room) to remove his tĕfillin,[13] but he would not let him—and he broke into tears. Whereupon Hyrcanus came out and said to the Sages: "Masters, it seems to me that father's mind is deranged."

"My son," Rabbi Eliezer called to him, "it is not my mind that's deranged but thine! For thou hast neglected the kindling of the (Sabbath) lights (at the proper hour)—for which the penalty can well be death [14]—and didst busy thyself with the tĕfillin—for whose use (on the Sabbath) there is only the penalty for transgressing the Sabbath rest." [15]

When the Sages saw that his mind was clear, they entered and sat down before him, at a distance of four cubits.[16] "Master," they asked him, "what is the law with regard to a round cushion, a ball, a shoe last, an amulet, or tĕfillin that were torn? (To wit: if they contract uncleanness, do their contents too) become unclean?"

"They do become unclean," he replied; "the objects are to be immersed in an immersion pool as they are. And be careful with such matters, for these are major laws [17] which were transmitted to Moses at Sinai." [18]

And they kept asking him about the law of cleanness, uncleanness, immersion pools. They would ask him, "Master, what about this?" and he would reply, "It is unclean." "What about that?" And he would reply, "It is clean." And he continued to reply "unclean" for the unclean and "clean" for the clean.

Now after that, Rabbi Eliezer said to the Sages: "I fear for the disciples of this generation, that they will be punished by death from Heaven."

"Master," they asked him, "what for?"

"Because," he replied, "they did not come and attend upon me."

Then he said to 'Aķiba ben Joseph " 'Aķiba, why didst thou not come and attend upon me?"

"Master," 'Aķiba replied, "I did not have the time."

Said Rabbi Eliezer to him: "I doubt if thou wilt die a natural death."—And some say that he said naught to him. Rather, when Rabbi Eliezer spoke in this way to his disciples, 'Aķiba's heart [19] suddenly melted within him.—

"Master," Rabbi 'Aķiba asked him, "what manner of death will be mine?"

" 'Aķiba," he replied, "thine will be the hardest of them all!"

Rabbi 'Aḳiba came forward and sat down before him and said to him: "Master, if so, teach me now."

He began, and taught him 300 laws about the *bright spot*.[20]

It was then that Rabbi Eliezer raised his two arms and laid them on his breast and cried: "Woe unto me! For my two arms that are like two Torah scrolls depart from the world!

> For if all the seas were ink,
> And all the reeds pens,
> And all men scribes,
> They could not write down
> All the Scripture and Mishnah I studied,
> Nor what I learned under the Sages in the academy.

Yet I carried away from my teachers no more than does a man who dips his finger in the sea; and I gave away to my disciples no more than a paintbrush takes from the tube. Moreover, I derived three hundred laws from *Thou shalt not suffer a sorceress to live*"[21]—and some say that Rabbi Eliezer said "Three thousand laws"—"but no one ever asked me about them except 'Aḳiba ben Joseph. For once he said to me: 'Master, teach me how one plants cucumbers (by magic) and how one uproots them.' I pronounced a certain word and the whole field was filled with cucumbers. 'Master,' he said to me, 'thou hast taught me how they are planted; teach me how they are uprooted.' I pronounced a certain word and all the cucumbers were gathered together in one place!"[22]

Said Rabbi Eleazar ben Azariah to him: "Master, what about a shoe (still) on the shoe last (which comes into contact with something unclean)?"

"It is clean," he replied.[23]

And so he continued to reply "unclean" for the unclean and "clean" for the clean—until his soul went forth pure.[24] Immediately Rabbi Eleazar ben Azariah rent his clothes and wept. And he came out and said to the Sages: "Masters, come and look upon Rabbi Eliezer,[25] for he is in a state of purity for the world to come, for his soul has gone forth pure."

After the Sabbath Rabbi 'Aḳiba came upon (his remains) being carried on the highway leading from Caesarea to Lydda. Forthwith he rent his clothes and tore at his hair—and his blood ran down to the ground. He kept crying out, weeping and exclaiming: "Woe unto me, my master, because of thee! Woe unto me, my teacher, because of thee! For thou hast left the whole generation fatherless!"

In the mourners' row he delivered the funeral oration and said: *"My father, my father, chariot of Israel and the horsemen thereof!* [26] (Many) coins do I have but no money changer to sort them out!" [27]

BEN 'AZZAI SAYS: BE QUICK TO CARRY OUT A MINOR COMMANDMENT AND FLEE FROM TRANSGRESSION.[28]

He used to say: If thou hast carried out one commandment and dost not regret having done so,[29] in the end it will lead to many commandments (to be carried out); if one commits one transgression and does not regret having transgressed, in the end it leads to many transgressions: [30] FOR ONE COMMANDMENT LEADS TO ANOTHER COMMANDMENT, AND ONE TRANSGRESSION LEADS TO ANOTHER TRANSGRESSION; FOR THE REWARD OF A COMMANDMENT (CARRIED OUT) IS A COMMANDMENT (TO BE CARRIED OUT), AND THE REWARD OF A TRANSGRESSION IS ANOTHER TRANSGRESSION.[31]

He used to say: Refrain (from sinning) of thine own accord and thou shalt be rewarded for thy restraint; and let not others make thee refrain and be rewarded for their restraining (thee).[32]

He used to say: Come down from where thou art two or three steps and take thy place: better is it for thee to be told to go up than to be told to come down, as it is said, *For better is it that it be said unto thee: Come up hither, than that thou shouldst be put lower in the presence of the prince, whom thine eyes have seen* (Prov. 25:7).[33]

There are three whose life is no life at all: to wit, he who depends for his food upon another, he who dwells in an attic,[34] and he whose wife rules over him.

And some say: He whose body is racked by suffering.

He used to say: It is easier to be king over the whole world than to sit and teach in the presence of men who put on linen.[35]

CHAPTER 26

RABBI 'Aḳiba says:
A hedge about honor—not [1] to be frivolous.
A hedge about wisdom—silence.
A hedge about vows—abstinence.
A hedge about holiness—purity.
A hedge about humility—fear of sin.[2]

He used to say:

Dwell [3] not amongst the heathen, lest thou learn their ways.

Break no bread with a priest who is an *'am ha-'areṣ,* lest thou commit sacrilege against holy things.

Be not reckless with vows, lest thou violate oaths.

Do not make a habit of eating at banquets, lest in the end thou wilt have eaten of what has been forbidden thee.[4]

Enter not into doubt, lest thou get into certain (sin).[5]

And do not quit the Holy Land, lest thou worship idols; for thus says David, *For they have driven me out this day that I should not cleave unto the inheritance of the Lord, saying: Go, serve other gods* (I Sam. 26:19). Now is it conceivable to thee that King David was an idol worshiper? But thus said David: He who leaves the Land of Israel and goes forth to another land is accounted by Scripture as though he worshiped idols.

He used to say: He who is buried in lands other than the Holy Land is as though he were buried in Babylonia.[6] He who is buried in Babylonia is as though he were buried in the Land of Israel.[7] He who is buried in the Land of Israel is as though he were buried under the altar: for the whole Land of Israel is fit to be the site of the altar. And he who is buried under the altar [8] is as though he were buried under the throne of glory, as it is said, *Thou throne of glory, on high from the beginning, thou place of our sanctuary* (Jer. 17:12).

HE USED TO SAY: THE 'AM HA-'AREṢ CANNOT BE A SAINT,[9] THE TIMID CANNOT LEARN, AND THE SHORT TEMPERED CANNOT TEACH.[10]

He used to say: Why do scholars die young? It is not because they are adulterous and not because they rob; but because they break off from studying Torah and engage in idle conversations, and then they do not begin where they left off.[11]

Rabbi Simeon ben Eleazar[12] says: Israel outside the Holy Land worship idols in all innocence.[13] Now, how so? If a heathen prepared a banquet in honor of his son, and sent for and invited all the Jews that were in the city, although they eat and drink of their own and their own servant stands by and pours for them, Scripture accounts it to them as though they had eaten of the sacrifices of the dead, as it is said, *And they call thee, and thou eat of their sacrifice* (Exod. 34:15).

RABBI ELIEZER OF MODA'IM SAYS: HE WHO PROFANES THE SABBATH[14] AND DESPISES THE FESTIVALS, AND ANNULS THE COVENANT IN THE FLESH,[15] AND IS CONTEMPTUOUS TOWARD THE TORAH[16]—EVEN THOUGH HE HAVE TORAH[17] AND GOOD WORKS TO HIS CREDIT—HAS NO SHARE IN THE WORLD TO COME.[18]

Rabbi 'Aḳiba says: If one weds a woman that is unfit for him, he transgresses five negative commandments:[19] *Thou shalt not take vengeance* (Lev. 19:19), *Nor bear any grudge* (ibid.), *Thou shalt not hate thy brother in thy heart* (Lev. 19:17), *But thou shalt love thy neighbor as thyself* (Lev. 19:18), *That thy brother may live with thee* (Lev. 25:36). (Moreover,) since he hates her, he desires her death and thus neglects the commandment to be fruitful and to multiply in the world.

He used to say: He who eats foods which do not agree with him transgresses three commandments,[20] in that he has despised himself, despised the foods, and recited a blessing improperly.

Rabbi Judah ben Il'ai says: When a son neglects to learn Torah from his father, and after the father's death goes and learns Torah from others, he is after flattery.[21]

Rabbi Eleazar[22] Haḳḳappar says: Be not like the lintel up high which men cannot touch with their hands, nor like the lintel up high which . . . ,[23] nor like the middle step against which feet are bruised.[24] Be rather like the threshold at the bottom, on which everyone treads: although in the end the whole edifice may be destroyed, the threshold remains in its place.

CHAPTER 27

RABBI YOSE SAYS: HE WHO HONORS THE TORAH IS HIMSELF HONORED BY MEN, AND HE WHO DISHONORS THE TORAH WILL HIMSELF BE DIS-HONORED BY MEN; [1] as it is said, *For them that honor Me I will honor, and they that despise Me shall be lightly esteemed* [2] (I Sam. 2:30).

ANOTHER interpretation. *For them that honor Me I will honor* refers to Pharaoh, king of Egypt, who treated with honor Him-that-spake-and-the-world-came-into-being. For when he went forth at the head of his retinue, his servants said to him: "It is worldwide practice for kings to go forth only after their retinue; but thou goest forth at the head of thy retinue!"

Said he to them: "Do I then go to encounter a king of flesh and blood? None other than the King of kings of kings, the Holy One, blessed be He, do I go to encounter!"

That is why the Holy One, blessed be He, treated him with honor and Himself only punished him, as it is said, *I have compared thee, O My love, to Mine own steed which charged against Pharaoh's chariots* (Cant. 1:9).

Rabbi Papias says: (At the Red Sea) the congregation of Israel was praising (God for what He did) against the horses and chariots of Pharaoh,[3] as it is said, *Thou hast trodden the sea with Thy horses* (Hab. 3:15).[4]

Rabbi Joshua ben Ḳorḥah says: When Pharaoh came into the sea, he came on a stallion, and the Holy One, blessed be He, revealed Himself to it as on a mare, as it is said, *To My mare* [5] *amongst Pharaoh's chariots* (Cant. 1:9).—

But did He not ride rather on a cherub, as it is said, *And He rode upon a cherub, and did fly; yea, He did swoop down upon the wings of the wind* (Ps. 18: 11)? In that event say: The cherub appeared to the horses of Pharaoh as a mare, and they all came into the sea.—

And they that despise Me shall be lightly esteemed refers to Sennacherib, king of Assyria. For it is said, *By thy servants hast thou taunted the Lord, and hast said: With the multitude of my chariots am I come up to the heights of the mountains, to the innermost parts of Lebanon; and I have cut down the tall cedars thereof, and the choice cypress trees thereof; and I have entered into his farthest height, the forest of his fruitful field* (Isa. 37: 24). That is why the Holy One, blessed be He, treated him with contumely and punished him by the hands of an angel only, as it is said, *And the angel of the Lord went forth and smote in the camp of the Assyrians a hundred and four score and five thousand; and when men arose early in the morning, behold, they were all dead corpses* (Isa. 37: 36).

RABBI ISHMAEL SAYS: IF ONE STUDIES IN ORDER TO TEACH, IT IS GRANTED HIM TO STUDY AND TO TEACH; BUT IF ONE STUDIES IN ORDER TO PRACTICE, IT IS GRANTED HIM TO STUDY, TO TEACH, AND TO PRACTICE.[6]

HE USED TO SAY: NOT THE WHOLE TORAH MUST THOU TAKE UPON THYSELF TO FINISH; YET THOU ART NOT AT LIBERTY TO WITHDRAW FROM IT: RATHER, HE THAT MORE AND MORE STUDIES, MORE AND MORE INCREASES HIS REWARD.[7]

RABBI ELEAZAR [8] BEN HISMA SAYS: THE LAWS OF BIRD OFFERINGS AND INTERPRETATIONS [9] OF THE LAWS OF THE MENSTRUANT—THESE, THESE ARE THE ESSENTIALS OF THE HALAKHA.[10] CALCULATIONS OF EQUINOXES AND GEMATRIA [11] ARE THE DESSERTS OF WISDOM.[12]

Rabbi Johanan ben Nuri says: The laws of purity and impurity,[13] of menstruation, of bird offerings—these, these are the essentials of the Torah.

He used to say: Setting a lavish table,[14] founding [15] courts of law, and maintaining them [16] bring good to the world.[17]

Rabbi Johanan ben Dahăbai says: If one says, "This law does not seem right," he has no share in the world to come.

RABBI ṬARFON SAYS: THE DAY IS SHORT, THE WORK IS PLENTIFUL, THE LABORERS ARE SLUGGISH, AND THE REWARD IS ABUNDANT; AND KNOW THAT THE REWARDING OF THE RIGHTEOUS IS IN THE AGE TO COME.[18]

He used to say: Do not remove thyself from the measure which hath no limit and the work which hath no end.[19] A parable: to what may this be likened? To one who keeps drawing up sea water and pouring it on dry land: the sea is not diminished and the dry land is not flooded.[20] If he should grow impatient, he is told: "Wretch! why dost thou grow impatient? Every day take thy reward, a golden denar!"

RABBI ELEAZAR [21] BEN SHAMMUAʿ SAYS: LET THE HONOR OF THY DISCIPLE BE AS DEAR TO THEE AS THINE OWN, AND THE HONOR OF THY COMPANION AS FEAR [22] OF THY MASTER, AND FEAR OF THY MASTER AS FEAR OF HEAVEN.[23]

Where are we told that the honor of one's disciple should be as dear to him as his own honor? Let all men learn from Moses our master, who said to Joshua, *Choose us out men* (Exod. 17:9). It is not said, "Choose me out men," but, *Choose us out men;* which teaches that Moses treated him as his equal: although he was his master and Joshua was his disciple, he treated him as his equal.

And how do we know that the honor of one's companion should be as dear to him as his master's? For it is said, *And Aaron said to Moses: O my lord* (Num. 12:11). Now, was not his brother younger than he? Nevertheless, Aaron treated him as his master.

And how do we know that the honor of one's master should be as dear to him as the honor of Heaven? For it is said, *And Joshua the son of Nun, the minister of Moses from his youth up, answered and said: My lord Moses, shut them in* (Num. 11:28): Joshua treated him as the equal of the Shekinah.[24]

Since at first they used to say, "There is grain in Judah and straw in Galilee and chaff in Transjordan," they later had to say "There is no grain in Judah, only straw; and there is no straw in

Galilee, only chaff; and in Transjordan there is neither the one nor the other." [25]

CHAPTER 28

RABBI Nathan says:
There is no love like the love of Torah.
There is no wisdom like the wisdom of the Land of Israel.

There is no beauty like the beauty of Jerusalem.

There are no riches like the riches of Rome.

There is no might like the might of Persia.

There is no harlotry like the harlotry of Arabs.

There is no arrogance like the arrogance of Elam.

There is no hypocrisy like the hypocrisy of Babylonia, as it is said, *And he said unto me: To build her a house in the land of Shinar* [1] (Zech. 5:11).

And there is no witchcraft like the witchcraft of Egypt.[2]

Rabbi Simeon ben Eleazar says: When a sage who lived in the Land of Israel leaves the Land, he deteriorates;[3] one who lives there is superior to him. But though the former has deteriorated, he is (still) superior to all the excellent men of other countries. A parable is told: to what may this be likened? To Indian iron which comes from overseas: although it has (now) become inferior to what it had been, it is (still) superior to all the excellent metals of other countries.[4]

Rabban [5] Simeon ben Gamaliel says: If one brings peace into his home, Scripture accounts it to him as though he had brought peace to everyone in Israel; but if one brings envy and contention into his home, it is as though he had brought envy and contention into Israel—for everyone is monarch in his home, as it is said, *That every man should bear rule in his own house* (Est. 1:22).

Rabban [5] Gamaliel says: By four things does the empire exist: [6] by its tolls, bathhouses, theaters, and crop taxes.

He used to say: Words of Torah are as hard to acquire as clothing of fine wool and as easy to destroy as linen clothing; words of folly and indecent speech are as easy to acquire and as hard to destroy as a sack: sometimes a man buys a sack in the market place for a *sela'* and goes on using it for four or five years.[7]

Rabbi Judah the Prince says: He who accepts the pleasures of this world shall be denied the pleasures of the world to come; but he who does not accept the pleasures of this world shall be granted the pleasures of the world to come.

He used to say: The righteous with whom it goes ill in this world, to what might they be likened? To a cook who prepares a feast for himself: although it is he who must take pains, he does not prepare the feast for others but for himself. But the wicked with whom it goes ill in this world, to what might they be likened? To a cook who prepared a feast for others: although it is he who must take pains, for himself he prepares naught, it is only for others.

He used to say: Let thy conduct in secret be (like) thy conduct in the open; [8] and what should not be heard, tell not to thy fellow.

HILLEL SAYS: [9]

DO NOT WITHDRAW FROM THE CONGREGATION.

PUT NO TRUST IN THYSELF UNTIL THE DAY OF THY DEATH.

DO NOT JUDGE THY FELLOW UNTIL THOU HAST STOOD IN HIS PLACE.

SAY NOT OF A THING WHICH CANNOT BE UNDERSTOOD THAT IN THE END IT WILL BE UNDERSTOOD.[10]

AND SAY NOT: "WHEN I HAVE LEISURE I WILL STUDY"—PERCHANCE THOU SHALT HAVE NO LEISURE.

He used to say: [11]

The more one eats, the more he eliminates.

The more flesh, the more worms and maggots.

But the more good works, (the more) one brings peace to himself.[12]

Rabbi Eleazar ben Shammua' says: There are three types of scholars: the hewn stone, the cornerstone, the polished [13] stone.[14]

The hewn stone: for example, the disciple who has studied

(only) Midrash: when a scholar comes to him and asks him about Midrash, he answers him. That is a hewn stone, for only one of its sides is exposed.[15]

The cornerstone: for example, the disciple who has studied (only) Midrash and Halakha: when a scholar comes to him and asks him about Midrash, he answers him; about Halakha, he answers him. That is a cornerstone, for only two of its sides are exposed.

The polished stone: for example, the disciple who has studied Midrash, Halakha, Agada, and Tosephta: when a scholar comes to him and asks about Midrash, he answers him; about Halakha, he answers him; about Tosephta, he answers him; [16] about Agada, he answers him. And that is a polished stone, for it has all its four sides exposed.

Rabbi Judah ben Il'ai says: He who makes the words of the Torah primary and worldly matters secondary will be made primary in the world to come; (but he who makes) worldly matters primary and the words of the Torah secondary will be made secondary in the world to come.[17] A parable is told: to what may this be likened? To a thoroughfare [18] which lies between two paths, one of flames and the other of snow. If one walks alongside the flames, he will be scorched by the flames; and if he walks alongside the snow, he will be frostbitten. What then is he to do? Let him walk between them and take care of himself in order not to be scorched by the flames and not to be frostbitten.

CHAPTER 29

RABBI SIMEON BEN ELEAZAR SAYS IN RABBI ME'IR'S NAME: DO NOT
APPEASE THY FELLOW IN THE HOUR OF HIS ANGER; DO NOT COMFORT
HIM IN HIS HOUR OF MOURNING; DO NOT QUESTION HIM [1] IN THE
HOUR OF HIS VOW; DO NOT COME TO HIS HOUSE ON THE DAY OF HIS
REVERSES; AND DO NOT STRIVE TO SEE HIM IN HIS HOUR OF MISFOR-
TUNE.[2]

HE used to say: If thou hast companions, some of whom
reprove thee and some of whom praise thee, love him
that reproves thee and hate him that praises thee: for
he who reproves thee brings thee to the life of the world to come,
while he who praises thee removes thee from the world.

He used to say: Wheresoever a man goes, his heart goes; wheresoever he stands, his heart stands; wheresoever he sits, things are
clarified for him.[3]

He used to say: He who is diligent over the words of the Torah
is given (agents) that are diligent in his behalf; but he who
neglects the words of the Torah is given over to (forces) that will
make him idle [4]—for example, wolves, lions, bears,[5] leopards,
panthers, serpents, robbers, or brigands come and surround him,
and they settle accounts with him, as it is said, *God hath His
chastisers on the earth* (Ps. 58: 12).

Abba Saul ben Nannas says: There are four types of scholars:
one studies himself but does not teach others; one teaches others
but himself does not study; one teaches himself and others; and
one teaches neither himself nor others.

One studies himself but does not teach others: for example,
when a person studies one order (of the Mishnah), or two or
three, and does not teach them to others, but himself is intent [6]
upon these studies and does not forget what he has learned. Such
is one who studies himself but does not teach others.

One teaches others but himself does not study: for example, when a person studies one order, or two or three, and teaches them to others, but himself is not intent upon these studies and (thus) forgets what he has learned. Such is one who teaches others but himself does not study.

One teaches himself and others: for example, when a person studies one order, or two or three, and teaches them to others; and himself is intent upon these studies and does not forget them—(so that) he masters them and they master them. Such is one who teaches himself and others.

One teaches neither himself nor others: for example, when a person studies one order two or three times [7] and does not teach it to others, and himself is not intent upon his studies and (thus) forgets what he learned. Such is one who teaches neither himself nor others.

Rabbi Hananiah ben Jacob says: If one is kept awake in the night by words of the Torah, it is a good sign for him; if by (idle) conversation, it is a bad sign for him.

Rabbi Jacob ben Hananiah says: [8] If one wakes in the night and the first words out of his mouth are not words of the Torah,[9] it would have been better for him if the afterbirth in which he lay [10] had been turned over his face, and he had never been born [11] and beheld the world.

Rabbi Eleazar [12] Hakkappar says: He who honors his fellow for the sake of wealth will in the end part from him in disgrace; but he who despises his fellow for the sake of some holy work [13] will in the end part from him in honor.

Now how do we know that he who honors his fellow for the sake of wealth will in the end part from him in disgrace? For thus we find concerning the wicked Balaam who honored Balak for the sake of his wealth, as it is said, *And Balaam answered and said unto the servants of Balak: If Balak would give me his house full of silver and gold* (Num. 22:19). And how do we know that he parted from him in disgrace? For it is said, *Therefore now flee thou to thy place. . . . But lo, the Lord hath kept thee back from honor* (Num. 24: 11).[14]

And how do we know that he who despises his fellow for the sake of some holy work will in the end part from him in honor? For thus we find concerning Moses our master, who despised Pharaoh for the sake of a holy work, as it is said, *And all these thy servants shall come down unto me, and bow down unto me, saying* (Exod. 11: 8).

—Was then Pharaoh [15] standing on a roof and Moses standing on the ground? (No!) But thus said Moses to Pharaoh: "Even if all thy servants who rise and bow down before thee at thy dais should stand and beseech me, I shall not hearken unto them."—

And how do we know that Moses parted from him in honor? For it is said, *And he called for Moses and Aaron by night, and said, Rise up, get you forth from among my people* (Exod. 12: 31).[16] "Are we then thieves," they demanded, "that we should go forth in the night? Wait rather until the Holy One, blessed be He, brings us the seven clouds of glory,[17] and we shall go forth with them in joy and broad daylight!" [18] As it is said, *On the morrow after the Passover the children of Israel went out in broad daylight* (Num. 33: 3).

It was with regard to the four categories of atonement that Rabbi Mattiah ben Ḥeresh went to call upon Rabbi Eleazar Haḳḳappar at Laodicea. And he asked him: "Hast thou heard what Rabbi Ishmael used to teach in regard to the four categories of atonement?"

"I have heard," Rabbi Eleazar replied, "but they are three, and along with each of these there must be repentance. One verse says, *Return, ye backsliding children, saith the Lord;* [19] *I will heal your backsliding* (Jer. 3: 22); a second verse says, *For on this day shall atonement be made for you, to cleanse you* (Lev. 16: 30); a third verse says, *Then will I visit their transgression with the rod, and their iniquity with strokes* (Ps. 89: 33); and a fourth verse says, *Surely this iniquity shall not be expiated by you till ye die* (Isa. 22: 14).

"Now how is all this to be understood?

"If a man transgressed a positive commandment and repented, he is forgiven on the spot, before he has so much as stirred from his place. Of such it is said, *Return, ye backsliding children.*

"If a man transgressed a negative commandment and repented, repentance suspends the sentence and the Day of Atonement atones. Of such it is said, *For on this day shall atonement be made for you.*

"If a man transgressed commandments punishable by extirpation or by death from the courts and repented, repentance and the Day of Atonement suspend the sentence and his sufferings during the remaining days of the year atone. And of such it is said, *Then will I visit their transgression with the rod.*

"But when one profanes the name of Heaven, there is no power either in repentance to suspend his sentence or in sufferings to cleanse him of his sins or in the Day of Atonement to atone. Rather, repentance and sufferings suspend the sentence, and death, along with these,[20] cleanses him of his sins. And of such it is said, *Surely this iniquity shall not be expiated by you until ye die.*" [21]

Isi ben Judah says: Why do scholars die before their time? It is not because they are adulterous and not because they rob, but because they despise themselves.[22]

Rabbi Isaac ben Phineas says: He who is master of Midrash but not of Halakha has not tasted the flavor of wisdom; he who is master of Halakha but not of Midrash has not tasted the flavor of fear of sin.

He used to say: He who is master of Midrash but not of Halakha is mighty but unarmed; he who is master of Halakha but not of Midrash is weak but armed; [23] he who is master of both is mighty and armed.

He used to say: Be careful about greeting fellow men; [24] enter not into the midst of controversy; strive not to be seen seated in the company of scholars; [25] AND BE A TAIL TO LIONS RATHER THAN A HEAD TO JACKALS.[26]

CHAPTER 30

RABBI NATHAN BEN JOSEPH SAYS: HE WHO FULFILLS THE WORDS
OF THE TORAH IN POVERTY WILL IN THE END FULFILL THEM IN RICHES;
BUT·HE WHO NEGLECTS THE WORDS OF THE TORAH IN RICHES WILL IN
THE END NEGLECT THEM IN POVERTY.[1]

HE used to say: Comforting mourners, visiting the sick,
and acts of loving-kindness bring good into the world.[2]
Rabbi Me'ir says: If one is in doubt whether or not
he has committed a transgression, Scripture [3] accounts it to him as
though he has certainly committed it. For example:

A man sins: if he later discovers that he has indeed sinned, he
must bring a sin offering at a sela' or [4] the tenth part of an *ephah*
at a *dupondium;* but if he remains in doubt whether he has
sinned or not, he must bring the value of the sacrilege and an
additional fifth thereof, and he must bring a trespass offering at
two sela'.[5]

Now then, which is the greater measure, the measure of reward
or the measure of punishment? [6] Surely the measure of reward!
Is there not therefore an inference to be drawn here? Thus:

When it is a matter of the lesser measure, of punishment, if one
is in doubt whether or not he committed a transgression, Scripture
accounts it to him as though he had certainly committed it; all the
more certain is it when it is a matter of the greater measure, of
reward, (that good works, even unpremeditated ones, will be rewarded!)

Rabbi Nathan ben Joseph says: If one commits a transgression
unwittingly, Scripture accounts it to him as though he had committed it deliberately. For example:

If unwittingly one killed a person and went into exile to a city
of refuge,[7] and the avenger of blood found him (outside the
city) and killed him,[8] he would be acquitted. If deliberately one
killed a person and the avenger of blood found him and killed
him, the avenger would be killed in turn.

Now then, which is the greater measure, the measure of reward or the measure of punishment? Surely the measure of reward! (Therefore:)

When it is a matter of the lesser measure, of punishment, if one commits a transgression unwittingly, Scripture accounts it to him as though he had committed it deliberately; all the more certain is it when it is a matter of the greater measure, of reward, (that good works, even unwitting ones, will be rewarded!)

Rabbi 'Aḳiba says: He who attaches himself to transgressors, although he does not do as they do, will receive punishment along with them; but he who attaches himself to those who carry out the commandments, although he does not do as they do, will receive reward along with them. For example:

Two men [9] bore witness against someone and said: "This man killed a person." They were found false and sentence was passed that they be put to death.[10] As they were led forth to the stoning place, someone [11] ran after them, crying, "I know something about this testimony." "Come, give thy testimony," he was told. Then he, too, was found false and he (too) was sentenced to die. As he was being led forth to the stoning place, he exclaimed: "Woe unto me! for had I not [12] come along, I would surely not have been sentenced to die. But now that I came along with the false witnesses, I am sentenced to die!" "Wretch!" they replied, "even if a hundred men were to come along after thee and be found false, they would all be put to death!"

Now then, which is the greater measure, the measure of reward or the measure of punishment? Surely the measure of reward! (Thus:)

If when it is a matter of the lesser measure, of punishment, he who attaches himself to transgressors, although he does not do as they do, will be punished; all the more certain is it when it is a matter of the greater measure, of reward, (that he who attaches himself to the righteous will be rewarded!)

Rabbi Simeon says: Such is the punishment of the liar, that even when he speaks the truth none believe him. For thus we find concerning the sons of Jacob who deceived their father: at first he believed them, as it is said, *And they took Joseph's coat, and killed a he-goat . . . and he knew it and said, It is my son's coat* (Gen. 37:31, 33); but in the end, albeit they spoke the truth to him, he did not believe them, as it is said, *And they told him, saying: Joseph is yet alive. . . . And his heart fainted, for he believed them not. . . . But when he saw the wagons, etc.* (Gen. 45:26 f.).

And some say: The Holy Spirit which had withdrawn from Jacob, our father, came back to rest upon him at that moment; for it is said, *And the spirit of Jacob their father revived (ibid.).*[13]

Rabbi 'Aḥai ben Josiah says:

He who purchases grain in the market place, to what may he be likened? To an infant whose mother died: although he is taken from door to door to other wet nurses, he is not satisfied.

He who buys bread in the market place, what is he like? He is as good as dead and buried.[14]

He who eats of his own is like an infant raised at its mother's breast.

He used to say: When a man eats at his own table, his mind is at rest. But a man's mind is not at rest if he eats even at his father's or his mother's or his children's table, or, needless to say, at a stranger's table.

CHAPTER 31

B Y [1] TEN WORDS [2] WAS THE WORLD CREATED. Now then, what purpose was there to this for the inhabitants of the world? [3] But this is to teach thee that he who puts one commandment into practice and he who keeps one Sabbath and he who sustains one soul [4] is accounted by Scripture as though he had sustained a whole world which was created by ten words; but he who commits one transgression and he who profanes one Sabbath and he who destroys one soul [4] is accounted by Scripture as though he had destroyed a whole world which was created by ten words.

For thus we find of Cain who killed his brother Abel, as it is said, *The voice of thy brother's blood*[5] *crieth unto Me* (Gen. 4:10): though he shed the blood of one, it is said *damim* ("bloods") in the plural. Which teaches that the blood of Abel's children and children's children and all his descendants to the end of all generations destined to come forth from him—all of them stood crying out before the Holy One, blessed be He.

Thus thou dost learn that one man's life is equal to all the work of Creation.

Rabbi Nehemiah says: How do we know that one man is equal to all the work of Creation? For it is said, *This is the book of the generations of Adam. In the day that God created man, in the likeness of God made He him* (Gen. 5:1),[6] and elsewhere it says, *These are the generations of the heaven and of the earth when they were created, in the day that the Lord God made earth and heaven* (Gen. 2:4): even as in the latter there was *creation* and *making*, so in the former there was *creation* and *making*. This teaches that the Holy One, blessed be He, showed to Adam[7] all the generations destined to come forth from him, standing and rejoicing[8] before him as it were.

And some say: God showed him only the righteous, as it is said, *All those that were written unto life in Jerusalem*[9] (Isa. 4:3).

Rabbi Joshua ben Ḳorḥah says: Lo, it says, *Thine eyes did see mine unformed substance, and in Thy book they were all written* (Ps. 139:16): this teaches that the Holy One, blessed be He, showed to Adam every generation and its teachers, every generation and its administrators, every generation and its leaders, every generation and its prophets, every generation and its heroes, every generation and its sinners, every generation and its saints; (and He told him that) in this generation so and so was destined to be king, in that generation so and so was destined to be a sage.[10]

Rabbi Eliezer, son of Rabbi Yose the Galilean, says: Nine hundred and seventy-four[11] generations before the world was created, the Torah was (already) written: it lay in the bosom of the Holy One, blessed be He, and recited the Song[12] along with the ministering angels, as it is said, *Then I was by Him, as a*

nursling; and I was daily all delight, playing before Him, and it
says, *Playing in His habitable earth, and my delights are with
the sons of men* (Prov. 8: 30 f.).

Rabbi Yose the Galilean says: Whatever the Holy One, blessed
be He, created in the world,[13] He created in man.[14] A parable: to
what may this be likened? If one takes a wooden tablet and tries
to draw many forms, he is hard put to it because he has no room
to make the drawings; but he who draws on the earth can go on
drawing many forms and spread them out.

But the Holy One, blessed be He—may His great name be
blessed forever and to all eternity!—in His wisdom and understanding created the whole world, created the heavens and the
earth, the beings on high and those down below, and formed in
man whatever He created in His world:

He created forests in the world and He created forests in man:
to wit, man's hair;

He created evil beasts in the world and He created evil beasts in
man: to wit, the vermin in man;

He created channels [15] in the world and He created channels
in man: to wit, man's ears; [16]

He created a wind in the world and He created a wind in man:
to wit, man's breath; [17]

A sun in the world and a sun in man: to wit, man's forehead; [18]

Stagnant waters in the world and stagnant waters in man: to
wit, man's rheum;

Salt water in the world and salt water in man: to wit, man's
tears; [19]

Streams in the world and streams in man: to wit, man's urine; [20]

Walls in the world and walls in man: to wit, man's lips; [21]

Doors in the world and doors in man: to wit, man's teeth; [22]

Firmaments in the world and firmaments in man: to wit, man's
tongue; [23]

Sweet waters in the world and sweet waters in man: to wit,
man's spittle;

Stars in the world and stars in man: to wit, man's cheeks; [24]

Towers in the world and towers in man: to wit, man's neck; [25]

Masts in the world and masts in man: to wit, man's arms; [26]

Pegs in the world and pegs in man: to wit, man's fingers;

Kings in the world and a king in man: to wit, man's heart; [27]

Clusters in the world and clusters in man: to wit, man's breasts; [28]

Counselors in the world and counselors in man: to wit, man's reins; [29]

Millstones in the world and millstones in man: to wit, man's stomach;

Mashing mills in the world and mashing mills in man: to wit, man's spleen;

Pits in the world and a pit in man: to wit, man's navel;

Flowing waters in the world and flowing waters in man: to wit, man's blood;

Trees in the world and trees in man: to wit, man's bones;

Hills in the world and hills in man: to wit, man's buttocks;

Pestle and mortar in the world and pestle and mortar in man: to wit, man's joints;

Horses in the world and horses in man: to wit, man's legs;

The angel of death in the world and the angel of death in man: to wit, man's heels; [30]

Mountains and valleys in the world and mountains and valleys in man: erect, he is like a mountain; recumbent, he is like a valley.

Thus thou dost learn that whatever the Holy One, blessed be He, created in His world, He created in man.

CHAPTER 32

TEN [1] GENERATIONS FROM ADAM TO NOAH.[2] NOW THEN, WHAT PUR-
POSE WAS THERE TO THIS FOR THE INHABITANTS OF THE WORLD? BUT
THIS IS TO TEACH THEE THAT ALTHOUGH ALL THE GENERATIONS WENT
ON PROVOKING HIM, HE DID NOT BRING UPON THEM THE WATERS OF THE
FLOOD—BECAUSE OF THE RIGHTEOUS AND SAINTS IN THEIR MIDST.

AND some say: So long as Methuselah was alive the flood
did not come down on the world; and even when Methuselah died it was still withheld from them for seven days
after his death, as it is said, *And it came to pass after the seven
days, that the waters of the flood were upon the earth* (Gen. 7: 10).

What purpose was served by these seven days? They were the
seven days of mourning for Methuselah the righteous which prevented the calamity from coming upon the world. That is why it
is said, *And it came to pass after the seven days.*

Another interpretation. *And it came to pass after the seven days*
teaches that the Holy One, blessed be He, fixed a time for them
after the hundred and twenty year limit,[3] in the hope that they
might repent. But they did not. And that is why it is said, *And it
came to pass after the seven days.*

Another interpretation. The verse teaches that the Holy One,
blessed be He, changed the order of the universe [4] for them, so
that the sun rose in the west and set in the east; perchance they
might understand and grow fearful and repent. But they did not.
That is why it is said, *And it came to pass after the seven days.*[5]

Another interpretation. The Holy One, blessed be He, set His
table for them and showed them a bounty like to that of the world
to come, so that themselves they might look closely to their ways
and say: "Woe unto us over this good which we are forfeiting!" [6]
—for they had corrupted their way upon the earth, as it is said,
*And God saw the earth, and, behold, it was corrupt; for all flesh
had corrupted their way upon the earth* (Gen. 6: 12).

Rabbi Eleazar ben Pĕraṭa says: Lo, it says, *My spirit shall not judge man in this world* (Gen. 6: 3). Said the Holy One, blessed be He: I shall not judge them until I have given them their reward in full.[7] As it is said, *They spend their days in prosperity, but then they go down to Sheol* (Job 21: 13).

Rabbi Yose the Galilean says: Lo, it says, *My spirit shall not judge man in this world*. Said the Holy One, blessed be He: I shall not judge equally the evil impulse along with the good impulse. When is that the case? Before their sentence has been decreed. But after their sentence is decreed, both are equal in guilt.[8]

He used to say: As to the righteous, from them the evil impulse is taken away and they are given the good impulse, as it is said, *My heart*[9] *is wounded within me*[10] (Ps. 109: 22); as to the wicked, from them the good impulse is taken away and they are given the evil impulse, as it is said, *Says transgression*[11] *to the wicked in the midst of his*[12] *heart, There is no fear of God before his eyes* (Ps. 36: 2).[13] Those betwixt and between are given the one impulse and the other: as for him who turns to the evil impulse, he is judged by the evil impulse; as for him who turns to the good impulse, he is judged by the good impulse; as it is said, *Because He standeth at the right hand of the needy, to save him from them*[14] *that judge his soul* (Ps. 109: 31).[15]

Rabbi Simeon ben Eleazar says: Lo, it says, *My spirit shall not punish man in this world*. Said the Holy One, blessed be He: I shall not punish them until I have paid the righteous their reward. When is that the case?[16] In this world. But in the world to come, says Scripture, *His breath goeth forth, he returneth to his dust in that very day*[17] (Ps. 146: 4).

Rabbi 'Akiba says: Lo, it says, *My spirit shall not judge man forever*. Said the Holy One, blessed be He: They did not take stock[18] of themselves that they are flesh and blood, but behaved with arrogant spirit toward Him on high. As it is said, *Yet they said unto God, Depart from us; for we desire not the knowledge of Thy ways* (Job 21: 14).

Rabbi Me'ir says: Lo, it says, (*My spirit*) *shall not judge*. Said the Holy One, blessed be He: That generation declared, "The

Lord does not judge: there is no judge of the world; God has abandoned the world!"

Rabbi [19] says: Lo, it says, *(My spirit) doth not judge.* Said the Holy One, blessed be He: They did not establish courts on earth, (but) I shall establish a court for them in heaven! [20]

CHAPTER 33

TEN [1] GENERATIONS FROM NOAH TO ABRAHAM.[2] NOW THEN, WHAT PURPOSE WAS THERE TO THIS FOR THE INHABITANTS OF THE WORLD? BUT THIS IS TO TEACH THAT ALL THOSE GENERATIONS KEPT PROVOKING HIM, AND THERE WAS NOT ONE [3] OF THEM THAT WALKED IN THE WAYS OF THE HOLY ONE, BLESSED BE HE, UNTIL ABRAHAM OUR FATHER CAME AND WALKED IN THE WAYS OF THE HOLY ONE, BLESSED BE HE, as it is said, *Because that Abraham hearkened to My voice, and kept My charge, My commandments, My statutes, and My laws* (Gen. 26:5): it is not written here *law,* in the singular, but *laws,* in the plural.[4]

WHERE did he learn them all? But this teaches that the Holy One, blessed be He, appointed the two reins of Abraham our father to act like two teachers, and they made him to understand and counseled him [5] and taught him wisdom every night, as it is said, *I will bless the Lord, who hath given me counsel; yea, in the night seasons my reins instruct me* (Ps. 16:7).[6]

Moreover, Abraham our father would first practice charity and then justice, as it is said, *For I have known him to the end that he may command his children and his household after him that they may keep the way of the Lord, to do charity and (then) justice* (Gen. 18:19). When two litigants would come before Abraham our father for judgment and one would say of his fellow, "He owes me a mina," Abraham our father would take out a mina of his own, give it to him, and say to them: "Draw up your claims before me." Then each would draw up his claims. In the event that the defendant was found owing the other a mina, Abraham would say to the one with the mina: "Give the mina to thy fellow." But if it was not so, he would say to them: "Divide the sum between you and depart in peace." [7]

King David on the other hand did not act in this manner. Instead he would first practice justice and then charity, as it is said, *And David executed justice and charity* [8] *unto all his people* (II Sam. 8:15). When litigants came for judgment before King David, he would say to them, "Draw up your claims." In the event that one was found owing his fellow a mina, [David would say to him, "Give it back to thy fellow." But if he could not do so, David would hand a mina of his own to the claimant and send him off] [9] in peace.

WITH TEN TRIALS WAS ABRAHAM OUR FATHER TRIED BEFORE THE HOLY ONE, BLESSED BE HE, AND IN ALL OF THEM HE WAS FOUND STEADFAST,[10] to wit:

Twice, when ordered to move on; [11]

Twice, in connection with his two sons; [12]

Twice, in connection with his two wives; [13]

Once, on the occasion of his war with the kings; [14]

Once, at the (covenant) between the pieces; [15]

Once, in Ur of the Chaldees; [16]

And once, at the covenant of circumcision.[17]

Now, what was the reason for all this? So that when Abraham our father comes to take his reward, the peoples of the world shall say: "More than all of us, more than everyone, is Abraham worthy of getting his reward!" And it is of him that Scripture says, *Go thy way, eat thy bread with joy, and drink thy wine with a merry heart, for God has already accepted thy works* (Eccl. 9:7).

Corresponding to the TEN trials with which Abraham our father was tried and in all of which he was found steadfast, the Holy One, blessed be He, performed TEN miracles for his children in Egypt.[18]

Corresponding to those (trials), the Holy One, blessed be He, brought TEN plagues on the Egyptians in Egypt.[19]

Corresponding to those, TEN miracles were wrought for Israel at the Red Sea.[20]

Corresponding to those, TEN plagues were brought upon the Egyptians in the Sea.[21]

The Egyptians thundered at Israel with their voices; in turn the Holy One, blessed be He, thundered at them with His voice, as it is said, *The Lord thundered from heaven, and the Most High gave forth His voice* (II Sam. 22:14).[22]

The Egyptians came against them with bows and arrows; in turn the Holy One, blessed be He, came against them with bows and arrows, as it is said, *Thy bow is made quite bare* (Hab. 3:9); it also says, *And He sent out His arrows, and scattered them* (Ps. 18:15).

The Egyptians came against them with swords; in turn the Holy One, blessed be He, came against them with swords and spears, as it is said, *And He sent out His arrows, and scattered them; and He shot forth lightnings, and discomfited them* [23] (*ibid.*). Now, "lightning" (*barak*) is none other than the sword, for it is said, *A sword, a sword, it is sharpened, and also furbished; it is sharpened that it make a sore slaughter, it is furbished that it may glitter* (*barak*) (Ezek. 21:14 f.).

The Egyptians vaunted themselves in shield and buckler; and in turn the Holy One, blessed be He, did likewise, as it is said, *Take hold of shield and buckler and rise up to my help* (Ps. 35:2).

The Egyptians came against them with spears; in turn the Holy One, blessed be He, came against them with a spear, as it is said, *At the shining of Thy glittering spear* (Hab. 3:11).

The Egyptians came with stones and slings, and the Holy One, blessed be He, was exalted over them with hailstones, as it is said, *At the brightness before Him, there passed through His thick clouds hailstones and coals of fire* (Ps. 18:13).

When [24] our ancestors stood at the Red Sea, Moses said to them: "Rise, go across!"

"We shall not go across," they declared, "until tunnels are made in the sea."

Moses took his rod and smote the sea, and tunnels were made in it, as it is said, *Thou hast stricken through with rods* [25] *the head of his rulers* (Hab. 3: 14). [26]

Said Moses to them: "Rise, go across!"

"We shall not go across," they declared, "until the sea is turned into a valley before us."

Moses took the rod and smote the sea, and it became a valley before them, as it is said, *He made a valley of the sea, and caused them to pass through* (Ps. 78: 13), and it is said, *As the cattle that go down into the valley, so didst Thou lead Thy people* (Isa. 63: 14).

Said Moses to them: "Rise, go across!"

"We shall not go across," they declared, "until it is cut asunder before us."

Moses took the rod and smote the sea, and it was cut asunder before them, [27] as it is said, *To Him who divided the Red Sea in sunder* (Ps. 136: 13).

Said Moses to them: "Rise, go across!"

"We shall not go across," they declared, "until it is turned into clay for our benefit."

Moses took the rod and smote the sea, and it became clay, [28] as it is said, *Thou hast trodden the sea with Thy horses, through the clay of mighty waters* (Hab. 3: 15).

Said Moses to them: "Rise, go across!"

"We shall not go across," they declared, "until it is made into a wilderness before us."

Moses took the rod and smote the sea, and it became a wilderness, [29] as it is said, *And He led them through the depths as through a wilderness* (Ps. 106: 9).

Said Moses to them: "Rise, go across!"

"We shall not go across," they declared, "until it is broken into many pieces before us."

Moses took the rod and smote the sea, and it was broken into many pieces, as it is said, *Thou didst break the sea in pieces by Thy strength* (Ps. 74:13).

Said Moses to them: "Rise, go across!"

"We shall not go across," they declared, "unless it is turned into rocks before us."

Moses took the rod and smote the sea, and it turned into rocks,[30] as it is said, *Thou didst shatter the heads of the sea monsters on the waters* (*ibid.*). Now on what are the heads of sea monsters dashed? Say surely, the heads of sea monsters would not be dashed save on rocks.

Said Moses to them: "Rise, go across!"

"We shall not go across," they declared, "until it is turned into dry land for us."

Moses took the rod and smote the sea, and it turned into dry land, as it is said, *He turned the sea into dry land* (Ps. 66:6); it also says, *But the children of Israel walked upon dry land in the midst of the sea* (Exod. 14:29).

Said Moses to them: "Rise, go across!"

"We shall not go across," they declared, "unless it is turned into walls before us."

Moses took the rod and smote the sea, and it turned into walls, as it is said, *And the waters were a wall unto them, on their right hand, and on their left* (*ibid.*).

Said Moses to them: "Rise, go across!"

"We shall not go across," they declared, "unless it is turned flask-shaped before us."

Moses took the rod and smote the sea, and it turned flask-shaped,[31] as it is said, (*The waters*) *stood upright like flasks containing liquids* (Exod. 15:8).—

As for the waters between the sundered paths,[32] a fire came down and lapped them up, as it is said, *When fire caused that which melts to disappear,*[32] *and the fire lapped up the waters; to make Thy name known to Thine adversaries* (Isa. 64:1).[34]—

And the flasks released oil and honey into the mouths of the babes and of this they took suck, as it is said, *And He made him to suck honey out of the crag* (Deut. 32:13).

Some say: Fresh water came forth for them from the sea, and this they drank in the midst of the sundered paths—for the waters of the sea are salty—for it is said, *flowing streams,* and "flowing streams" are none other than sweet waters, as it is said, *A well of living waters, and flowing streams from Lebanon* (Cant. 4:15).

With the clouds of glory [35] over them lest the sun overpower them, Israel crossed, so as not to be discomfited.

Rabbi Eliezer says: The deep arched over them and under it Israel went across, so as not to be discomfited.

Rabbi Eliezer and Rabbi Simeon say: The upper and lower waters tossed the Egyptians up and down, as it is said, *And the Lord tossed the Egyptians up and down in the midst of the sea* (Exod. 14:27).

CHAPTER 34

WITH TEN TRIALS OUR ANCESTORS TRIED THE HOLY ONE, BLESSED BE HE, IN THE WILDERNESS,[1] to wit, *In the wilderness, at Arabah, over against Suph, in the neighborhood of Paran and Tophel, and Laban, and Hazeroth, and Di-zahab* (Deut. 1:1).

IN *the wilderness,* where they made the golden calf, as it is said, *They made a calf in Horeb* (Ps. 106:19).

At Arabah, where they clamored for water,[2] as it is said, *And the people thirsted there for water* (Exod. 17:3). Some say: This refers to the idol of Micah.[3]

Over against Suph is a reference to their being rebellious at the Red Sea.[4] Rabbi Judah says: They were rebellious at the sea, they were rebellious in the sea, as it is said, *But they were rebellious at the sea, even in the Red Sea* (Ps. 106:7).

In the neighborhood of Paran refers to the incident of the spies, as it is said, *And Moses sent them from the wilderness of Paran* (Num. 13:3).

And Tophel refers to the slanderous words which they uttered over the manna.[5]

And Laban refers to the controversy of Korah.[6]

And Hazeroth refers to the incident of the quail.[7]

These are seven. And elsewhere it says, *And at Taberah,*[8] *and at Massah,*[9] *and at Kibroth-hattavah* [10] *ye made the Lord wroth* (Deut. 9:22).

And Di-zahab: Said Aaron to them: "Enough for you is the sin of the gold which you brought for the calf!" [11]

Rabbi Eliezer ben Jacob says: For this iniquity there is enough to punish Israel from now until the dead are resurrected.

By [12] TEN names of praise was the Holy One, blessed be He, called, to wit: Lord,[13] YHWH,[14] God (*Elohim*), Deity (*'Ĕloah*), Thy God, Your God, Mighty (*El*), I AM,[15] Almighty, [16] Hosts.[17]

Said Rabbi Yose: I disagree as regards Hosts, for it is said, *That captains of the hosts shall be appointed at the head of the people* (Deut. 20:9).[18]

By [19] TEN names of contempt was idolatry called, to wit: abominations,[20] idols,[20] molten images,[21] graven images,[21] false gods,[22] Asherim,[23] sun images,[23] shapes,[24] wickedness,[25] teraphim.[25]

TWO marks [26] occur in the Torah in a short section, and that short section is, *And it came to pass, when the ark set forward, that Moses said. . . . And when it rested, he said,* etc. (Num. 10:35 f.).

Rabban Simeon ben Gamaliel says: In the future this section will be lifted from its (present) place and written down elsewhere.[27]

It is the same [28] with the verse, *And Jonathan, the son of Gershom, the son of Manasseh* [29] (Jud. 18:30). For was he then the son of Manasseh? Was he not the son of Moses? [30] But it is because his actions were not like those of his father Moses that he was associated with Manasseh.[31]

Similarly,[32] with the verse, *These are the two anointed ones, that stand by the Lord of the whole earth* (Zech. 4:14). This is a reference to Aaron and the Messiah, but I cannot tell which is the

more beloved. However, from the verse, *The Lord hath sworn,
and will not repent: Thou art a priest for ever after the manner
of Melchizedek* [33] (Ps. 110:4), one can tell that the Messianic
King is more beloved than the righteous priest.

Scripture reads, *The boar out of the wood (y'r) doth ravage it*
(Ps. 80:14), but it is written, *The boar out of the river (y'r) doth
ravage it.* [34]

The boar out of the wood doth ravage it refers to the Roman
Empire. [35] For when Israel do not do the will of God, the nations
appear to them like *the boar out of the wood*: even as the boar of
the forests kills people and injures folk and smites men, so too, so
long as Israel do not do the will of God, the nations kill them
and injure them and smite them.

But so long as Israel do the will of God the nations do not rule
over them. (Then the nations are) like *the boar out of the river*:
even as the boar of the rivers kills no people and harms no folk,
so too, so long as Israel do His will, no nation or people kills them
or harms them or smites them.

That is why it is written, [36] *The boar out of the river.*

There are TEN dotted passages in the Torah, [37] as follows:
The Lord judge between me and thee (Gen. 16:5). The (second) letter *y* of *bynyk* (*and thee*) is dotted to teach that Sarah
spoke to Abraham of Hagar only. [38] Some say: (She spoke to him)
of those who stir up quarrels "between me and thee." [39]

Again, *And they said unto him, Where is Sarah* (Gen. 18:9).
The letters *'*, *y*, and *w* of *'lyw* (*unto him*) are dotted to teach that
they knew her whereabouts but inquired after her (nonetheless). [40]

Again, *And he knew not when she lay down, nor when she
arose* (Gen. 19:33). The letter *w* of the first [41] *bkwmh* (*when-she-
arose*) is dotted to teach that he was unaware of the getting up of
the younger daughter only. [42]

Again, *And Esau ran to meet him, and embraced him, and fell
on his neck, and kissed him* (Gen. 33:4). The whole word *wyškhw*
(*and-he-kissed-him*) is dotted to teach that he did not kiss him

sincerely. Rabbi Simeon ben Eleazar says: This kiss was sincere, but all the others were not sincere.[43]

Again, *And his brethren went to feed their father's flock in Shechem* (Gen. 37:12). The particle *'t*[44] is dotted to teach that they did not go to tend the flock, but to eat, drink, and make merry.[45]

Again, *All that were numbered of the Levites, whom Moses and Aaron numbered* (Num. 3:39). The word *Aaron* is dotted; why is that? This teaches that Aaron was not included in the number.[46]

Again, *Or be in a journey afar off* (Num. 9:10). The letter *h* of *rḥwḳh (afar off)* is dotted to teach that it is not necessarily a journey far off, but even as far off as beyond the threshold of the Temple court.[47]

Again, *And we have laid waste even unto Nophah, which reacheth unto Medeba* (Num. 21:30). The letter *r* of *'šr (which)* is dotted; why is that? This teaches that they destroyed the people but did not destroy the cities.[48]

Again, in *And a several tenth part* (Num. 29:15) of the first festival day of the Feast of Booths, the word *'šrwn (tenth part)* is written with the letter *w* dotted;[49] why is that? This teaches that there must be no more than one tenth part.[50]

Finally, in *The secret things belong unto the Lord our God; but the things that are revealed belong unto us and to our children for ever* (Deut. 29:28), the words *unto us and to our children* and the letter *'* of *'d (for)* are dotted; why is that? [This teaches that in this world they are not revealed to us, but they will be revealed to us in the age to come.[51]

Now why are all these passages dotted?][52] But this is what Ezra said: If Elijah comes and says to me, "Why didst thou write in this fashion?"[53] I shall say to him: "That is why I dotted these passages." And if he says to me, "Thou hast written well," I shall remove the dots from them.

In ELEVEN instances the word *hy'* ("she," "it") is written in the Torah with a *y*.[54]

The first is *And the king of Bela—it (hy') is Zoar* (Gen. 14:2).
(The others are:)

*Said he not himself unto me: She is my sister? And she (hy'),
even she herself said: He is my brother* (Gen. 20:5).

*When she was brought forth, she (hy') sent to her father-in-
law, saying* (Gen. 38:25).

And if any beast, of which (hy') ye may eat, die (Lev. 11:39).

And it (hy') have turned the hair white (Lev. 13:10).

But if the priest look on it . . . but it (hy') be dimmed (Lev.
13:21).

And she (hy') see his nakedness (Lev. 20:17).

She (hy') profaneth her father (Lev. 21:9).

(The remaining instances are in the chapter) on jealousy:

*She being defiled secretly . . . neither she (hy') be taken in the
act* [55] (Num. 5:13); *Or if the spirit of jealousy come upon him,
and he be jealous of his wife, and she (hy') be not defiled* (Num.
5:14).[56]

TEN descents did the Shekinah make to the world:[57]

Once in the Garden of Eden, as it is said, *And they heard the
voice of the Lord God walking in the garden* (Gen. 3:8).

Once in the generation of the Tower of Babel, as it is said, *And
the Lord came down to see the city and the tower* (Gen. 11:5).

Once in Sodom, as it is said, *I will go down now and see
whether they have done altogether according to the cry of it,
which is come unto Me* (Gen. 18:21).

Once in Egypt, as it is said, *And I came down to deliver them
out of the hand of the Egyptians* (Exod. 3:8).

Once on the Red Sea, as it is said, *He bowed the heavens also,
and came down* (II Sam. 22:10).

Once at Sinai, as it is said, *And the Lord came down upon
Mount Sinai* (Exod. 19:20).

Once in the pillar of the cloud, as it is said, *And the Lord came
down in a cloud* (Num. 11:25).

Once in the Temple, as it is said, *This gate shall be shut, it shall*

*not be opened . . . for the Lord, the God of Israel, hath entered
in by it* (Ezek. 44:2).

And one will take place in the future, in the days of Gog and
Magog, as it is said, *And His feet shall stand that day upon the
mount of Olives* (Zech. 14:4).[58]

By TEN ascents the Shekinah withdrew from one place to the
next:

From the ark cover to the cherub;

From the cherub to the threshold of the house;

From the threshold of the house to the two cherubim;

From the two cherubim to the roof of the Sanctuary;

From the roof of the Sanctuary to the wall of the Temple court;

From the wall of the Temple court to the altar;

From the altar to the city;

From the city to the Temple mount;

And from the Temple mount to the wilderness.

From the ark cover to the cherub, as it is written, *And He rode
upon a cherub, and did fly* (II Sam. 22:11).

From the cherub to the threshold, as it is written, *And the glory
of the Lord mounted up from the cherub to the threshold of the
house* (Ezek. 10:4).

From the threshold of the house to the two cherubim, as it is
written, *And the glory of the Lord went forth from off the
threshold of the house, and stood over the cherubim* (Ezek. 10:18).

From the cherubim to the roof of the Sanctuary, as it is written,
It is better to dwell in a corner of the housetop [59] (Prov. 21:9).

From the roof to the wall of the Temple court, as it is written,
And, behold, the Lord stood beside a wall made by a plumbline
(Amos 7:7).

From the wall of the Temple court to the altar, as it is written, *I
saw the Lord standing beside the altar* (Amos 9:1).

From the altar to the city, as it is written, *Hark! the Lord
crieth unto the city* (Micah 6:9).

From the city to the Temple mount, as it is written, *And the*

*glory of the Lord went up from the midst of the city, and stood
upon the mountain* (Ezek. 11:23).

And from the Temple mount to the wilderness, as it is written,
It is better to dwell [60] *in a desert land* (Prov. 21:19).

And once when it withdrew upward on high, as it is written,
I will go and return to My place (Hos. 5:15).[61]

By TEN names were prophets called,[62] to wit: ambassador,[63]
trusted,[64] servant,[65] messenger,[66] visionary,[67] watchman,[68] seer,[69]
dreamer,[70] prophet,[71] man of God.[72]

By TEN names was the Holy Spirit [73] called, to wit: parable,[74]
metaphor,[75] riddle,[76] speech,[77] saying,[78] glory,[79] command,[80]
burden,[81] prophecy,[82] vision.[83]

By TEN names was gladness called, to wit: joy,[84] gladness,[84]
rejoicing,[85] singing,[86] dancing,[87] jubilation,[88] delight,[89] cheerfulness,[90] glory,[91] exultation.[92]

TEN were called living, to wit:

(The Holy One, blessed be He,) as it is said, *But the Lord God
is the true God, He is the living God* (Jer. 10:10).

The Torah was called life, as it is said, *She is a tree of life to
them that lay hold upon her* (Prov. 3:18).

Israel was called alive, as it is said, *But ye that did cleave unto the
Lord your God are alive every one of you this day* (Deut. 4:4).

The righteous man was called life, as it is said, *The fruit of the
righteous is a tree of life* (Prov. 11:30).

The Garden of Eden was called living, as it is said, *I shall walk
before the Lord in the lands of the living* (Ps. 116:9).

Trees were called life, as it is said, *The tree of life also in the
midst of the garden* (Gen. 2:9).

The Land of Israel was called living, as it is said, *And I will
set glory in the land of the living* (Ezek. 26:20).

Acts of loving-kindness were called life, as it is said, *For Thy
loving-kindness is better than life; my lips shall praise thee* (Ps.
63:4).

Sages were called life, as it is said, *The teaching of the sage is a fountain of life* (Prov. 13:14).

Water was called living, as it is said, *In that day . . . living waters shall go out from Jerusalem* (Zech. 14:8).[93]

CHAPTER 35

TEN [1] MIRACLES WERE WROUGHT FOR OUR ANCESTORS IN JERUSALEM:

NO WOMAN EVER MISCARRIED BECAUSE OF THE SMELL OF THE SACRED FLESH; [2]

NO man was attacked (by demons) in Jerusalem;
No man ever met with an accident in Jerusalem;
No fire ever broke out in Jerusalem;
No structures ever collapsed [3] in Jerusalem;
No man ever said to his fellow: "I haven't found an oven in Jerusalem to roast the paschal sacrifices";
No man ever said to his fellow: "I haven't found a bed to sleep in in Jerusalem";
NO MAN EVER SAID TO HIS FELLOW: "TOO STRAIT IS THE PLACE FOR ME,[4] THAT I SHOULD LODGE IN JERUSALEM." [5]

TEN things were said of Jerusalem: [6]
Jerusalem's houses do not become unclean through leprosy; [7]
It is not to be declared a condemned city; [8]
Neither beams nor balconies nor sockets may project there over the public thoroughfare lest, by overshadowing,[9] they give passage to corpse uncleanness;
The dead may not be lodged there overnight; [10]
The bones of a dead man may not be carried through it; [11]
No place is made available there for a resident alien; [12]
No graves may be kept up there excepting the graves of the house of David, and of Huldah the prophetess, which were there since the days of the early prophets.—[13] And when (all other)

graves were cleared away, why were these not cleared away? They say: There was a tunnel here which gave passage to the uncleanness into the brook of Kidron.[14]—

No plants may be planted there; neither gardens nor orchards may be cultivated there,[15] excepting rose gardens, which were there since the days of the early prophets;

Neither geese nor chickens may be raised there nor, needless to say, pigs; [16]

No dunghills may be kept there because of uncleanness;

No trial of a stubborn and rebellious son [17] may be held there— such is the view of Rabbi Nathan—for it is said, *Then shall his father and his mother lay hold on him, and bring him out unto the elders of his city, and unto the gate of his place* (Deut. 21:19), and this (Jerusalem) is not *his* [18] *city,* this is not *his place;*

No houses may be sold there save [19] from the ground up; [20]

The sale of houses is not valid there for longer than twelve months; [21]

No payment for a bed [22] is accepted there—Rabbi Judah says: Not even payment for beds [and] [23] coverings; [24]

The hides of the sacrificial beasts are not for sale there. What was done with them? Rabban Simeon ben Gamaliel says: They were given to the innkeepers. The guests would stay indoors and the innkeepers out of doors. The guests resorted to an evasion [25] by buying painted [26] sheep whose hides were worth four to five sela', and these were left as compensation for the men of Jerusalem.[27]

One verse says, *The place which the Lord shall choose in one of thy tribes* (Deut. 12:14), and another verse says, *Out of all your tribes* (Deut. 12:5).

In one of thy tribes refers to the tribes of Judah and Benjamin.

Out of all your tribes refers to Jerusalem, in which all Israel share.

What was contained in the portion of Judah? The Temple mount, the Temple treasuries, and the Temple courts.

And what was contained in the portion of Benjamin? The

Sanctuary, the Porch, and the chamber of the Holy of Holies.

And a triangular strip extended (from the portion of Judah into the portion of Benjamin), and upon it was the altar built. Benjamin was found worthy and was made host for the Almighty,[28] as it is said (concerning Benjamin), *And He dwelleth between his shoulders* (Deut. 33:12).[29]

Said Joshua at that time:[30] "I know that the Temple is to be set up on the border between Judah and Benjamin; I shall go (therefore) and prepare the pasture of Jericho."[31]

Now who enjoyed its advantages all those years?[32] The descendants of the Kenite, the father-in-law of Moses, as it is said, *And the children of the Kenite, Moses' father-in-law, went up out of the city of palm trees*[33] (Jud. 1:16).

They[34] said: "When the Holy One, blessed be He, reveals his Shekinah, He will richly reward Jethro and his descendants."

Now how did the descendants of Jethro make their living? By pottery work, for it is said, *And the families of scribes that dwelt at Jabez . . . these are the Kenites that came of Hammath, the father of the house of Rechab* (I Chron. 2:55), and it says, *These are the potters, and those that dwelt among plantations,* etc. (I Chron. 4:23).[35] They had been people of importance, householders, owners of fields and vineyards, but for the sake of the service of the King of kings of kings, the Holy One, blessed be He,[36] they gave up everything and went off. Where did they go to? To Jabez, to study Torah; and (thus) they became God's people.[37]

At that time Jabez—the good and worthy man,[38] the man of truth and saint—was sitting and expounding the Torah, as it is said, *And Jabez called on the God of Israel, saying: Oh that Thou wouldst bless me indeed. . . . And God granted him that which he requested*[39] (I Chron. 4:10).

TEN MIRACLES WERE WROUGHT FOR OUR ANCESTORS IN THE TEMPLE:[40]

NEVER WAS A FLY SEEN IN THE SLAUGHTERHOUSE;[41]

NEVER DID THE HIGH PRIEST SUFFER UNCLEANNESS ON THE DAY OF

ATONEMENT—excepting Rabbi Ishmael ben Ḳimḥiṭ:[42] He went out to converse with a certain hegemon, and spittle flew from the hegemon's mouth and landed on Ishmael's clothes;[43] so his brother came in and served as High Priest in his place.[44] Their mother thus beheld them both High Priests on that day. When the Sages saw her, they asked: "What merit was thine?" And she replied: "Never did the rafters of my house see the hair of my head."[45]

Never was a man attacked (by demons) in Jerusalem; no man was ever harmed or met with an accident in the Temple;

NO WOMAN EVER MISCARRIED BECAUSE OF THE SMELL OF THE SACRED FLESH;

Never did the priests impair[46] the sacrifices;

When they ate excessively of the meat of the sacrifices, they drank the waters of Siloah and the meat would be digested in their bowels the way food is (ordinarily) digested;

NEVER WAS A DEFECT FOUND IN THE 'OMER[47] OR IN THE TWO LOAVES[48] OR IN THE SHOWBREAD;[49]

When an earthenware vessel broke,[50] the fragments disappeared on the spot;[51]

NO WIND PREVAILED OVER THE PILLAR OF SMOKE. When the pillar of smoke rose from the altar of the burnt offering, it rose straight upward like a staff until it reached the heavens; and when the pillar of incense rose from the golden altar, it entered straightaway into the chamber of the Holy of Holies.

THE PEOPLE STOOD PRESSED TOGETHER YET BOWED DOWN AND HAD ROOM ENOUGH.[52] On the occasion when Israel went up to worship their Father who is in heaven, while they were sitting, they sat crowded together and no one could force a finger between them; yet when they bowed down, they bowed down and had room enough.

The greatest miracle of all was this: Even if a hundred men bowed down[53] at one time, the minister of the synagogue did not need to call out and say: "Make room for your brethren!"

Miracles were wrought in the Temple court: Even if all Israel entered the Temple court, the Temple court held them.

The greatest miracle of all was this: While Israel were standing up for the prayer, they were crowded together and no one could force a finger between them; yet when they bowed down, space was formed between them of fully a man's height.

Rabban Simeon ben Gamaliel says: In the future Jerusalem will be the gathering place of all the nations and all the kingdoms, as it is said, *And all the nations shall be gathered unto it, to the name of the Lord, to Jerusalem* (Jer. 3:17). Now elsewhere it says, *Let the waters under the heaven be gathered unto one place* (Gen. 1:9). Even as the gathering spoken of in the latter instance refers to the assembling of all the waters of Creation in one place, so the gathering spoken of here refers to the assembling of all the nations and kingdoms in one place,[54] as it is said, *And all the nations shall be gathered unto it.*

CHAPTER 36

THE [1] men of Sodom will neither live (in the world to come) nor be brought to judgment,[2] for it is said, *Now the men of Sodom were wicked and sinners against the Lord exceedingly* (Gen. 13:13):

were wicked toward one another;

and sinners as regards unchastity;

against the Lord refers to the profaning of the Name;

exceedingly, in that by their transgressions they had in mind (to rebel against God).[3]

Such is the view of Rabbi Eliezer.

Rabbi Joshua says: They shall be brought to judgment,[4] for it is said, *Therefore the wicked shall not stand in the judgment, nor sinners in the congregation of the righteous* (Ps. 1:5)—in the congregation of the righteous they do not stand, but they do stand in the congregation of the wicked.

Rabbi Nehemiah says: Even into the congregation of the wicked they do not come, as it is said, *Let sinners [5] cease out of the earth, and let the wicked be no more* (Ps. 104:35).

Young children of the wicked (who died in their minority) [6] will neither live (in the world to come) nor be brought to judgment, as it is said, *For behold, the day cometh; it burneth as a furnace; and all the proud, and all that work wickedness, shall be stubble; and the day that cometh shall set them ablaze, saith the Lord of hosts, that shall leave them neither root nor branch* [7] (Mal. 3:19). Such is the view of Rabbi Eliezer.

Rabbi Joshua says: They shall enter (into the world to come), [8] and of them Scripture says, *He cried aloud, and said thus: Hew down the tree, and cut off its branches, shake off its leaves, and scatter its fruit* (Dan. 4:11), and continues, *Nevertheless leave the stump of its roots in the earth, even in a band of iron and brass* (Dan. 4:12). Here (in Malachi) *roots* are spoken of, and there (in Daniel) *roots* are spoken of: Even as in the Daniel passage, where roots are mentioned, Scripture speaks of the tree itself (being hewn down), so in the Malachi passage, where roots are mentioned, Scripture speaks of the (wicked) man himself. [9]

"If so," (said Rabbi Eliezer to him,) "how am I to interpret *That shall leave them neither root nor branch?*"

"That there will be found no merit for them [10] on which to base any claims for reward," [11] (he replied).

Others say: They shall enter (into the world to come), [12] and it is of them that the verse says, *One shall say: I am the Lord's; and another shall call himself by the name of Jacob; and another shall subscribe with his hand unto the Lord, and (another) surname himself by the name of Israel* (Isa. 44:5):

One shall say: I am the Lord's is a reference to the thoroughly righteous.

And another shall call himself by the name of Jacob is a reference to the young children of the wicked. [13]

And another shall subscribe with his hand unto the Lord is a reference to the wicked who forsook their ways and turned away from them and repented.

And (another) surname himself by the name of Israel is a reference to the proselytes amongst the Gentiles. [14]

Korah and his company will neither live (in the world to come) nor be brought to judgment, as it is said, *And the earth closed upon them, and they perished from among the assembly* (Num. 16:33)—such is the view of Rabbi Eliezer.[15]

Rabbi Joshua says: They shall enter (into the world to come),[16] and of them it says, *The Lord killeth, and maketh alive; He bringeth down to the grave, and bringeth up* (I Sam. 2:6). (Now) in the Korah chapter the *grave* is spoken of: *So they, and all that appertained to them, went down alive into the grave* (Num. 16:33); and in the Samuel passage, too, the *grave* is spoken of. Even as in the latter passage, where the grave is spoken of, it is said, *He bringeth down and bringeth up*, so in the Korah passage, where the grave is spoken of, it is implied that (though) they went down, they are destined to come up again.

Said Rabbi Eliezer to him: "How then dost thou interpret *And the earth closed upon them, and they perished from among the assembly?*"

"From among the assembly they perished," he replied, "but from the world to come they did not perish."

And the Generation of the Wilderness will neither live (in the world to come) nor be brought to judgment, for it is said, *In the wilderness they shall be consumed, and there they shall die* (Num. 14:35); [17] it says also, *Wherefore I swore in My wrath, that they should not enter into My rest* (Ps. 95:11). Such is the view of Rabbi Eliezer.

Rabbi Joshua says: They shall enter (into the world to come),[18] and of them it says, *Gather My saints together unto Me; those that have made a covenant with Me by sacrifice* [19] (Ps. 50:5).

Said Rabbi Eliezer to him: "How dost thou interpret *Wherefore I swore in My wrath,* etc.?"

"That," he replied, "refers to the spies [20] and all the wicked of that generation."

Said Rabbi Joshua to Rabbi Eliezer: "And how dost thou interpret *Gather My saints together unto Me?*"

"That," Rabbi Eliezer replied, "refers to Moses and Aaron and all the saints of that generation of the tribe of Levi."

Rabbi [21] Yose the Galilean says: They shall not enter (into the world to come), as it is said, *In this wilderness they shall be consumed, and there they shall die;* it says also, *And they shall break the heifer's neck there in the valley* (Deut. 21:4): even as the word *there* used in the latter instance, in connection with the broken-necked heifer, implies that it shall be dead and not stir from its place, so the word *there* used in our instance implies that they shall die and not stir from their place.

But the Sages countered: Is it only in connection with the wicked that the word *there* is used; is not the word used in connection with the righteous? Verily it is said, *There they buried Abraham and Sarah his wife* (Gen. 49:31); and it says, *In my grave which I have digged for me in the land of Canaan, there shalt thou bury me* (Gen. 50:5); and it says, *And Miriam died there, and was buried there* (Num. 20:1), *And Aaron the priest went up . . . and died there* (Num. 33:38); and it says, *So Moses the servant of the Lord died there in the land of Moab, according to the word of the Lord* (Deut. 34:5)!

Others [22] say: They shall enter (into the world to come), and of them it says, *Go and cry in the ears of Jerusalem, saying . . . I remember for thee the affection of thy youth* (Jer. 2:2).

The Ten Tribes will neither live (in the world to come) nor be brought to judgment, for it is said, *And the Lord rooted them out of their land . . . and cast them into another land, as it is this day* (Deut. 29:27).

Rabbi Simeon ben Judah says: Even as the day departs and does not return, so shall they not return.

Rabbi 'Akiba says: Even as the day [23] is now overcast and now bright again, so shall their darkness be made bright.[24]

Rabban Gamaliel says: Scripture says, *That your days may be multiplied, and the days of your children* (Deut. 11:21), and also, *The fathers shall not be put to death for the children* (Deut. 24:16): so long as the father's days are prolonged, the son's days are prolonged; when the father's days are not prolonged, the son's days are not prolonged.[25]

Rabbi Yose the Galilean supports [26] the view of Rabbi Eliezer [27] and Rabban Gamaliel supports the view of Rabbi Joshua.[28]

SEVEN have no share in the world to come, to wit:

Scribes, elementary teachers, (even) the best of physicians, judges in their native cities, diviners,[29] ministers of the court, and butchers.[30]

THREE kings and FOUR commoners have no share in the world to come: [31]

The three kings are Jeroboam, Ahab, Manasseh.

The four commoners are Balaam, Doeg, Ahitophel, and Gehazi.

Rabbi Judah says: Not Manasseh, for he repented, as it is said, *And he prayed unto Him, and He was entreated of him, and heard his supplication, and brought him back to Jerusalem into his kingdom* (II Chron. 33:13).[32]

Said the Sages to him: "Had Scripture read, *And brought him back to Jerusalem* and no more, we might have held with thy view. But Scripture reads, *into his kingdom:* to his kingdom he was brought back, but into the world to come he was not brought."

Rabbi Me'ir says: Absalom (too) has no share in the world to come.

Rabbi Simeon ben Eleazar says: Jeroboam, Ahab, Manasseh, Basha, Ahaziah, and all the kings of Israel who were wicked, have no share in the world to come.

Rabbi Johanan ben Nuri says: So, too, he that pronounces God's name according to its consonants [33] has no share in the world to come.

He used to say: He who makes a (mere) song of the Song of Songs,[34] or whispers charms over a wound, or spits over a wound and recites, *I will put none of the diseases upon thee, which I have put upon the Egyptians; for I am the Lord that healeth thee* [35] (Exod. 15:26) has no share in the world to come.[36]

And the Sages say: Any scholar who studied (Torah) and (then) withdrew has no share in the world to come, as it is said,

Because he hath despised the word of the Lord . . . that soul
shall utterly be cut off (Num. 15:31); it says also, *What un-*
righteousness have your fathers found in Me, that they are gone
far from Me (Jer. 2:5).

Rabbi Me'ir says: He who has in his city a study house and does
not frequent it, has no share in the world to come.[37]

And Rabbi 'Aḳiba says: So, too, he that does not make it a habit
to attend upon scholars has no share in the world to come.

CHAPTER 37

THERE are SEVEN created things, one superior to the
other:[1]

He created the firmament on high.[2]

Superior to the firmament are the stars He created, for they
give light to the world.

Superior to the stars are the trees He created: for trees bear
fruit, while the stars bear no fruit.

Superior to the trees are the winds[3] He created: for winds[3] go
hither and yon, while trees do not stir from their spot.

Superior to the winds[3] are the beasts He created: for beasts
work and eat, while winds neither work nor eat.

Superior to the beasts is man whom He created: for in man
there is understanding, while in beasts there is no understanding.

Superior to man are the ministering angels He created: for the
ministering angels go from one end of the world to the other,
while human beings are not like that.

SIX things were said of human beings; in three they are like
the beasts and in three they are like the ministering angels.

In three they are like the beasts: They eat and drink like the
beasts, they reproduce and multiply like the beasts, they excrete
like the beasts.

In three they are like the ministering angels: They have understanding like the ministering angels, they walk erect like the ministering angels, and they converse in the holy tongue [4] like the ministering angels.

SIX things were said of the demons; in three they are like human beings and in three they are like the ministering angels.

In three they are like human beings: They eat and drink like human beings, they reproduce and multiply like human beings, and they die like human beings.

In three they are like the ministering angels: They have wings like the ministering angels, they know what will happen like the ministering angels, and they go from one end of the world to the other like the ministering angels.

And some say: They also change their appearance to any likeness they please; and they see, but themselves are not seen.

There are SEVEN types of Pharisee: [5] the *škmy* Pharisee,[6] the *nkp'y* Pharisee,[7] the *mkṣw'y* Pharisee,[8] the *mkwb'y* Pharisee,[9] the Pharisee who had a trade,[10] the Pharisee (who says:) . . . ,[11] the Pharisee who masters his evil impulse,[12] and the Pharisee out of fear (of God).[13]

SEVEN things in large quantity are harmful but in small quantity are beneficial: wine, work, sleep, riches, cohabitation, hot water, and blood-letting.

With [14] SEVEN things the Holy One, blessed be He, created His world,[15] to wit: knowledge, understanding, might, lovingkindness and compassion, judgment, and decree.[16]

Corresponding to (the SEVEN things) with which the Holy One, blessed be He, created His world, He created (SEVEN persons)—the Three Patriarchs and the Four Matriarchs:

The Three Patriarchs: Abraham, Isaac, and Jacob.

The Four Matriarchs: Sarah, Rebecca, Rachel, and Leah.

SEVEN qualities minister before the throne of glory, to wit: wisdom, righteousness, justice, loving-kindness and compassion, truth, and peace; [17] as it is said, *And I will betroth thee unto Me for ever; yea, I will betroth thee unto Me in righteousness, and in justice, and in loving-kindness, and in compassion. And I will betroth thee unto Me in faithfulness; and thou shalt know the Lord* (Hos. 2:21 f.).[18]

Rabbi Me'ir says: Why does the verse say, *And thou shalt know the Lord?* To teach that whosoever has in himself all these qualities knows the will of God.

There are SEVEN levels (to the universe), to wit: the upper level (of the heavens), the lower level, the world's atmosphere, and the four upper spheres.[19]

Rabbi Me'ir says: There are SEVEN heavens, to wit: the Velum,[20] the Firmament,[21] the Skies,[22] the Habitation,[23] the Dwelling Place,[24] the Foundation,[25] the Clouds.[26]

Corresponding to these He called the earth by SEVEN names,[27] to wit: Earth,[28] Land,[29] Ground,[30] Dry Ground,[31] Dry Land,[32] World,[33] Abode.[34]

Why was it called World (*tebel*)? Because it is rich (*metubbelet*)[35] in everything.

Another interpretation:[36] Because it is accustomed to store up but unaccustomed to give up.[37]

SEVEN distinctions set off one righteous man from the other:[38]

The wife of one is comelier than his fellow's;

His sons are finer than his fellow's;

If both eat from the same dish, one tastes according to his conduct and the other tastes according to his conduct;

If both dip stuff into the same kettle, for the one it comes up handsome, for the other it comes up ugly;

(One is also distinguished from the other) by his wisdom, by his understanding, and by his stature, as it is said, *One righteous man excels his friend; but the way of the wicked leadeth them astray* (Prov. 12:16).

SEVEN rules of interpretation Hillel the Elder expounded before the Bĕne Bathyra, to wit: *a fortiori,*[39] analogy,[40] deduction from one verse,[41] deduction from two verses,[42] (inference) from general and particular,[43] from particular and general,[44] similarity elsewhere,[45] deduction from context. These are the seven rules which Hillel the Elder expounded before the Bĕne Bathyra.[46]

SEVEN QUALITIES CHARACTERIZE THE CLOD AND SEVEN THE WISE MAN:

THE WISE MAN DOES NOT SPEAK BEFORE HIM THAT IS GREATER THAN HE IN WISDOM OR IN AGE; HE DOES NOT BREAK INTO HIS FELLOW'S SPEECH; HE IS NOT IN A RUSH TO REPLY; HE ASKS WHAT IS RELEVANT AND REPLIES TO THE POINT; HE SPEAKS OF FIRST THINGS FIRST AND OF LAST THINGS LAST; OF WHAT HE HAS NOT HEARD HE SAYS: "I HAVE NOT HEARD," AND IS NOT ASHAMED (TO ADMIT IT); [47] AND HE ACKNOWLEDGES WHAT IS TRUE.

AND CORRESPONDINGLY, THE OPPOSITES APPLY TO THE CLOD.[48]

THE WISE MAN DOES NOT SPEAK BEFORE HIM THAT IS GREATER THAN HE IN WISDOM OR IN AGE: Such was Moses. For it is said, *And Aaron spoke all the words which the Lord had spoken unto Moses, and did the signs in the sight of the people* (Exod. 4:30). Who indeed was qualified to speak, Moses or Aaron? Surely Moses! for Moses heard (the words) from the mouth of the Almighty, while Aaron heard them (only) from the mouth of Moses. But thus thought Moses: Shall I then speak while my older brother is standing by? He therefore said to Aaron: "Speak thou." That is why it is said, *And Aaron spoke all the words which the Lord had spoken unto Moses.*

HE DOES NOT BREAK INTO HIS FELLOW'S SPEECH: Such was Aaron. For it is said, *Then* [49] *Aaron spoke. . . . Behold, this day have they offered their sin offering, and their burnt offering . . . and there have befallen me such things as these* (Lev. 10:19): He kept quiet until Moses finished what he wanted to say, and Aaron did not say to him, "Cut thy words short." Only afterward did he say to Moses: *"Behold, this day they have brought their offerings,* although we are in mourning!" [50]

Some say: Aaron drew Moses aside out of the midst of the congregation and said to him: "Moses my brother, if of tithes, which are of lesser sanctity, a mourner is forbidden to eat, how much more should a mourner be forbidden to eat of sin offerings which are of higher sanctity!" Forthwith Moses agreed with him, as it is said, *And when Moses heard that, it was well-pleasing in his sight* (Lev. 10:20) and in the sight of the Almighty too.

Similarly [51] with the verse *And Moses* [52] *was angry with Eleazar and with Ithamar, the sons of Aaron* (Lev. 10:16). Hence it has been said: When a person prepares a feast for his disciples, he turns his face to the oldest only; but when he gets angry, he gets angry only with the youngest; [53] for it is said, *And he was angry with Eleazar and with Ithamar,* (while the expression *sons of Aaron*) teaches that Aaron, too, was the object of his anger.

Aaron was older than Moses, and greater than Aaron was the Holy One, blessed be He.[54] Why,[55] therefore, did He not speak with Aaron? Because he had no sons to stand in the breach. For had his sons Eleazar and Ithamar stood in the breach, no sin would have affected Nadab and Abihu.

The same applies [56] to Abraham, our father. When he was praying in behalf of the men of Sodom, the Holy One, blessed be He, said to him: *If I find in Sodom fifty righteous . . . then I will forgive all the place for their sake* (Gen. 18:26). It was manifest and foreknown to Him-that-spake-and-the-world-came-into-being that had there been present in Sodom three [57] or five righteous men, iniquity would not have affected it. Yet the Holy One, blessed be He, waited until Abraham finished what he wanted to say, and only then answered him; as it is said, *And the Lord went His way when He had left off speaking to Abraham* (Gen. 18:33): God, as it were, said to him: "Now, I shall depart"; as it is said, *And the Lord went His way . . . then Abraham returned unto his place* (ibid.).[58]

HE IS NOT IN A RUSH TO REPLY: Such was Elihu ben Barachel the Buzite. For it is said, *I am young, and ye are very old; wherefore I held back, and durst not declare you mine opinion. I said: Days should speak, and multitude of years should teach wisdom* (Job 32:6 f.). This teaches that Job's friends sat and kept quiet in the presence of Job. When he stood up, they stood up; when he sat down, they sat down; when he ate, they ate; when he drank, they drank.[59] Finally he asked their permission and (spoke up) cursing his day, as it is said, *After this opened Job his mouth and cursed his day . . . and said: Let the day perish when I was born, and the night wherein it was said: A man-child is brought forth* (Job 3: 1 ff.).

Let the day perish when my father came to my mother and she said to him: "I have conceived."

And how do we know that they did not respond out of turn? For it is said:

Then Job answered and said (Job 3:2 and *passim*); *Then answered Eliphaz the Temanite, and said* (Job 4:1, etc.); *Then answered Bildad the Shuhite, and said* (Job 8:1, etc.); *Then answered Zophar the Naamathite, and said* (Job 11:1, etc.); *Then Elihu the son of Barachel the Buzite answered and said* (Job 32:1). Scripture arranged them one by one only in order to make known to all the inhabitants of the world that the wise man does not speak before him that is greater than he in wisdom, does not break into his fellow's speech, and is not in a rush to reply.

HE ASKS WHAT IS RELEVANT: Such was Judah, who said, *I will be surety for him* (Gen. 43:9).

Asking what is not relevant was Reuben. For it is said, *And Reuben said unto his father: Thou shalt slay my two sons* [60] (Gen. 42:37).

HE SPEAKS OF FIRST THINGS FIRST: Such was Jacob.[61] Some say: Such was Sarah.[62]

AND OF LAST THINGS LAST: For example, the men of Haran.[63]

HE ACKNOWLEDGES WHAT IS TRUE: Such was Moses, for it is said, *And the Lord said unto me: They have well said that which they have spoken* (Deut. 18:17).[64]

So too the Holy One, blessed be He, acknowledged what was true, as it is said, *And the Lord spoke unto Moses, saying: The daughters of Zelophehad speak right* (Num. 27:6 f.).

CHAPTER 38

SEVEN KINDS OF CALAMITY COME UPON THE WORLD FOR SEVEN
CLASSES OF TRANSGRESSION: [1]

IF SOME TITHE AND SOME DO NOT, FAMINE AS A RESULT OF DROUGHT
COMES;

IF SOME GIVE THE HEAVE OFFERING AND SOME DO NOT, FAMINE AS A
RESULT OF TUMULT [2] COMES;

IF SOME SET ASIDE THE DOUGH OFFERING AND SOME DO NOT, AN ALL-
CONSUMING FAMINE COMES;

IF (ALL) DETERMINE NOT TO TITHE, THEY HOLD BACK THE HEAVENS
FROM BRINGING DOWN DEW AND RAIN, AND MEN TOIL BUT CANNOT
PROVIDE FOR THEMSELVES.

RABBI Josiah says: For neglect of the dough offering, no
blessing comes upon the fruits, and men toil but cannot
provide for themselves. For neglect of the heave offerings
and tithes, the heavens are held back from bringing down dew and
rain, and the people are handed over to the government.

PESTILENCE COMES UPON THE WORLD for neglect of the harvest
gleanings, the forgotten sheaf, the corner of the field, and poor
man's tithe.[3]

There was once a (poor) woman who dwelt in the neighborhood [4] of a landowner. Her two sons went out to gather gleanings,
but the landowner did not let them take any. Their mother kept
saying: "When will my sons come back from the field; perhaps I
shall find that they have brought something to eat." And they
kept saying: "When shall we go back to our mother; perhaps we
shall discover that she has found something to eat."

She found that they had nothing and they found that she had
nothing to eat. So they laid their heads on their mother's lap and
the three of them died in one day.

Said the Holy One, blessed be He: "Their very existence you
take away from them! By your life! [5] I shall make you, too, pay
for it with your very existence!"

And so indeed it says, *Rob not the weak, because he is weak, neither crush the poor in the gate; for the Lord will plead their cause, and despoil of life those that despoil them* (Prov. 22:22 f.).

THE SWORD COMES UPON THE WORLD [6] FOR THE DELAY OF JUSTICE, FOR THE PERVERSION OF JUSTICE, AND BECAUSE OF THOSE THAT TEACH THE TORAH NOT IN ACCORDANCE WITH THE HALAKHA.[7]

Now when Rabban Simeon ben Gamaliel and Rabbi Ishmael [8] were taken off to be slain, Rabban Simeon ben Gamaliel kept turning the matter over in his mind, saying: "Woe unto us that we are being slain like Sabbath breakers, like idol worshipers, like the unchaste, and like bloodshedders!"

Said Rabbi Ishmael ben Elisha to him: "By thy leave, may I say something before thee?"

"Speak," he replied.

Said Rabbi Ishmael: "Perhaps when thou didst settle down to dinner, poor folk came and stood at thy door, and thou didst not let them come in and eat?"

"By Heaven!" Rabban Simeon protested, "I did not act that way. On the contrary, I had doormen sitting at the entrance; when the poor came, the doormen would bring them in to me and the poor used to eat and drink with me and recite a blessing in the name of Heaven." [9]

"Perhaps," Rabbi Ishmael asked him, "when thou didst sit holding a discourse on the Temple mount and all the hosts of Israel sat before thee, thy thoughts puffed up with pride?"

"Ishmael, my brother," he replied, "a person must be prepared to receive his punishment." [10]

Now they both kept appealing to the executioner. Rabbi Ishmael said to him: "I am a priest, son of a High Priest; kill me first and let me not behold the death of my fellow."

And Rabban Simeon said: "I am a prince, son of a prince; [11] kill me first and let me not behold the death of my fellow."

Said the executioner to them: "Cast lots."

So they cast lots and the lot fell upon Rabban Simeon ben

Gamaliel (to die first). Whereupon the executioner took his sword and cut off Rabban Simeon's head.

Rabbi Ishmael ben Elisha took hold of it and held it to his breast, and kept weeping and crying out, "O holy mouth, O faithful mouth! O holy mouth, O faithful mouth! O mouth that uttered beautiful gems and precious stones and pearls! Who hath laid thee in the dust! Who hath filled thy tongue with dust and ashes! Of thee the verse says, *Awake, O sword, against My shepherd, and against the man that is near unto Me*" (Zech. 13:7).

Before he could finish his lament,[12] the executioner took the sword and cut off his head. And of them the verse said, *My wrath shall wax hot, and I will kill you with the sword; and your wives shall be widows, and your children fatherless* (Exod. 22:23).

Since the verse says, *And I will kill you with the sword,* do I not [13] know that the wives will become widows? But (Scripture here tells us that) they will be widows and yet not widows: for no witnesses shall be found for them to permit them to re-wed—as in Bettar, from which not a soul escaped to testify that the married women might now remarry.[14]

And since the verse says, *And your wives shall be widows,* do I not [15] know that the children will be fatherless? But (Scripture implies that) they will be fatherless and yet not fatherless: for their property shall remain under title of their fathers, and the children will not be permitted to take possession or to transact business with it.

EXILE COMES UPON THE WORLD FOR IDOLATRY, FOR UNCHASTITY, FOR BLOODSHED, AND FOR NEGLECT OF THE YEAR OF RELEASE OF THE LAND.[16]

FOR IDOLATRY, as it is said, *And I will destroy your high places . . . and you will I scatter among the nations* (Lev. 26:30, 33). Said the Holy One, blessed be He, to Israel: "Since you desire idolatry, I shall indeed exile you to a place where there is idolatry!" That is why it is said, *And I will destroy your high places . . . and you will I scatter among the nations.*

FOR [17] UNCHASTITY: why is that? Said Rabbi Ishmael, son of Rabbi Yose: So long as Israel abandon themselves to unchastity, the

Shekinah withdraws from their midst. For it is said, *That He see no unseemly thing in thee, and turn away from thee* (Deut. 23:15).

[FOR BLOODSHED: why is that? For it is said, *So ye shall not pollute the land wherein ye are; for blood, it polluteth the land* (Num. 35:33).] [18]

FOR [19] NEGLECT OF THE YEAR OF RELEASE OF THE LAND: how do we know that? For it is said, *Then shall the land be paid her sabbaths* (Lev. 26:34). Said the Holy One, blessed be He, to Israel: "Since you did not release the land, it will release you; the number of months which you did not release it, it will release itself." That is why it is said, *Even then shall the land rest, and repay her sabbaths. As long as it lieth desolate it shall have rest; even the rest which it had not in your sabbaths, when ye dwelt upon it* (Lev. 26:35).

CHAPTER 39

FIVE shall obtain no forgiveness: He that is forever repenting,[1] he that sins excessively,[2] he that sins in a righteous generation,[3] he that sins with the intention to repent, and he who has on his hands (the sin of) profaning the Name.[4]

Because of his sin it is not granted to man [5] to know what likeness is on high; and were it not for that, the keys would have been handed over to him and he might have known what heaven and earth were created with.[6]

He [7] used to say: EVERYTHING IS FORESEEN and everything is revealed, yet everything happens according to man's will.

HE [8] USED TO SAY:

> EVERYTHING IS GIVEN AGAINST A PLEDGE
> AND A NET IS CAST OVER ALL OF LIFE: [9]
> THE SHOP IS OPEN,
> THE SHOPKEEPER EXTENDS CREDIT,
> THE LEDGER LIES OPEN,
> THE JUDGE IS IN ATTENDANCE,
> THE COLLECTORS MAKE THE ROUNDS

AND CONTINUALLY,

EVERY DAY,

EXACT PAYMENT OF MAN

EITHER WITH HIS CONSENT OR WITHOUT IT.

The [10] repentance of the wicked puts off (punishment) even though their sentence has been sealed.

The prosperity of the wicked ends in misfortune.

Power buries its possessors.

Repentance suspends (judgment) and the Day of Atonement atones.

Repentance atones along with [11] the day of death, and the day of death atones when there has been repentance.[12]

The [13] wicked are paid (at once) but to the righteous credit is extended:

The wicked are paid (at once) as though they were men who cheerfully carried out the teachings of the Torah and in whom nothing evil was ever found.

But to the righteous credit is extended as to men who carried out the teachings of the Torah grudgingly and in whom nothing good was found.

To each a little is given, but the greater part is laid aside for them.[14]

He [15] used to say:

Everyone goes off and departs naked; [16]
Oh! would that the departure might be like the arrival!

Rabbi Me'ir says:[17] BELOVED IS MAN, FOR HE WAS CREATED IN THE IMAGE OF GOD, AS IT IS SAID, FOR IN THE IMAGE OF GOD MADE HE MAN (Gen. 9:6). BELOVED ARE ISRAEL, FOR THEY WERE CALLED CHILDREN OF GOD, AS IT IS SAID, YE ARE THE CHILDREN OF THE LORD YOUR GOD (Deut. 14:1). BELOVED ARE ISRAEL, FOR TO THEM WAS GIVEN THE PRECIOUS IMPLEMENT [18] WITH WHICH THE WORLD WAS CREATED, AS IT IS SAID, FOR I GIVE YOU GOOD DOCTRINE; FORSAKE YE NOT MY TORAH (Prov. 4:2).

Rabbi Eliezer bar Zadok says: To what may the righteous be likened in this world? To a tree which stands in a clean place but whose foliage extends out into an unclean place. What do men say? "Cut off this foliage from the tree so that it may be entirely clean, as it should be." To what may the wicked be likened in this world? To a tree which stands in an unclean place but whose foliage extends out into a clean place. What do men say? "Cut off this foliage from the tree so that the tree may be entirely as it should be, unclean."

By SIX names is the lion called: *'ǎri*,[19] *kĕfir*,[20] *labi*,[21] *layiš*,[22] *šahal*,[23] *šahaṣ*.[24]

By SIX names is the serpent [25] called: [*nahaš*,] *šaraf* ("fiery serpent"),[26] *tannin*,[27] *ṣif'oni* ("basilisk"),[28] *'ef'eh* ("viper"),[29] *'akšub* ("asp").[30]

By SIX names is Solomon called: [Solomon,] Jedidiah,[31] Kohelet,[32] Ben Jakeh,[33] Agur,[33] Lemuel.[34]

CHAPTER 40

FOUR things a man does, and he enjoys their fruits in this world while the stock is laid up for him in the world to come,[1] to wit: honoring father and mother, acts of lovingkindness, establishing peace between man and his fellow man, and the study of Torah, which is equal to them all.

There are FOUR things for doing which a man shall be punished in this world and in the world to come, to wit: idolatry, unchastity, bloodshed, and slander, which outweighs them all.[2]

Virtue has stock and has fruits, as it is said, *Say ye of the righteous that it shall be well with him; for they shall eat the fruit of their doings* (Isa. 3: 10).

Transgression has stock but has no fruits, as it is said, *Woe unto the wicked! It shall be ill with him; for the work of his hands shall be done to him* (Isa. 3: 11).

Some say: Transgressions do have fruits, as it is said, *Therefore they shall eat of the fruit of their own way, and be filled with their own devices* (Prov. 1: 31).

If [3] one leads the multitudes to virtue, through him transgression shall not come to pass, lest his disciples inherit the world to come and he go down to Sheol; as it is said, *For Thou wilt not abandon my soul to the netherworld* (Ps. 16:10). But one who causes the multitudes to sin shall be given no opportunity to repent, lest his disciples go down to Sheol and he inherit the world to come; as it is said, *A man that is laden with the blood of any person shall hasten his (own) steps unto the pit* (Prov. 28:17).

If one says, "I shall sin and then repent," he is given no opportunity to repent. (If one says) "I shall sin and the Day of Atonement will atone," then the Day of Atonement does not atone. (If one says) "I shall sin and the day of death will purge me of sin," the day of death does not purge him of sin.

Rabbi Eliezer son of Rabbi Yose says: If one sins and repents and continues uprightly, he is forgiven before he stirs from the spot. But if one says, "I shall sin and then repent," he is forgiven up to three times, but no more.[4]

THERE [5] ARE FOUR TYPES OF MEN:

ONE WHO SAYS "MINE IS MINE AND THINE IS THINE" [6]—THE COMMONPLACE TYPE. SOME SAY: THAT'S THE SODOM TYPE.

"MINE IS THINE AND THINE IS MINE"—THE 'AM HA-'AREṢ.[7]

"MINE IS THINE AND THINE IS THINE"—THE SAINT.

"THINE IS MINE AND MINE IS MINE"—THE WICKED.

There [8] are FOUR types of disciples:

One wishes that he might study and that others might study too—the liberal.

(One wishes) that he might study but not others—the grudging.

(One wishes) that others should study but not he—the commonplace type. Some say: that's the Sodom type.

(One wishes) that neither he nor others should study—that's the thoroughly wicked.

There are FOUR types among those that frequent the study house:[9]

One takes his place close to (the sage) [10] and is rewarded;[11]

one takes his place close to (the sage) and is not rewarded. One takes his place at a distance (from the sage) and is rewarded; one takes his place at a distance and is not rewarded.

One engages in discussion and is rewarded; one engages in discussion and is not rewarded. One sits and keeps quiet and is rewarded; one sits and keeps quiet and is not rewarded.

If one takes his place close to (the sage) in order to listen and learn, he is rewarded.

If one takes his place close to (the sage) so that men might say, "There's so-and-so drawing close to and sitting down before a sage," he is not rewarded.

If one takes his place at a distance so that he might honor someone greater than he, he is rewarded.

If one takes his place at a distance so that men might say, "So-and-so has no need of a sage," he is not rewarded.

If one engages in discussion in order to understand and learn, he is rewarded.

If one engages in discussion so that men might say, "So-and-so engages in discussion in the presence of sages," he is not rewarded.

If one sits and keeps quiet in order to listen and learn, he is rewarded.

If one sits and keeps quiet so that men might say, "There's so-and-so sitting quietly in the presence of sages," he is not rewarded.

THERE [12] ARE FOUR TYPES AMONG THOSE THAT SIT IN THE PRESENCE OF THE SAGES:

THERE'S ONE WHO IS LIKE A SPONGE, THERE'S ONE WHO IS LIKE A SIFTER, THERE'S ONE WHO IS LIKE A FUNNEL, AND THERE'S ONE WHO IS LIKE A STRAINER.

ONE IS LIKE A SPONGE: For example, the staunch disciple who sits before the Sages and studies Scripture and Mishnah, Midrash, Halakha, and Agada. Even as the sponge soaks up everything, so he soaks up everything.

ONE IS LIKE A SIFTER: For example, the bright disciple who sits before the scholars and studies Scripture and Mishnah, Midrash,

Halakha, and Agada. Even as the sifter holds back the coarse flour and collects the fine flour, so he holds back the bad and collects the good.

ONE IS LIKE A FUNNEL: For example, the witless disciple who sits before the scholars and studies Scripture and Mishnah, Midrash, Halakha, and Agada. Even as the funnel takes in at one end and lets out at the other, so does he—everything which comes to him goes in one ear and out the other: one word after another slips through and is gone.

ONE IS LIKE A STRAINER: For example, the wicked disciple who sits before a sage and studies Scripture and Mishnah, Midrash, Halakha, and Agada. Even as the strainer lets pass the wine and retains the lees, so he lets pass the good and retains the bad.

Rabbi Eliezer ben Jacob calls him [13] "Perforated horn, a ḳiṭṭuʻah." [14]

A ḳiṭṭuʻah, what is that? It's (like) a child to whom pearls are given, and then he is given bread; so he throws away the pearls and keeps the bread. Then they give him an earthenware vessel; so he throws away the bread and keeps the earthenware vessel. In the end there is nothing in his hand but an earthenware vessel.

On the subject of disciples Rabban Gamaliel the Elder spoke of FOUR kinds: An unclean fish, a clean fish, a fish from the Jordan, a fish from the Great Sea. [15]

An unclean fish: who is that? A poor youth [16] who studies Scripture and Mishnah, Halakha and Agada, and is without understanding.

A clean fish: who is that? That's a rich youth who studies Scripture and Mishnah, Halakha and Agada, and has understanding. [17]

A fish from the Jordan: who is that? That's a scholar who studies Scripture and Mishnah, Midrash, Halakha, and Agada, and is without the talent for give and take.

A fish from the Great Sea: who is that? That's a scholar who studies Scripture and Mishnah, Midrash, Halakha, and Agada, and has the talent for give and take.

There are FOUR types (of evil): [18] There's the seeing and the seen, the seen but unseeing, the seeing but unseen, the unseeing and unseen.

The seeing and the seen: for example, wolves, lions, bears, leopards,[19] panthers, serpents, brigands, and robbers. These see and are seen.

The seen but unseeing: for example, sword, bow, spear, knife, stick, and switch.[20] These are seen but unseeing.

The seeing but unseen: that's the affliction of an evil spirit.

The unseen and unseeing: that's the affliction of bowel sickness.

Of FOUR Sages: [21]

If one sees Rabbi Johanan ben Nuri in his dream, let him look forward to fear of sin; [22] if Rabbi Eleazar ben Azariah, let him look forward to greatness and riches; [23] if Rabbi Ishmael, let him look forward to wisdom; [24] if Rabbi 'Akiba, let him fear calamity.[25]

Of THREE scholars: [26]

If one sees Ben 'Azzai in his dream, let him look forward to saintliness; [27] if Ben Zoma, let him look forward to wisdom; [28] if Elisha ben 'Abuyah, let him fear calamity.[29]

Of THREE prophetic books: [30]

If one sees the Book of Kings in his dream, let him look forward to greatness and riches; if Isaiah, let him look forward to consolation; if Jeremiah, let him fear calamity.

Of THREE Holy Writings: [31]

If one sees the Book of Psalms in his dream, let him look forward to humility; if Proverbs, let him look forward to wisdom; if Job, let him fear calamity.

> When [32] death comes to the wicked—how good for
> them, how good for the world!
> When it comes to the righteous—how bad for
> them, how bad for the world!
>
> When sleep overcomes the wicked—how good for
> them, how good for the world!

When it overcomes the righteous—how bad for
them, how bad for the world!

When leisure comes to the wicked—how bad for
them, how bad for the world!
When it comes to the righteous—how good for
them, how good for the world!

Let [33] no man stand naked facing the chamber of the Holy of
Holies.

If [34] one enters a privy, let him turn his face neither to the east
nor to the west, but sideways. Nor should he uncover himself
standing up, but sitting down. Nor shall a man wipe himself with
his right hand, but with his left.

Now why was it said that a man should not wipe himself with
his right hand, but with his left? Rabbi Eliezer says: Because with
the right hand the words of the Torah are pointed at.[35] Rabbi
Joshua says: Because one eats and drinks with it.

IF [36] LOVE DEPENDS ON SOME SELFISH END,[37] WHEN THE END FAILS,
LOVE FAILS; BUT IF IT DOES NOT DEPEND ON A SELFISH END, IT WILL
NEVER FAIL. A LOVE WHICH DEPENDED ON A SELFISH END WAS THE LOVE
OF AMNON FOR TAMAR.[38] A LOVE WHICH DID NOT DEPEND ON A
SELFISH END WAS THE LOVE OF DAVID AND JONATHAN.[39]

EVERY [40] CONTROVERSY WHICH IS FOR THE SAKE OF HEAVEN WILL
IN THE END ENDURE; BUT ONE WHICH IS NOT FOR THE SAKE OF HEAVEN
WILL NOT ENDURE IN THE END. A CONTROVERSY FOR THE SAKE OF
HEAVEN WAS THE CONTROVERSY OF HILLEL AND SHAMMAI.[41] A CON-
TROVERSY WHICH WAS NOT FOR THE SAKE OF HEAVEN WAS THE CON-
TROVERSY OF KORAH AND HIS COMPANY.[42]

EVERY [43] ASSEMBLY WHICH IS FOR THE SAKE OF HEAVEN WILL IN THE
END ENDURE; BUT ONE WHICH IS NOT FOR THE SAKE OF HEAVEN WILL
NOT ENDURE IN THE END. What kind of assembly was for the sake of
Heaven? For example, the assembly of Israel before Mount
Sinai.[44] And what kind was not for the sake of Heaven? For
example, the assembly of the Generation of Dispersion.[45]

CHAPTER 41

RABBI SIMEON SAYS: THERE ARE THREE CROWNS, TO WIT, THE
CROWN OF TORAH, THE CROWN OF PRIESTHOOD, AND THE CROWN OF
ROYALTY; BUT THE CROWN OF A GOOD NAME MUST ACCOMPANY [1] THEM
ALL.[2]

THE CROWN OF PRIESTHOOD: what is there to be said of it?
Even if one were to offer all the silver and gold in the
world, he could not be given the crown of priesthood, for
it is said, *And it shall be unto him,*[3] *and to his seed after him, the
covenant of an everlasting priesthood* (Num. 25:13).

THE CROWN OF ROYALTY: (what is there to be said of it?) Even
if one were to offer all the silver and gold in the world, he could
not be given the crown of royalty, for it is said, *And David My
servant shall be their prince for ever* (Ezek. 37:25).

Not so, however, THE CROWN OF TORAH: the toil of Torah—anyone who wishes to take it on may come and do so, as it is said,
Ho, every one that thirsteth, come ye after water [4] (Isa. 55:1).

Do thou toil away over the words of the Torah and do not engage in idle matters.

Once as Rabbi Simeon ben Yoḥai went about visiting the sick,
he found a certain man, afflicted and laid up with bowel sickness,
uttering blasphemies against the Holy One, blessed be He.

"Wretch!" Rabbi Simeon cried, "thou shouldst be beseeching
mercy for thyself, and thou utterest blasphemies!"

Said the man: "May the Holy One, blessed be He, remove the
sickness from me and lay it on thee!"

(Thereupon) Rabbi Simeon exclaimed:[5] "Well has the Holy
One, blessed be He, done with me,[6] for I neglected [7] the words
of the Torah and engaged [8] in idle matters."

A story of Rabbi Simeon ben Eleazar.

He was once coming from Migdal Eder,[9] from his master's
house, making his way leisurely along the seashore on his ass,

when he saw a certain man who was exceedingly ugly. "Wretch!" Rabbi Simeon called to him, "how ugly thou art! Are all thy townspeople perchance as ugly as thou?"

"What can I do?" the man answered; "go to the craftsman who made me and say to him: How ugly is this vessel which Thou hast made!"

No sooner did Rabbi Simeon perceive that he had acted amiss than he got down from the ass and prostrated himself before the man. "I beg of thee," he said, "forgive me."

Said the man: "I shall not forgive thee until thou hast gone to the craftsman who made me and said: How ugly is this vessel which Thou hast made!" (And the man went on ahead.)

Rabbi Simeon ran after him for three miles.

The townspeople came forth to meet Rabbi Simeon and hailed him, "Welcome Rabbi!"

Said the man to them: "Whom are you calling Rabbi?"

"Him that is coming along behind thee," they replied.

"If that's a rabbi," he said to them, "may there be no more like him in Israel!"

"Heaven forbid!" they exclaimed. "What did he do to thee?"

"Thus and so he did to me," he told them.

Said they: "Nevertheless, forgive him."

"Well," he said, "I forgive him, but only on condition that he shall not act in this manner again."

That day Rabbi Simeon entered his great study house and held forth as follows: [10]

"At all times let a man be supple as the reed and not rigid as the cedar:

"A reed, when all the winds come and blow upon it, bends with them; when the winds are still, the reed is again upright in its place. And the end of this reed? Its good fortune is to be used as the pen that writes the Torah scroll.

"The cedar, however, does not remain standing in its place: for as soon as the south wind blows, it uproots it and tears it down. And the end of the cedar? Loggers come upon it and chop it up and use it to cover the housetops with—and what remains, they cast to the flames."

This is why it is said: Let a man be supple as the reed and not rigid as the cedar.

THREE things were said of men: one gives charity, may blessing come upon him; superior to him is one who lends his funds; superior to all is one (who forms a partnership with the poor) on terms of half the profits (for each), or on terms of sharing what remains.[11]

There are THREE types of scholar: One who can ask questions and offer answers is wise; inferior to him is one who can ask questions but not offer answers; inferior to both is one who can neither ask questions nor offer answers.

THREE kinds of sweat are good for the body: the sweat of the sick man, the sweat of the bathhouse, the sweat of labor.

Sweat during sickness restores health.

Sweat of the bathhouse [makes one strong.

As for the sweat of labor,] [12] there is nothing like it.

There are six kinds of tears, THREE beneficial and THREE harmful:

Tears because of grief,[13] because of smoke, and because of the privy are harmful.

Tears because of drugs, because of laughter, and because of herbs [14] are beneficial.

THREE things were said of earthenware vessels:

They soak up, they do not discharge, and they do not cause whatever is in them to rot.

THREE things were said of glass vessels:

They neither soak up nor discharge; they reveal whatever is in them; in a hot place they are hot, in a cold place, cold.

On FOUR occasions cohabitation is harmful:

On returning from a journey, on quitting the surgeon,[15] on recovering from sickness, and on coming out of prison.

If one takes upon himself these FOUR things, he is accepted as an Associate: [16]

Not to go to the cemetery; [17] not to raise small cattle; [18] not to give heave offering or tithe to a priest who is an *'am ha-'areṣ;* [19] not to fix foods requiring levitical purity [20] in the company of the *'am ha-'areṣ;* [21] and [22] to eat (even) profane foods in a state of cleanness.[23]

[THREE returned to their place of origin: Israel, the silver of Egypt, and the heavenly writing.[24]

Israel dwelt beyond the river, as it is said, *Your father dwelt of old time beyond the river, even Terah, the father of Abraham,* etc. (Josh. 24:2). And how do we know that they returned to their place of origin? For it is said, *But because that our fathers had provoked the God of heaven, He gave them into the hand of Nebuchadnezzar . . . who . . . carried the people away into Babylon* (Ezra 5:12).]

The silver of Egypt returned to its place of origin. For it is said, *And they despoiled the Egyptians* (Exod. 12:36), and it says, *And Joseph gathered up all the silver* (Gen. 47:14). And it says, *And it came to pass in the fifth year of King Rehoboam, that Shishak, King of Egypt, came up . . . and took away the treasures of the house of the Lord,* etc. (II Chron. 12:2, 9).

The heavenly writing returned to its place of origin, as it is said, *Wilt thou set thine eyes upon it? it is gone; for it certainly makes itself wings, like an eagle that flieth toward heaven* [25] (Prov. 23:5).

RABBI JUDAH BEN TEMA SAYS: [26] BE STRONG AS THE LEOPARD, SWIFT AS THE EAGLE, FLEET AS THE GAZELLE, AND BRAVE AS THE LION, TO DO THE WILL OF THY FATHER WHO IS IN HEAVEN.

He used to say: Do thou love Heaven, be in awe of Heaven, tremble and rejoice [27] at all the commandments.

(He used to say:) If thou hast done thy fellow a slight wrong, let it be a serious matter in thine eyes; but if thou hast done thy fellow much good, let it be a trifle in thine eyes. And if thy fellow hath done thee a slight favor, let it be a great thing in thine eyes; if thy fellow hath done thee a great evil, let it be a little thing in thine eyes.

[Be [28] like a vessel coated with pitch and be not like a funnel or tube.]

A sponge and vessel coated with pitch: Such are scholars.[29]

A funnel and tube: Such are the wicked.[30]

Be like the bottle which has no opening to let in air; [31] learn to accept pain; and forgive insult to thee.

There are FIVE things which (first) were made and (later) hidden away,[32] to wit:

The tent of meeting and the furnishings therein; the ark, and the broken tables of the Commandments in it; [33] the jar of manna; [34] the cruse of the anointing oil; [35] the rod (of Moses); [36] Aaron's staff, its almond blossoms and flowers; [37] the priestly vestments; and the vestments of the anointed priest.[38]

But the mortar of the house of Abṭinas,[39] the table,[40] the candle-stick,[41] the curtain of the ark,[42] and the plate [43] still lie in Rome.[44]

Once, as Rabbi Ṭarfon sat teaching his disciples, a bride passed by in his presence. He ordered that she be brought into his house, and said to his mother and his wife: "Wash her, anoint her, have her outfited, and dance before her, until she goes on to her husband's house." [45]

The following, the Sages declared, have no share in the world to come: Five were kings.[46] And six had a hankering for greatness: Cain, Korah, Balaam, Ahitophel, Doeg, and Gehazi.[47]

Rabbi Yose says: (At Judgment) those altogether righteous shall not be put through a purgatory; [48] those altogether wicked shall not be put through a purgatory. Who then will be put through a purgatory? Those betwixt and between.—*I beseech Thee, O Lord, deliver my soul* (Ps. 116:4) from the torment [49] of Gehenna.— [50]

The School of Shammai says: Those betwixt and between shall go down into Gehenna, be purged there, be singed,[51] and come up therefrom; as it is said, *And I will bring the third part* [52] *through the fire, and will refine them as silver is refined, and will try them as gold is tried* (Zech. 13:9).

The School of Hillel says: Those betwixt and between shall not behold Gehenna at all, for it is said, *For Thy loving-kindness is good to them that are without life;* [53] *my lips shall praise Thee* (Ps. 63:4); and it says, *And spare them* [54] *according to the greatness of Thy mercy* (Neh. 13:22), so that they are delivered from the torments of Gehenna.[55]

WHATSOEVER THE HOLY ONE, BLESSED BE HE, CREATED IN HIS WORLD, HE CREATED FOR HIS OWN GLORY ONLY, AS IT IS SAID, EVERYONE THAT IS CALLED BY MY NAME, HIM I CREATED FOR MY GLORY, I HAVE FORMED HIM, YEA, I HAVE MADE HIM (Isa. 43:7). It says also, THE LORD SHALL REIGN FOR EVER AND EVER (Exod. 15:18).[56]

SAID RABBI HANANIAH BEN ʿAḲASHYA: IT PLEASED THE HOLY ONE, BLESSED BE HE, TO GRANT MERIT TO ISRAEL; THAT IS WHY HE GAVE THEM TORAH AND COMMANDMENTS IN ABUNDANCE, AS IT IS SAID, THE LORD WAS PLEASED FOR HIS [57] RIGHTEOUSNESS' SAKE TO MAKE TORAH GREAT AND GLORIOUS (Isa. 42:21).[58]

CHAPTER I

1. See the more compact beginning in PA 1: 1. "At Sinai," lit., "from Sinai," i.e. from Him who revealed Himself at Sinai. Cf. ARNB, p. 1.

2. The Hebrew word under discussion might be either "covered him" or "covered it."

3. I.e. no special purification took place. R. Yose and R. 'Akiba differ on the relation of Exod. 24: 15 f. to Exod. 19 f. Yose takes the account in Exod. 24: 15 f. to have occurred after the revelation of the Ten Commandments reported in Exod. 19 f. The latter he takes to have occurred on the sixth day of the "third month." According to his interpretation, then, after the revelation of the Commandments Moses went up into the mount; for six days the cloud covered him; on the seventh day God called him.

'Akiba on the other hand regards Exod. 19 f. as a repetition of the account in Exod. 19 f. According to his interpretation, Moses went up into the mount on the first day of the "third month." For six days the cloud covered the mount; and on the seventh day of the month God revealed the Commandments to all the people. Thus, on the seventh day God really called unto all the people; and the clause reporting that on the seventh day God "called unto Moses" means only that on that day Moses was singled out from among all Israel for special distinction. Cf. MMKJV, pp. 278 ff.

4. This question assumes Yose's interpretation of Exod. 24: 16.

5. The same expression, "with awe, with fear, with dread, and with trembling," occurs again twice in Ch. 6, where behavior in the presence of scholars is prescribed. Such conduct is reported also in connection with receiving emperors' edicts; cf. S. Lieberman in JQR, 35, 7 f.

6. Literally, "from their youth."

7. Cf. ARNB, p. 2.

8. For the reading "middleman" cf. L. Finkelstein, *Tarbiz* (1950), p. 96.

9. See Exod. 29, Lev. 8.

10. See Exod. 29: 35, Lev. 8: 33.

11. See Num. 19. Rashi notes on Num. 19: 2 that the heifer prepared by Eleazar was associated with the name of Moses. For the expression "heifer of purification" cf. Num. 19: 9.

12. Even a High Priest who is the son of a High Priest requires anointing. Cf. ARNB, p. 1.

13. Exod. 30: 31 reads: *This shall be a holy anointing oil unto Me throughout your generations.*

14. Cf. PA 1: 1, ARNB, p. 2.

15. For the Elders were no longer.

16. Cf. Jer. 7: 25a.

17. PA 1: 1, ARNB, p. 2.

18. The root of the Hebrew for "copied out" may also be taken to mean "to be strong, mature, old," hence "to consider maturely." Cf. ARNB, pp. 2 f.

19. The Hebrew for "copied out" and the Hebrew for "interpret" both have a common literal meaning, "to remove, move away, set aside." On the other hand, cf. *Mabo,* pp. 126 f.; ARNB, p. 3.

20. Literally, "Originally they used to say."

21. Reading *šehayu* rather than *šehem hayu;* cf. ARNS, p. 2, n. 20; addenda to ARNS, p. 150.

22. Text erroneously, "Men of the Great Assembly." Cf. ARNS, p. 2, n. 22.

23. The point is that such verses had to be interpreted, for the sentiments they expressed seemed of a sensual nature and contrary to the spirit of Scripture. See e.g. Num. 15:39, which contradicts Eccl. 11:9a.]

24. Cf. ARNB, p. 3.

25. The lesson derived from Moses' impatience is resumed in the paragraph beginning, "Now is there not an inference." Having quoted Num. 31:14, however, the text proceeds with a discussion of a problem in this biblical passage; see the next note.

26. The homily that follows (as Professor Lieberman points out to me) is an attempt to explain why Moses was justified in his anger. The question the homilist wants to answer is: why should Moses have been angry at the sparing of the women? He had not instructed the Israelites in advance to slay the women along with the men; cf. Deut. 20:13 f. Moreover, even in Num. 31:17 he condemns only one class of women. If so, why should Moses have been angry that they had *saved all the women?* And the answer given is that these women were indeed guilty of seducing Israel, *through the counsel of Balaam* (v. 16). [However, the alleged "if so" (*'im ķēn*) is represented by the abbreviation *'ķ,* which might easily have been miswritten for *wķ,* that is, the abbreviation for "etc." In this case the preceding paragraph should end with the quotation from Num. 31:14 f., and the following paragraph begin with "To what does this verse refer . . ."—the text thus yielding an admirably simple context. J.O.]

27. "Compartment, tent of prostitution"; cf. Jastrow, p. 1323. See Wertheimer, 2, 114, n. 1.

28. See *Legends, 3,* 380 ff. and *6,* 134 f.

29. Hebrew *ķal waḥomer;* see below, Ch. 37, p. 154.

30. The rendering of this dictum is not altogether certain; cf. ARNB, p. 3.

31. Cf. ARNB, p. 3.

32. Literally, "man, the first"; see *Legends, 5,* 78.

33. Text: "in peace." For the reading adopted cf. MMKJV, p. 269, n. 31; *Mabo,* p. 116. God visited on His creatures exactly what they deserved, even as He had foretold Moses. Cf. ARNB, p. 3.

34. Although God had said nothing about *touching* the tree.

35. Strictly speaking, of course, this statement was made by Eve, but it is attributed to Adam because presumably she said what Adam had told her. Cf. ARNB, p. 4.

36. Note indeed that Scripture does not say that the serpent *gave* Eve the fruit; merely that when Eve saw that the fruit was good she *took* of it and ate. Cf. ARNB, p. 5.

37. Cf. ARNB, pp. 5 f.

38. See addenda to ARNS, p. 135. "Wand" is here a euphemism for "phallus."

39. That is, "wolf, ravenous beast."

40. Here in the sense of "altar." Cf. Tg on Isaiah, *ad loc.,* and S. Spiegel in AMJV (Heb. vol.), pp. 501 f.

41. See below, p. 14. Cf. ARNB, p. 117.

42. On the woman's covering her head, see also I Cor. 11: 1–16. Cf. SLC, pp. 31 ff., 72; LGJV (Heb. vol.), pp. 267 f. (I owe this last reference to Professor Lieberman.)

43. See above, n. 34.

44. Cf. ARNB, p. 3.

45. *nitkalkel;* ARNB, p. 5, reads "cursed." Cf. B. Ta'anit, 15b, bottom.

46. Cf. *Legends, 5,* 79, n. 22.

47. See *Legends, 5,* 134, n. 4.

48. The following paragraphs refer to the psalms sung by the Levites in the Temple on the respective days of the week. See Bialoblotzki in AA, p. 59. The account of Creation in Gen. 1 should be consulted for the whole passage. The relevance of the whole section at this point, however, is not altogether clear; it seems to have been inserted because in the previous paragraph creation (of Adam) had been discussed, and shortly Adam's Sabbath is to be referred to.

49. Perhaps, "and He will (always) possess."

50. That is, He chose the heavens, "above the firmament," as His abode.

51. Cf. *Mabo,* pp. 173 f. and Tur-Sinai in MMKJV (Heb. vol.), p. 84.

52. See *Legends, 1,* 44 ff.

53. The words *did eat and drink* are taken not literally but as an expression for rejoicing, as though they had eaten and drunk; cf. Tg Onkelos on the verse.

54. That is, why was Adam created on the sixth day, after all the others?

55. Cf. ARNB, pp. 6 f.

56. According to Finkelstein, *Tarbiz* (1950), p. 98, the original reading of the last clause refers to loose sexual relations.

57. Cf. ARNB, pp. 7 f.

58. Cf. *Mabo,* p. 117.

59. That is, he divorced her. On the parable, cf. HJP, p. 136, n. 86.

60. Cf. ARNB, p. 8.

61. Adam, Eve, Cain, and his sister; literally, "Two mounted their couch and four came down."

62. Adam, Eve, Cain, and his twin, and Abel and his two twins. See also Jubilees, 4: 1, 8, and Antt, 1.ii.1.

63. The three decrees are: (1) *in toil,* etc.; (2) *thorns also,* etc.; (3) *eat the herb.*

64. And in that way showed that he repented of his sin.

65. See *Legends, 5,* 116 f.

66. That is, he was caught by his horns which extended beyond his hoots.

67. On the first Sabbath.

68. After Adam and Eve had sinned.

69. So the MSS (cf. ARNS, p. 7, n. 93) and *editio princeps,* the reference being to Adam. ARNS, "the serpent." See the next note.

70. That is, unless God punished Adam for his transgression, He would not be maintaining justice, and thus the world would be destroyed.

71. Cf. above, p. 10, where the serpent is described as planning the death of Adam so that *he,* rather than Adam, might be king of the universe.

72. These words merely introduce the passage which is quoted; the proof text is v. 17. Frequently in midrashic texts only a part of the biblical citation is furnished, although the comment and elaboration apply to other words in the passage which have not been included.

73. Literally, "written."

74. After the curses against the serpent and Eve. That is, if Adam had not been punished, the requirements of justice would have been neglected. Cf. above, n. 70.

75. Cf. ARNB, pp. 22 f.

76. See *Legends*, *1*, 66; *5*, 88 f.

77. There is no apparent connection between this paragraph and the preceding one; the "hence" is not to be taken literally.

78. Note *hands,* not *hand.*

79. The last two verses are not essential for the present discussion. They strike a note, however, on which homilists were fond of closing.

CHAPTER 2

1. Cf. ARNB, p. 12.

2. In the sense of flirting words (L.G.).

3. The Oral Law. See further, Strack, p. 3.

4. These are what the New Testament calls "phylacteries"—leather receptacles worn on the arm and forehead, containing biblical passages (Exod. 13: 1–10, 11–16, Deut. 6: 4–9, 11: 13–21) on parchment. See JE, *10*, 21 ff. Professor Ginzberg called my attention to Mekilta, ed. Lauterbach, *1*, 157, where a Sage speaks of his grandfather's těfillin; apparently they were saved as "heirlooms."

5. See GJP, p. 70, n. 23.

6. See addenda to ARNS, p. 136; "three days" is not clear; cf. n. 8.

7. [Text, "nothing," but the underlying word, *kělum,* is probably miswritten for *kelim,* "utensils"; so in fact the Epstein MS. ARNS, *ad loc.,* n. 13. J.O.]

8. According to Scripture a woman is forbidden contact with her husband during the menstrual period (cf. Lev. 15: 19), but by decree of the Sages, even after the discharge ceases she has to wait another seven consecutive days to see that no further issue of blood occurs; and in these days as well she is still forbidden to her husband.

9. "In my clothes" should very likely be deleted; cf. ARNS, p. 9, n. 14.

10. Cf. ARNB, pp. 12 f.

11. The verse in Canticles and the comment have been introduced because of the interpretation which follows.

12. The word "minor" must not be pressed too literally, for the examples that follow are all biblical commands. "Minor" is probably understood in the sense of "what may seem of minor consequence to one."

13. Cf. MHG, Numbers, ed. Fisch. p. 153; but "tender" (*ha-rakkot*) may be miswritten for "many" (*ha-rabbot*), as Professor Ginzberg suggested to me.

14. See Lev. 15: 16.

15. See Num. 15: 18–21.

16. See Deut. 18: 4.

17. See above, n. 13.

18. Cf. ARNB, pp. 9 ff.

19. Cf. ARNS, p. 9, n. 29.

20. This is not clear. Professor Ginzberg suggested that perhaps the meaning is that when Moses received the command, he went back to inform his wife of it, but kept apart from her. It may be, however, that the words were mistakenly added in imitation of the phrase below, "He started back," which is the same in Hebrew as our phrase here.

21. This sentence is not altogether clear at this point. [That is, by keeping away from his wife, Moses followed God's judgment as implied in the Deut. passage just quoted. J.O.] Note the reading in ARNB, p. 10.

22. So *editio princeps*.

23. This is taken as proof that the tables had been created during the first six days, for it was then that God worked. For other creations at that time, not spoken of in the biblical account, see *Legends, 1*, 83.

24. Text, "like the work."

25. See Exod. 32.

26. Professor Ginzberg suggested to me that the word *ḥāsidah* ("pious") in the text be slightly emended to read *ḥāsudah* ("gracious").

27. The expression "inference" is not to be pressed too literally either in the parable or in the application which follows. What is meant is simply that by reasoning independently the steward (and Moses) reached a wise conclusion. Cf. ARNS, p. 11, n. 48.

28. Hebrew, *ḳĕṭubbah*.

29. Our text reads, *niftĕrennah,* but the word may require a slight emendation; cf. *Mabo*, pp. 127 f. According to the parable, if the betrothal deed is not handed to the bride, there will be no evidence that she had been betrothed, and in the absence of a *ḳĕṭubbah* the king would not have legal grounds to condemn her to death, the penalty for unfaithfulness; thus he might marry her later. Hence the steward destroyed the betrothal deed, as ARNB, p. 10, specifically states. Cf. Wertheimer *1*, 173. See however, *Mabo, ibid*. On the status of a *ḳĕṭubbah*-less marriage reflected in our parable, see also JMC, p. 8.

30. Not actually of course, but in the sense that all the commandments are implicit in the Ten Commandments.

31. Text: "and *he* brought—or, turned—them (i.e. Israel) back to good." Perhaps, however, the statement by Moses closes with the words "and break them"; and the following clause is the homilist's comment, "And Moses led Israel back to good," i.e. he led them to mend their ways so that they would not be fatally separated from God.

32. The comment which follows is evidently intended to explain the *before your eyes* of Deut. 9:17, as Professor Ginzberg suggested (cf. Elijah Wilna, *ad loc*.). Moses smashed the first tables publicly lest Israel doubt that he had ever brought them down. [The reading of the text seems perfectly clear, requiring no emendation of any kind either in grammar or in wording: " 'Rather, I shall take hold of them and break them.' But he (Moses) did make them (the tables, that is the Ten Commandments) good again (by inscribing them on new tables), lest Israel say," etc. J.O.]

33. [In this and the five following homilies the point is made that Moses broke the tables by God's command rather than "of his own accord," except that in each homily a different scriptural passage is cited to prove the point. J.O.]

34. It is not clear how the verse cited as proof text supports the statement. On the writing disappearing cf. Tg (Jonathan) *ad* Deut. 9:17.

35. Deut. 34:11, *which the Lord sent him to do.*

36. Note the expression *before your eyes* in Deut. 9:17.

37. One word follows in the text, *lbwr'y*, "to my creator" (?). On an expression which may be related to our difficult text, see Deut. R. 3:15. Professor Ginzberg suggested that because of homoeoteleuton a line was omitted between the words *šeyakol* and *lebor'i*, and Text should read, *"What he can* hold onto. This teaches that Moses was so told by the mouth of the Almighty and Moses held on *as it were* to his (*sic*) Creator."

38. According to BY (on the basis of Rashi in B. Měnahot, 99a), the proof text is in the conclusion of Deut. 10:2, (*which thou didst break,*) *and put them in the ark.* Since God instructed Moses to store the broken tables in the ark, He evidently approved of Moses' actions. More likely, however, there is simply a play on words here, R. Me'ir interpreting *'ašer* ("which") as *yě-'ašer* (= *yišar*) *kohăka,* "May thy strength hold firm, more power to thee."

39. In this way the king who had been mortally sick (see II Kings 20:1 ff. and Isa. 38:1 ff.) demonstrated his wholly unqualified trust in God. Cf. *Legends, 6,* 369, n. 90.

40. See, however, B. Běrakot, 10b, and cf. *Tarbiz, 14,* 143.

41. Cf. ARNB, pp. 8 f.

42. See above, p. 17.

43. Literally, "If so, why does the verse say"—i.e. since Job is described as one that feared God and shunned evil, for what purpose were the words *wholehearted and upright* added?

44. The word for "wholehearted" (*tam*) also means "perfect," and being perfect is here understood as being circumcised. Cf. M. Nědarim 3:11.

45. The image of God is of course perfect, and so long as one is uncircumcised he is not perfect.

46. The Hebrew *šalem* also means "whole, perfect." On Shem equaling Melchizedek cf. *Legends, 5,* 226, 268.

47. Since he was the eldest son, the narrative in the Bible should have spoken of him first.

48. The proof seems to lie in a play on the immediately preceding words (*šětum ha-'ayin*), interpreted as "whose eye was *perfect*"; see also Septuagint and cf. above, n. 44. There is perhaps also a play euphemistically on the word *'ayin.*

49. The Hebrew for "in favor" is the same as for "goodly"; see the verse on Moses.

50. The second syllable of *Michtam* (*tam*) suggests the word play; see n. 44 above.

51. "Signet" is *hotam,* and again the play is on the syllable *tam.*

52. Cf. ARNB, p. 13.

53. Perhaps the text should read "and not even," i.e. God is even mightier than all the mighty in the world; cf. ARNS, p. 13, n. 71. For the hedge involved see below, n. 55.

54. MT does not read "Lord."

55. The hedge of the prophets is this, that they employed some metaphor in the description of God who, strictly speaking, is beyond description and comparison.

56. Cf. ARNB, p. 13.

57. The term *minuṯ* is used here to designate heresy or heterodox doctrine.

58. Finkelstein, *Mabo*, suggests "to the house of"; cf. his discussion, *ibid.*, p. 129.

59. Literally, "thither."

60. This seems to be a doublet of what precedes; note the change to second person.

61. Cf. *Mabo*, p. 129.

62. Cf. ARNB, p. 14.

63. The prayer beginning with the words *Šĕma' Yiśra'el* ("Hear, O Israel"; cf. Deut. 6:4). For the prayer see *Daily Prayer Book* (N.Y., 1931), pp. 40 ff., and CPB, pp. L ff.

64. Although it might be argued (cf. Rashi *ad* B. Bĕraḵoṯ, 4b, top) that from the point of view of the biblical text (Deut. 6:7) what R. Simeon b. Gamaliel describes would be permitted, the Sages by their ordinances declared that one is not to recite the evening Shema after midnight, nor the morning Shema before sunrise. For a different interpretation of the last sentence of the chapter cf. *Mabo*, pp. 26 ff.

CHAPTER 3

1. Cf. ARNB, pp. 14 f.

2. Literally, "wise"; cf. Ginzberg, *Commentary*, *3*, 188.

3. Cf. G. Allon in *Tarbiz* (1950), pp. 86 f.; *Tolĕḏoṯ*, pp. 316 ff.

4. A very small coin; cf. Jastrow, p. 1219, *s.v.*

5. Cf. ARNB, p. 16.

6. Literally, "give."

7. Literally, "furuncular."

8. Hebrew, *yeṣer ha-ra'*. See *Aspects*, chs. 15–16.

9. Cf. ARNB, pp. 16 f.

10. Cf. ARNB, p. 16.

11. Cf. ARNS, p. 15, n. 11.

12. On *zuz* cf. Jastrow, p. 385, *s.v.*; for the penalty imposed by R. 'Aḳiba cf. M. Baba Ḳamma 8:6. See SLC pp. 39 ff.; n. 66.

13. The Roman *As*; cf. Jastrow, p. 57.

14. Cf. ARNB, p. 15.

15. For this restoration see ARNS, n. 22, *ad loc.*; cf. ARNB, p. 15.

16. Cf. ARNB, p. 39.

17. See addenda to ARNS, p. 137.

18. The numerical value of *daleṯ*, the fourth letter of the Hebrew alphabet, is 4; the play on words is suggested by the word *dalṯoṯai*.

19. Cf. ARNB, p. 16.

20. Cf. ARNB, pp. 15 f.

21. A denarius; cf. Jastrow, p. 302.

22. Instead of shrouds. On burial in reed mats see also I. E. S. Edwards, *The Pyramids of Egypt* (Pelican Books, 1949), p. 36.

23. The story was apparently introduced because of the discussion of charity; this may have suggested the tale of a saint who had assisted a poor person during a famine. Moreover, the sowings spoken of are reminiscent of Eccl. 11:6; see n. 28.

24. This was a form of oath.

25. Cf. *Mabo,* p. 147.

26. See below, Ch. 31, p. 125, and n. 4, p. 204; cf. addenda to ARNS, p. 155.

27. On 22 as a round number see *Legends,* 7, 483 f. (L.G.).

28. The whole of the preceding chapter, except for the opening paragraph, is out of place and properly should form part of the discussion in the next chapter on "acts of loving-kindness."

CHAPTER 4

1. PA 1:2, ARNB, p. 18.

2. Cf. ARNB, p. 22.

3. Because in the verse just quoted the "burnt offering" has been singled out after the general term "sacrifice," the homily then proceeds to explain *why* the burnt offering is so distinguished.

4. It was after this offering that the Lord answered him and came to Israel's rescue.

5. Cf. S. Lieberman in AA, pp. 75 ff.

6. It was customary to greet brides with exclamations of praise; cf. B. Kĕtubbot, 17a.

7. Cf. ARNB, p. 22.

8. For this reading see ARNS, p. 19, n. 10.

9. Cf. AA, p. 80, n. 10.

10. The root of this word in Hebrew is *bny,* which is here combined with *binyata,* Aramaic for "network"; cf. Jastrow, p. 177.

11. Cf. ARNB, p. 23.

12. Literally, "As (or, for) it is said"; the proof text obviously belongs to the statement "The first time Eve was brought forth from Adam." Cf. the reading on this anecdote and homily in MHG, Genesis, ed. Margulies, p. 88.

13. I.e. this time only did God bring forth a bride for the man from himself.

14. The whole passage is obviously out of place and properly should be included in the discussion of "acts of loving-kindness" below, pp. 34 f. Cf. ARNB, p. 22.

15. Cf. ARNB, pp. 18 f.

16. This comment on the verse in Hag. is irrelevant to the principal discussion here.

17. Cf. ARNB, p. 22.

18. Cf. *Aspects,* p. 312; *Tolĕdot,* pp. 30 f.

19. See Dan. 10:11.

20. The bracketed sentence has been added from the wording of our passage in *Exempla,* p. 133, called to my attention by Professor Ginzberg; cf. MHG, Gen., ed. Margulies, p. 308.

21. I.e. among the acts of worship by means of which Daniel served God.

22. The following story of the war with Rome in the first century is properly part of the discussion of temple service. Cf. ARNB, pp. 19 ff.

23. As a token of subjection.

24. The reference is to Florus and Cestius Gallus. Cf. *Essai,* pp. 284 f.

25. Cf. Antt, *15,* 3.

26. So MSS reading. Cf. ARNS, p. 23, n. 55. Cf. also TR, *3*, 190. Text: "up to until."

27. Cf. below, Ch. 35, p. 143. MSS add at this point "under any circumstance" (cf. ARNS, p. 23, n. 57), on which see TR, *3*, 190.

28. Cf. ARNS, p. 23, n. 58.

29. Cf. ARNS, p. 23, n. 62; BY, *ad loc.* But perhaps, as Professor Ginzberg suggested, the original reading was *beṭ talmuḍ.* For the expression cf. P. Kěṭubboṭ 13:1, 35c.

30. I.e. the Temple. Lebanon frequently occurs in rabbinic sources as a term for the Temple. Its service was said to wash Israel clean (i.e. white, *laḥan*) of iniquity.

31. Rome.

32. See also the story in Josephus, *Jewish War* (Loeb Classics ed.), III, viii, 9.

33. Cf. *Thesaurus, 3,* 1327.

34. Cf. Löw in Krauss, LW, *2,* 587 (I owe this reference to Professor Ginzberg).

35. See *Legends, 6,* 393 f.

36. See also Baruch 10:18.

37. The reading should probably be "Holy of Holies"; cf. ARNS, p. 24, n. 86; addenda to ARNS, p. 165.

38. Cf. Jastrow, p. 919, *s.v. ně'imah.*

39. This whole discussion was no doubt introduced into this chapter because it had opened with a statement of *three* things on which the world stands. Cf. ARNB, p. 17.

CHAPTER 5

1. On *pěras,* see E. Bickerman in HTR (1951), pp. 153 ff.

2. PA 1:3, where the last clause, however, does not appear. Cf. ARNB, pp. 25 f.

3. Cf. *Ha-Perushim,* p. 43. ARNB omits "from the Torah."

4. On these sects see JE, *3,* 284 f.; *10,* 630 ff.; 9, 661 ff.

5. Cf. *Mabo,* pp. 35 f. for an alternate reading: "after Boethus who used . . . all his life—not because he was," etc. Cf. *Ha-Perushim,* p. 43.

6. Literally, "of arrogant disposition."

7. See the articles in JE referred to in n. 4, above.

8. This is the only story in our sources on the origin of these two sects. Cf. ARNB, p. 26, and see *Mabo,* pp. 35 ff.

CHAPTER 6

1. PA 1:4; ARNB, p. 27.

2. Literally, "appointed, designated."

3. Cf. ARNB, p. 28.

4. The following paragraph seems to be an interpretation of "Sit in the very dust."

5. Cf. above, Ch. 1, n. 5. See also *Mabo,* pp. 29 f.

6. Cf. ARNB, p. 28.

7. Cf. ARNB, pp. 29 f.

8. Literally, "read."

9. The parenthetical statement seems to be a second version of the answer 'Aḳiba received to his question; cf., however, ARNB, p. 29.

10. I.e. he wrote out the alphabet for him. *'Aleph* is the first letter in the Hebrew alphabet, *beṭ* the second, *taw* the last.

11. In talmudic times children began their study of Scripture with this book; see Lev. R. vii, 3 (at the end of the section).

12. Law, legal decision.

13. In studying Scripture 'Aḳiba inquires into the reason of every letter, every A and B; cf. e.g. B. Měnaḥoṭ 29b.

14. So MSS (cf. ARNS, p. 29, n. 22) and *editio princeps;* ARNS: "wood." [This may well have been the original reading. J.O.]

15. Apparently the straw [or the wood; n. 14] was also used by 'Aḳiba for fuel.

16. The conclusion is unintelligible and anticlimactic as it stands, and may indeed be a gloss. Cf., however, the corresponding passage in ARNB toward the end of ch. 12.

17. See addenda to ARNS, p. 138; *Mabo,* p. 135.

18. Literally, "a city of gold"; i.e. on the tiara was engraved an outline of the city of Jerusalem.

19. On the career of R. 'Aḳiba see further JE, *1,* 304 ff.

20. Cf. ARNB, 30 f.

21. Literally, "at his hosts'."

22. Literally, "skipped, leaped"; the expression seems to mean "he advanced farther up (to the front)."

23. Cf. ΛΕΤ, p. 163.

24. I.e. to offer the exposition.

25. On R. Eliezer see JE, *5,* 113 ff.

26. This would suggest that the name was Ṣiṣiṭ Hakkesef, i.e. "Ṣiṣiṭ of the Silver"; see ARNS, p. 31, n. 56; *Mabo,* p. 135. But there may perhaps be a play on words based on the resemblance of *kesef* to *keseṭ* ("cushion"), on which one reclines.

27. See Deut. 25: 5 f.

28. The explanation is based on the assumption that the name Naḳdimon is related to the root *nḳd,* understood here in the sense of "to shine clearly."

29. In Aramaic *kalba sabbi'a* (Hebrew *keleḇ śaḇea'*) means "a dog satiated."

30. These were members of a party most active in conducting the revolt against Rome in the first century. See JE, *12,* 639 ff. See also above, p. 35.

31. See above, Ch. 3, n. 27.

32. I.e. they destroyed the provisions. See also Josephus, *War,* v, i, 4 and Tacitus, *Histories* (Loeb Classics ed.), v, 12. Cf. ARNB, p. 31.

33. To store up food in the event of a prolonged siege.

34. See Jastrow, p. 1066, *s.v. 'iggul.*

35. So according to the reading in the MSS (cf. ARNS, p. 33, n. 80) and *editio princeps.* For the meaning, cf. S. Spiegel in LGJV, p. 345 and nn. 16–18. See further n. 36 below. ARNS, "and grind them with saws" (?).

36. I owe the understanding of this sentence (and references) to Professor Lieberman, who further calls my attention to M. Makširin 1: 6 to illustrate how the besieged used to hide food on which they would be able to sustain themselves.

37. Cf. Josephus, *War*, VI,iii,3.

38. Text, "them." Cf. ARNB, p. 20.

CHAPTER 7

1. PA I: 5; ARNB, p. 33.

2. Cf. ARNB, p. 33.

3. Cf. *Mabo,* pp. 31 f. Cf. ARNB, p. 33.

4. The Hebrew word for tamarisk consists of the same consonants (*'šl*) as the verb "to ask" (*š'l*).

5. Cf. ARNB, p. 33 f.

6. Literally, "to him." The context suggests that the reference is to the master of the house.

7. Cf. *Mabo,* pp. 140 f.

8. Literally, "even if she is one's own wife, and needless to say with his fellow's wife."

9. Cf. PA I: 5.

10. Cf. ARNB, p. 35.

CHAPTER 8

1. From Yose ben Joezer and Joseph ben Johanan; see above, pp. 40, 46; cf. PA I: 4, 6.

2. PA I: 6; ARNB, p. 38.

3. Cf. ARNB, p. 39.

4. Literally, "fixed, permanent."

5. "Mishnah" is here used as the generic term for the three branches of the Oral Law—Midrash, Halakha, Agada—studied in the rabbinic academies. Cf. AT, *1,* 475 ff.

6. So also Aknin, SM, p. 11; but cf. ARNS, p. 35, n. 3.

7. For a different view held by R. Me'ir see above, p. 28.

8. Cf. ARNB, p. 40.

9. I.e. methods and principles of logical deduction and reasoning.

10. See *Mabo,* pp. 18 f.

11. Cf. ARNB, p. 40.

12. "Band" (Hebrew, *'aggudah*) is here taken to mean a group of three, a triad, held together.

13. Literally, "accepted" (*mitkabbel*).

14. *šeggozĕrin gĕzerah* (so ARNS and Aknin, SM, p. 87): literally, "who make a decision, who decide." (I owe the understanding of this expression in the present context to Professor Lieberman, who calls my attention also to the reading of our passage in *Yalkut Makiri,* Malachi, p. 52.) Mal. 3: 16 having been quoted, a midrash on the verse is introduced, although it is not germane to our present discussion. The midrash wishes to contrast those who are of a decisive character, with those who are indecisive, who keep weighing and debating matters in their hearts. The former are helped by God to carry out their decision; the latter, says our midrash, are not helped, and in the end an angel comes and strikes them down. Cf. B. San-

hedrin, 19b. (I am grateful to Rabbi Dov Zlotnick for urging upon me this interpretation of the ARNA passage.) For a more liberal attitude toward those who do
not carry out good intentions, see ARNB, p. 40, and cf. Lev. R. 34: 8.

15. Perhaps this should be translated, "Shall we go and release the prisoners
and ransom the captives?"

16. Text, *lamaḏ* ("studied"), should most likely read *'amaḏ*.

17. Cf. ARNB, pp. 41 f.

18. I.e. the house of prostitution where the girl was held. On "the harlots' apartment" cf. above Ch. 1, n. 27.

19. Cf. Jastrow, p. 1454, *s.v. raḥan*.

20. The phrase "because of unchastity" seems awkward, but see BY, *ad loc.*

21. Literally, "didst."

22. This sentence is not clear.

23. Restoration according to ARNS, pp. 37 f., n. 29.

24. See Lev. 15: 16.

25. On forbidden foods that defile see Lev. 17: 15; Maimonides, *Book of Cleanness*, v,iii,1 (YJS, *8*, 263 f.). Cf. below, Ch. 16, n. 13.

26. In this instance the text adds *'et*, the sign of the accusative, which does
not occur in MT.

27. Cf. Tur-Sinai in MMKJV (Heb. vol.), p. 85.

28. This section on the saintliness of beasts was very likely added as a kind of
climax to the discussion of JUDGE EVERYONE. In the previous comments some inci-
dents in the lives of saintly folk had been reported; to these was later appended
the present discussion on the saintliness of the very beasts of saints in ages past.

CHAPTER 9

1. PA 1: 7; cf. ARNB, p. 35.

2. Cf. ARNS, p. 38, n. 2; the reading in addenda to ARNS, p. 139; and in Aknin,
SM, p. 13.

3. Cf. ARNS, p. 38, n. 3.

4. See Lev. 14: 34 f.

5. But see *Mabo*, p. 121.

6. See also below, Ch. 34, p. 136.

7. Text, "one." In B. 'Arakin, 15a, where the reading is "two," Israel is described as having been of little faith both on approaching and on emerging from
the Red Sea. Cf. ARNS, p. 39, n. 6; addenda to ARNS, p. 155.

8. Exod. 16: 19 ff.

9. Exod. 16: 26 f.

10. Exod. 16: 3, 13.

11. Num. 11: 4.

12. Exod. 15: 23 f.

13. Exod. 17: 1 ff.

14. Where the golden calf was made; see Exod. 32 and Ps. 106: 19.

15. Num. 13 f.

16. The two verses prove the grievous character of the last trial, the trial of
slander, because only in connection with it did the Lord punish them, as is stated
in Num. 14: 22 f. and 14: 37.

17. The subject of the trials has been introduced at this point because of the discussion of slander, one punishment for which (see the following section) is plagues of leprosy.

18. The subject of the conversation is described below.

19. Verse 10 continues, *And when the cloud was removed from over the Tent, behold, Miriam was leprous*, etc.

20. See addenda to ARNS, p. 139.

21. Cf. *Mabo*, pp. 188 f.; ARNB, p. 116.

22. I.e. on us, Moses and Aaron, our own flesh and blood; see the next note below.

23. The proof text is in the closing words of the verse, *of whom the flesh is half consumed;* this suggests the thought that when Miriam was afflicted, her brothers—also of the flesh of Amram—were afflicted too.

24. The reference to Amos 1:9, Professor Ginzberg suggested to me, is based on the agadic interpretation of *brotherly* as referring to Moses and Aaron; cf. B. Horayot, 12a.

25. A magical act by means of which the person cut out for himself, as it were, a precinct over which evil or demonic spirits could have no influence. See JMS, p. 121.

26. See further, *Legends, 3,* 255 ff.

27. Text, "as meek as." Cf. ARNS, p. 41, n. 35; addenda to ARNS, p. 156.

28. Cf., however, ARNS, p. 41, n. 36; ARNB, Ch. 16, p. 36.

29. Literally, "slander."

30. Text adds *ma'al;* cf. MT.

31. Text: *lĕhaḵṭiro;* cf. MT.

32. Literally, "in two parts, twelve by twelve miles." See *Legends, 6,* 358, n. 30.

33. Cf. MT.

34. So MT; *text,* "Shemaiah."

35. Cf. ARNB, p. 36.

36. Literally, "even for Torah." See HUCA, *19,* 101 f. Cf., however, *Mabo*, pp. 19 ff., 135, 245.

37. Cf. ARNB, p. 37.

38. A characteristic agadic thought; see further below, Ch. 39, p. 162.

CHAPTER 10

1. From Joshua ben Peraḥyah and Nittai the Arbelite; cf. above, Ch. 8, n. 1.

2. For this translation cf. Gen. R., ed. Theodor, p. 519, to which Professor Ginzberg called my attention.

3. PA 1:8; cf. ARNB, p. 43.

4. Text, literally, "word, thing." See, however, Aknin, SM, p. 14.

5. Literally, "which they asked me"; but cf. the reading in Aknin, SM, p. 14, for the whole clause.

6. The following discussion seems to be the comment on WHEN THERE ARE LITIGANTS STANDING, etc.

7. Cf. ARNB, p. 43.

8. That is, Judah ben Ṭabbai. According to a tradition (cf. DM, p. 37) Judah ben Ṭabbai was originally president (*Naśi*) of the Sanhedrin. He was asked to re-

sign (or did so of his own accord) in favor of his colleague, Simeon ben Sheṭaḥ, because he (Judah) had given a wrong decision in a capital offense. See also *Mabo*, p. 14.

9. On the Hebrew expression *yaraḏ 'aḏ lĕ-ḥayyaw* cf. Jastrow, p. 455, *s.v.* *ḥayyim.*

10. Cf. GJP, pp. 170 ff.

11. Cf. *Mabo*, pp. 149 f., for the suggestion that the clause be understood as "for high office is hard to put on; and even as it is hard to put it on, so is it difficult to take it off."

12. Cf. ARNB, p. 43.

13. PA 1:9 (more succinctly): AND BE CAREFUL IN THY WORDS; PERCHANCE THROUGH THEM THEY MAY LEARN TO LIE.

14. Text, literally, "and add to thee falsehood because of the deceivers." The words "because of the deceivers" may perhaps be a gloss to the expression, "they that hear hear." Cf. the statement in ARNB, p. 42 (where it is attributed to Judah b. Ṭabbai).

CHAPTER 11

1. From Judah ben Ṭabbai and Simeon ben Sheṭaḥ.

2. PA 1:10; ARNB, p. 44. On this saying see *Tolĕḏoṭ*, pp. 329 f.

3. See Exod. 31:16. Cf. ARNB, p. 44, in the name of R. Eliezer ("even as Israel was commanded concerning the Torah," etc.).

4. Such funds could be used to remunerate Temple laborers. Cf. ARNB, p. 44, in the name of R. Yose, and ARNB, p. 45, in the name of R. Eliezer.

5. R. Dostai here suggests that such misfortune might well be a punishment for neglecting to work during the week. Cf. ARNB, p. 45, in the name of R. Me'ir.

6. Cf. ARNB, p. 44, in the name of R. Eliezer.

7. Cf. ARNB, p. 44, in the name of R. Yose.

8. I.e. any manner of work.

9. Cf. ARNB, p. 45, in the name of Rabbi (Judah the Prince).

10. Cf. *Mabo*, p. 181. Professor Ginzberg suggested to me that the proof text refers to the fact that Jacob's death occurred *after* he had finished commanding his sons—because so long as he was engaged in a task death was powerless over him; cf. the immediately preceding words of the verse.

11. In the text the next two sentences occur in reverse order. But the second sentence is actually an objection to Yose's view: how explain the sudden death of one engaged in work! Cf. ARNB, pp. 44 f.; *editio princeps* omits entirely the sentence about standing on the rooftop or seashore.

12. The following seems to belong to a homily the first part of which is wanting; cf. ARNS, p. 45, n. 18. Or perhaps it should be connected with R. Ṭarfon's statement above.

13. In other words, children too. The verse reads literally "the people."

14. Cf. *Legends*, *3*, 192 f.

15. Cf. ARNB, p. 46.

16. Cf. the reading in ARNB, p. 46.

17. Comp. below, Ch. 25, p. 110.

18. Cf. ARNB, p. 47.

19. A measure; cf. Jastrow, p. 625, *s.v.*

20. Translation conjectural; cf. JC, *3*, 25, n. 12; *Tolĕḏoṯ*, p. 340, n. 119. MSS (quoted in ARNS, p. 47, n. 33) and Aknin, SM, p. 16, read "chief (prince) of the banquet"; cf. Sirach 32: 1 and see SJ, 2, 84 f.

21. Professor Obermann suggests that this may mean that they open the door for him upon his arrival and escort him upon his departure.

22. PA 1: 11 (with some additions and omissions); cf. ARNB, p. 47 and see *Mabo*, pp. 150 f.

23. Cf. ARNB, p. 47. See Wertheimer, 2, 99, n. 3.

24. I.e. heresy. See also JE, *1*, p. 404, col. 2.

25. Cf. the reading in ARNB, p. 47.

CHAPTER 12

1. From Shemaiah and 'Abṭalyon.

2. PA 1: 12–14; cf. ARNB, pp. 48, 56, 54.

3. Cf. ARNB, p. 48.

4. Cf. ARNB, pp. 49 f.

5. On an additional clause, "his head aching violently," cf. *Mabo*, p. 122.

6. For the bracketed phrases cf. ARNS, p. 49, n. 10, and addenda to ARNS, p 163. Text, literally, "Why did Israel weep for Aaron thirty days? Because Aaron rendered judgment strictly according to the truth. How do we know this? He did not say to a man that 'thou hast acted offensively,'" etc. Cf. ARNB, p. 50.

7. Aaron reconciled husbands to their wives when they fell out with each other. On Aaron as peacemaker see *Legends*, *3*, 328 f.

8. Text, *kohănim gĕḏolim* (according to Professor Ginzberg), is not to be taken in a technical sense, i.e. as "High Priests."

9. Note the reading in ARNB, p. 51, line 13.

10. Cf. ARNB, p. 51.

11. Text, *bĕḵaf;* MT: *bĕṯoḵ ḵaf.*

12. Text, literally, "although."

13. On this meaning for *samaḵ* cf. e.g. GS, *1*, 94. The verb, however, may signify the same as in Ch. 36, below, p. 148: "base a claim (for reward)." In our passage the thought is that the souls of the wicked shall have no resting place.

14. Translation conjectural; cf. *Thesaurus, 3,* 1354, col. 2, and notes *ad loc.;* see Saadia, p. 257. For other interpretations cf. Rashi in B. Šabbaṯ, 152b, and Jastrow, p. 387, *s.v. zum.*

15. Cf. Job 28: 23.

16. Frequently identified with Torah, but here with Moses, since it was he who taught it to Israel.

17. On the death of Moses see further, *Legends, 3,* 463 ff.

18. Cf. ARNB, p. 49.

19. Cf. ARNB, pp. 48 f.

20. Cf. above, p. 56.

21. Namely, *Blessed be the glory of the Lord from His place.* See Ezek. 3: 12.

22. In the immediately preceding verse the prophet speaks of Seraphim, in the plural; this suggests the thought that the angels recite their praises in groups, not as individuals.

23. Cf. ARNB, p. 52.

24. Scripture describes them as *of one language and one speech*. See Gen. 11: 1–9.

25. See below, Ch. 36, p. 147; ARNB, p. 64. On Sodom's sin of rebellion see *Aspects*, pp. 219 f.

26. Text, *mĕkappeaḥ;* here perhaps in the sense of "subjecting someone." Cf. TG Onkelos on Gen. 12: 5. Professor Ginzberg suggested that we read *mekareḇ*. See also *Thesaurus, 12,* 6063, col. 2, n. 1.

27. Text, "Abraham."

28. Cf. ARNB, pp. 53, 54.

29. This is not clear (but Professor Obermann suggests that the passage would be intelligible if *śĕḵar* is taken in the sense of employer's "wages"): perhaps we have here a reference to some doctrine which would teach that even in this life what a man enjoys is the divine reward for his own actions only.

30. Cf. ARNB, p. 54.

31. Text, "me." Cf. ARNS, p. 53, n. 55. The thought seems to be that in the present situation also no comforting is possible. Cf. the reading in ARNB, p. 54; addenda to ARNS, pp. 142 f.

32. Cf. S. Bialoblotzki in AA, p. 40. Cf. ARNB, p. 53.

33. ARNS (cf. p. 54, n. 57) suggests omission of "in my lifetime."

34. Text for this sentence seems doubtful. [It may well be based on a reading *uḵśe-'ēni*, "and not being for myself," rather than that of *uḵśe-'āni;* for a case of the same variance, see below, Ch. 38, n. 13. J.O.]

35. Cf. ARNB, p. 54.

36. Cf. ARNS, p. 54, n. 60; addenda to ARNS, pp. 141, 143.

37. Hillel. Cf. ARNB, p. 55.

38. Perhaps to be translated, *"in* the world to come."

39. For this exclamation of Hillel's, at the water-drawing festivities in the Temple, see B. Sukkah, 53a.

40. Cf. Ginzberg's note in OT, p. 272, n. 71.

41. For these two maxims cf. PA 5: 22 f., and on the authority of the last maxim, see GJP, p. 160, n. 113. Cf. ARNB, p. 55.

42. Cf. ARNB, pp. 55 f.

43. A measure; see Jastrow, p. 947.

44. I.e. he informed them that the maxim applied only to such things as the study of Torah and the performance of religious duties.

45. PA 2: 6. The last word in the text should probably be emended according to the reading of the Oxford MS; cf. ARNS, p. 55, n. 69, and *editio princeps*. On the saying see HJP, p. 137, n. 87. Cf. ARNB, p. 56.

46. I.e. in Aramaic. Actually the previous maxim is also in Aramaic and so are the two before that one. On the maxims now quoted see above, p. 62.

47. Cf. above, p. 62. Cf. ARNB, p. 57.

48. Cf. ARNB, p. 57; MHG, Lev., ed. Rabinowitz, p. 241 (cf. *Mabo*, p. 152). See SHY, *1*, p. 16.

49. Cf. above, n. 8; see, however, *Mabo*, p. 152.

50. See Num. 18: 8 ff., Deut. 18: 4. The heave offering must be prepared and eaten in a state of purity.

51. [This could be said only of an object having a receptacle, e.g. an oven. J.O.]

52. By neglecting to study with and observe the Sages, the priest had fallen into error concerning the two Lev. passages just cited. See also *Tolĕḏoṯ*, p. 62.

53. Cf. ARNB, p. 56.

54. See MTJM, pp. 354 f. For an interpretation of "crown" as Torah see PA 4: 5 (R. Zadok). Cf. ARNB, p. 56.

CHAPTER 13

1. PA 1: 15; ARNB, p. 47.

2. Perhaps, "he is not to do so occasionally, but to do so regularly," i.e. one should attend a study house regularly and listen to the exposition of the Sages.

3. Cf. ARNB, p. 47.

4. Cf. ARNB, pp. 47 f.

5. I.e. that it was four oxen he prepared for the angels.

6. The two consonants, D and N (the *dalet* and *nun* of the Hebrew alphabet), make up the word *punish* in the verse just cited (*dan*); they are also contained in the word *'Adonai* (Lord), one of the names of God.

7. One of the mystical names of God; cf. JMS, p. 95.

8. According to the Midrash (cf. Gen. R. 44: 19, ed. Theodor, p. 442) the proof text in the Hebrew, from "to go" up to "by great terrors" (excluding the word "nation" once) adds up to 72 letters.

9. Cf. ARNB, p. 48.

CHAPTER 14

1. PA 2: 8; ARNB, p. 66. Cf. *Mabo*, p. 41.

2. Cf. ARNB, pp. 57 f.

3. According to the Rabbis, God spoke to the prophets only because Israel of their generation merited it; cf. Meḵilta, ed. Lauterbach, *1*, p. 13; N. N. Glatzer in RR (1946), pp. 132 f. See further, *Mabo*, p. 137.

4. It was a particular distinction to be invited to intercalate the year; cf. B. Sanhedrin, 10b–11a; ARNB, p. 57.

5. See JE, 7, 238.

6. Various branches of the Oral Law; see Strack, pp. 3 ff. "Supplements" (cf. addenda to ARNS, p. 143) were a kind of agadic midrash, as Professor Ginzberg pointed out to me, referring to GS, 2, 566, n. 28. Nevertheless, cf. TR, 2, 7 ff.

7. Various fine points in the interpretation of the Written and Oral Laws. "Scribes" is a term for the early, pre-Tannaite Sages.

8. For examples of such rules see below, Ch. 37, p. 154.

9. PA 2: 8; cf. ARNB, pp. 58, 66.

10. Cf. Eccl. 4: 12.

11. Cf. AC, 2, 374 and n. 8.

12. Our text places here the exclamation "Happy the disciple," etc., which apparently belongs at the end of the next paragraph. Cf. addenda to ARNS, p. 158.

13. See n. 12 above.

14. PA 2: 8; cf. ARNB, pp. 58 f.

15. Literally, "a good heart."

16. On the addition of this clause see below, R. Eleazar's statement on the EVIL WAY; cf. also the reading in *editio princeps*.

17. On the rabbinic view of the heart, see *Aspects*, pp. 255 ff.

18. PA 2: 9; cf. ARNB, p. 59.

19. R. Johanan realized that R. Eleazar would succeed in consoling him and therefore he prepared to go to the bathhouse, a luxury normally forbidden to a mourner. The phrase "Take my clothing," etc. was suggested (according to Professor Ginzberg) by the reference to II Sam. 12: 20, where it is said that David terminated the mourning for his son by bathing and putting on his clothes.

20. For the correct reading of this clause see MHM, *3*, 522 f. Text: "he studied Torah, Scripture (*mikra*), Prophets, Holy Writings, Mishnah, Halakhot, and Agadot."

21. On the soul as a trust cf. *Legends*, *5*, 255, n. 259; Josephus, *War*, III, viii, 5.

22. Cf. addenda to ARNS, p. 143.

23. Literally, "the public baths" (Greek, *demosia*). Emmaus was famous for its springs and the luxurious life there. Cf. ARNB, p. 59; SHY, *1*, 5. See JE, *s.v.*

24. The famous coastal city where after the destruction of the Temple R. Johanan ben Zakkai established his academy and court. See above, p. 36.

25. On Eleazar ben 'Arak see JE, *5*, 96 f.

CHAPTER 15

1. Each of the disciples described in the last chapter.

2. PA 2: 10; ARNB, p. 59.

3. Cf. below, p. 82; ARNB, p. 60.

4. Aknin, SM, p. 51, reads, "his fellow."

5. This is not clear. Perhaps (so one of the commentators) the meaning is that false testimony even over a farthing must be avoided despite any sacrifice involved for oneself in bearing true testimony.

6. Cf. ARNB, pp. 60 f. and see *Mabo*, pp. 44 ff.

7. Literally, "what dost thou need?"

8. Text, *hălakah*, here in the general sense of a rule on any branch of human knowledge.

9. According to rabbinic tradition Hillel was the *Naśi* of the Sanhedrin in his time (*ca.* 30 B.C.E.–10 C.E.).

10. I.e. in Palestine.

11. Cf. ARNB, pp. 61 f.

12. '*Aleph, bet*, and *gimmel* are the first three letters of the Hebrew alphabet.

13. Hillel agreed that the man had indeed been answering correctly, but he went on to indicate that without the support of tradition one could hardly be sure of the truth of anything. Note, however, the suggested reading by R. Elijah Wilna in accordance with B. Šabbat, 31a; but cf. ARNB, p. 61.

14. Cf. ARNB, p. 61.

15. See above, Ch. 6, n. 11.

16. So according to addenda to ARNS, p. 144.

17. Gamaliel (I) was the grandson of Hillel.

18. Cf. ARNB, p. 62.

19. I.e. R. Eliezer ben Hyrcanus.

20. PA 2: 10; ARNB, p. 62. Cf. ARNS, p. 59, n. 2; *Mabo,* p. 42.

CHAPTER 16

1. PA 2: 11; cf. ARNB, p. 62.

2. Cf. above, p. 78; ARNB, p. 63.

3. I.e. unchastity.

4. Cf. ARNB, p. 36.

5. The wife of Potiphar; see Gen. 39.

6. And hence will not permit her to carry out her evil plans. "Wickedness" refers here to illicit love.

7. Text: *'rm'y* (MHG, Gen., ed. Margulies, p. 670, *'army*), which is used often to mean "pagan" (cf. supplement to AC, p. 435 and GJP, pp. 80, 167) but may well mean here something like "stranger"; i.e. she threatened Joseph that she would exile him to a far off land (cf. Tanhuma Wayyeṣe, 7) and reduce him to the status of strangers, who generally have no rights and are helpless; hence Joseph's answer. Cf. B. Bĕraḵot, 8b, where the term *'Ăramiṭ* is explained as *giyyorta,* "proselyte" (fem.); note the reading recorded in DS, *ad loc.* shγa, p. 165, paraphrases Joseph's answer as "God protects all the strangers who are in an alien land" (lit., "in a land they know not"). Professor Obermann suggests that "strangers" (*gerim*) in Joseph's answer is intended here in the sense of "proselytes," the implication being that Joseph, having been made a "pagan" (*'arma'i*), would of course return to his former faith, and thus be a "proselyte."

8. Cf. *Mabo,* p. 153.

9. Cf. MLBT, pp. 194 f.

10. For the expression cf. Dan. 3: 8.

11. Literally, "between them."

12. This has all the earmarks of contemporary polemics against so-called Jewish separatism; cf. Tacitus, *History,* v, v, and see Pauly-Wissowa, suppl., *5,* 42.

13. Literally, "from the flesh of carrion, *ṭĕrefah,* and creeping things."

14. I.e. R. Eliezer b. Hyrcanus.

15. In quoting I Sam. 25: 41 (which cf.) the girl indicates by implication her willingness to marry her uncle. Text reads "disciple" (sing.), perhaps merely a *scriptio defectiva.*

16. I.e. asking for her *explicit* permission; a woman cannot be married against her wish.

17. Cf. PJT, pp. 87 f., n. 2.

18. Cf. ARNB, p. 63; *Mabo,* p. 138.

19. Cf. TG Jonathan, *ad loc.* See also ARNB, p. 36.

20. The text for the next line or so is awkward but the idea is clear: the foolish actions which characterize human life are due to the evil impulse in man; beasts, however, free of the evil impulse, always know instinctively how to take care of themselves. Cf. ARNB, p. 63. On the evil impulse see *Aspects,* Ch. 15.

21. Literally, "It is said to a person, when the child is lying in his cradle, the man wants to kill thee, he wishes to pull out his hair from him."

22. Cf. below, p. 103, for the same expression.

23. Cf. *Legends, 5,* 84 f., 93.

24. Cf. *Aspects*, pp. 280 ff.

25. Cf. ARNB, p. 63.

26. Cf. below, Ch. 41, n. 21.

27. See above, Ch. 2, n. 57.

28. *ma ṭa'am*, literally, "what is the reason, i.e. the scriptural support"; but the reading is doubtful; cf. *Mabo*, pp. 47 ff. As the text reads, *ma ṭa'am* refers back to the closing phrase of Lev. 19:18, *I am the Lord*, i.e. what does this mean? The answer given is that *I am the Lord* = I the Lord have created him.

29. Cf. *editio princeps*; see also the readings in *Mabo, loc. cit.*

30. In answering the question of what the *I am the Lord* of Lev. 19:18 means, the homilist makes use of the biblical idiom, a phrase from Isa. 45:8. For other examples of such use of the biblical idiom see e.g. above, pp. 28 f.; below, p. 113 and n. 3 *ad loc.*; p. 143 and n. 4. *ad loc.*

31. Cf. ARNB, p. 53; *Mabo* pp. 47 ff.

32. Cf. *Mabo*, p. 139.

33. [In agadic literature the solemn formula *'ăni YHWH*, "I (am) the Lord," is very frequently said to imply a divine pledge of reward for the righteous and a threat of punishment for the wicked; see the material adduced in Yalḳuṭ Šim'oni, Lev., sections 586–91, and cf. Rashi, *ad* Exod. 6:2. J.O.]

34. Cf. SPG, 2, 206 f.

CHAPTER 17

1. PA 2:12; ARNB, p. 65.

2. Cf. above, pp. 78, 82; ARNB, p. 65.

3. Cf. above, p. 82; G. Allon in *Tarbiz* (1950), p. 90 and n. 26.

4. See *Legends*, *3*, 397.

5. Cf. ARNB, p. 65; *Legends*, *3*, 396 ff. Acting as interpreter (*turgeman*; see JE, *8*, 521) would make it clear to all that henceforth Joshua held first place.

6. For lack of adequate clothing she used her long hair to cover herself.

7. Literally, "If you don't keep it"—*haser*; "if you give alms"—*hesed*. In either case the idea is that charity is the preserver (literally, salt) of wealth. Presumably, Naḳdimon had not practiced sufficient charity to save his wealth.

8. The wealth of one household was tied up with that of the other.

9. See above, Ch. 2, n. 28.

10. *Ba'al*, the power (literally, the master, the lord) or spirit or angel that reveals things by means of a dream; cf. AMJV, p. 177 (Heb. vol.), n. 7.

11. See HUCA, *19*, 99 ff.

12. I.e. the "Eighteen" benedictions which next to the Shema (see above, p. 25 f.) constitute the most important section in the daily prayers. Though called "Eighteen," it has actually nineteen benedictions. See JE, *11*, 270–82.

13. See also Jonah 4:2. The verse in the text does not correspond exactly either to Joel 2:13 or Jonah 4:2; the copyist seems to have quoted from memory.

14. PA 2:13; cf. ARNB, p. 64.

15. Cf. addenda to ARNS, p. 144.

16. One who treats the teachings of Scripture and the tradition skeptically and frivolously; Hebrew form, *'appiḳoros*.

17. PA 2:14 (with some deviations); cf. ARNB, p. 66.

CHAPTER 18

1. I.e. even as R. Johanan ben Zakkai described the individual distinctions of his disciples (see above, p. 74), so R. Judah described those of his masters.

2. Literally, "rings (upon) rings." The meaning is that R. 'Akiba not only systematized the body of tradition which he had acquired, but formulated this tradition in abstract general rules; cf. HJP, p. 95 and notes.

3. In the following paragraphs the compiler incorporates additional matter bearing on R. Eleazar ben Azariah. The R. Joshua mentioned here is Joshua ben Hananiah.

4. I.e. whose turn was it to preach? As a result of the rather arbitrary nature of the patriarch Gamaliel II (ca. 100), a revolt occurred in the rabbinic academy and the scholars demanded his resignation from the presidency (of the academy). In his place they elected R. Eleazar ben Azariah. Subsequently, however, the scholars and Gamaliel were reconciled, and they reinstated him; in order not to offend R. Eleazar, who was asked to relinquish the office, it was arranged that he preach one Sabbath every month, while R. Gamaliel preached on the others. Hence R. Joshua's question.

5. I.e. perhaps the difference of opinion among the scholars endangers the stability of the Law. Such a fear in fact led to Gamaliel's difficulty with the Sages, and R. Eleazar's sermon therefore had a timely relevance.

6. Moses.

7. Cf. addenda to ARNS, p. 145.

8. The text is awkward, but Professor Ginzberg suggested that the meaning seems to be that R. Yose is praiseworthy for his modesty, a quality which had been emphasized at Mount Sinai; he in turn praised the other Sages for exemplifying the same virtue.

9. R. Me'ir was a famous scribe.

10. I.e. few laws have come from him, but these few are of utmost trustworthiness. The word for "little" is literally a small measure (*kab*).

11. Literally, "subsequently, eventually."

12. For the understanding of this term I am indebted to Professor Ginzberg, who refers also to MHG, Exod., p. 55. Cf. Midrash Ruth Zuta, p. 53.

CHAPTER 19

1. PA 3: 1 (with some deviations); cf. ARNB, p. 69. See *Mabo*, p. 67.

2. Cf. ARNB, p. 69.

3. Cf. PA, 3: 1.

4. Cf. Sirach 10: 11.

5. Cf. *editio princeps* and addenda to ARNS, p. 158. ARNS: "and dwelt in all of them."

6. So too the reading in Aknin, SM, p. 86. The text adds, "of what thou hast taught us," which ARNS suggests omitting; cf. ARNS, p. 70 and n. 11, *ad loc*. If the clause is retained, perhaps the meaning is "Teach us (again) one of the things thou didst teach us (previously)."

7. For example, at the seams; cf. TR, *3*, 76.

8. Literally, "a round cushion . . . a phylactery which was torn, which thou didst tell us, what are they?" The text is somewhat awkward; the point of the question, however, seems to be, did R. Eliezer still maintain his views?

9. Literally, "They are unclean." See also below, Ch. 25, pp. 108 f. On the principle underlying this view cf. the discussion of Rashi and Tosafot in B. Sanhedrin, 68a, and M. Kelim 23:1. According to Rabbi Eliezer, what is within objects like a cushion, etc., is regarded as part of the object as a whole; if, therefore, something of corpse uncleanness came into contact with the outer covering or container, even though it were torn open, the whole object becomes unclean, including what is within. This seems to be the first point R. Eliezer is making (for a contrary view see M. Kelim, 23:1). In line with his reasoning, R. Eliezer then insists that in order to be made clean the whole object is to be immersed as it is, i.e. we do not consider the contents as constituting an interposing element (*ḥoṣeṣ*) preventing the water of the immersion pool from purifying the object as a whole. For further discussion of the passage cf. *Mabo*, pp. 190 ff. and TR, *3*, 76.

10. *Hălakot kěbu'ot;* cf. below, p. 108, for the reading *hălakot; gědolot; Mabo,* p. 191.

CHAPTER 20

1. Cf. PA. 3:5; ARNB, p. 68.

2. Cf. addenda to ARNS, p. 145; *Mabo*, p. 124.

3. But cf. *Mabo*, p. 124.

4. Reading *ya'eb* (S. Lieberman, JQR, *36*, 345, n. 113). Text seems to read *yk'* or perhaps *yb'*.

5. Cf. Lieberman, *op. cit.; Tolědot*, p. 41.

6. For a different reading in MHG, Deut., cf. ARNS, p. 71, n. 7.

7. So ARNS, p. 72, n. 8, and addenda to ARNS, p. 145. Text: "He used to say." The verse in Canticles and the first comment thereon seem to have been added as further discussion on the Deut. verse just interpreted, *because thou didst not serve the Lord thy God . . . therefore shalt thou serve thine enemy,* etc.

8. Cf. *Aspects*, pp. 87 f.; Allon in *Tarbiz, 21*, pp. 106 ff.

9. Text, "refers to Moses when"; cf. ARNS, p. 72, n. 11; Azulai, p. 244b. On Dathan and Abiram see *Legends*, *2*, 281.

10. Text, "many"; *editio princeps*, "those many." The same reading occurs in DR, p. 59.

11. See *Legends*, *2*, 280.

12. Four words follow in our text which are unintelligible: "they are guilty in judgment, they are guilty now" (?); see also the reading in *editio princeps*.

13. Removed from his own people he was thus far from his *own vineyard*.

14. Literally, "and brought it upon Israel that their carcasses fall."

15. In this connection the vineyard is taken as a metaphor for heave offerings and tithes.

CHAPTER 21

1. PA 3:10; ARNB, p. 73.

2. On the connection between reciting the Shema and the study of Torah cf. Ginzberg, *Commentary, 1*, 136 f.

3. For this reading cf. ARNS, p. 74, n. 5; Aknin, SM, p. 94. Text, "neglects the whole Torah."

4. I.e. when is that season when thy king will be free? In typical midrashic fashion, once Eccl. 10:17 has been quoted, another comment is added, in this case the verse being interpreted as a reference to the "distant future." On this passage see also HYKP, pp. 116 f.

5. See Maimonides, *Epistle to Yemen*, ed. Halkin, pp. 82 f. (and trans., p. XVI).

6. Literally, "for"; the verse is not strictly a proof text, but a quotation to reinforce the idea that one must always study.

7. Cf. Tertullian, *De spectaculis*, III.

8. Cf. ARNS, p. 74, n. 15; DR, p. 19, n. 6.

9. See above, p. 41; JE, *1*, 304 f.

10. Cf. Ginzberg, *Commentary*, *3*, 223.

CHAPTER 22

1. PA 3:9; cf. ARNB, p. 69.

2. Cf. PA 3:17; ARNB, p. 75.

3. PA 1:16.

4. Cf. PA 1:17 and ARNB, p. 70, and note variants. On the identity of Simeon cf. Ginzberg in JJLP, p. 288, n. 108.

CHAPTER 23

1. PA 4:1 (with some variants); cf. ARNB, p. 72.

2. PA 4:14; the last clause is a quotation from Prov. 3:5.

3. PA 4:3, where Ben 'Azzai is presumably the authority. Cf. *Mabo*, p. 78.

4. Cf. *Mabo*, pp. 155 f.

5. PA 4:20 (with slight variants), in the name of Elisha ben 'Abuyah; cf. ARNB, pp. 88 f.

6. *Editio princeps* (so too Aknin, SM, p. 134): R. Simeon b. Gamaliel. Cf. addenda to ARNS, p. 159.

7. Cf. ARNB, p. 88.

8. Literally, "she flings herself upon him and he flings himself upon her."

9. In B. Kiddušin, 30a f., these verses are quoted in connection with Torah study.

10. On the Torah compared to healing drugs cf. Sifre Deut., 85 (ed. Friedmann, 82b).

11. Literally, "So too." The connection of this paragraph with the preceding one is not clear.

12. The expression in the text is not altogether clear; the meaning seems to be that the contents of the Torah ought to be classified into groups and then the groups logically related to each other.

CHAPTER 24

1. On the series of sayings of Elisha b. 'Abuyah cf. *Mabo*, p. 80.

2. Cf. ARNB, p. 77.

3. On the expression "headlong" see above, p. 85.

4. Bacher, AT, *1*, 432, n. 5, calls attention to the Roman proverb *"in succum et sanguinem."*

5. See Sirach 25: 3.

6. See, however, Ruth Rabba 6: 4 for a different attitude of Elisha's toward this view.

7. Cf. ARNB, p. 68.

8–9. So the text literally, which makes no sense. Aknin, SM, p. 134, has the following reading: "even as glass vessels cannot be mended unless restored to their original state, so gold vessels cannot be mended unless restored to their original state." The passage is no doubt awkward but perhaps is to be translated as follows: "even as gold vessels can be mended if they have been broken, so (reading *kk* rather than *wkl*) glass vessels: (but) they cannot be mended, if they have been broken, unless they be restored to their original state." The expression "unless they be restored to their original state" refers principally to the idea underlying the parable, that is, the scholar who has "forgotten what he learned" (broken with his tradition) may recover it (be forgiven) if he repents thoroughly; cf. P. Ḥagigah 2: 1, 77b, and B. Ḥagigah, 15a.

10. According to Sifre Deut., 188, such confusion is a transgression of a negative commandment (Deut. 19: 14).

11. Review is like a protecting wall.

12. Note that Deut. 4: 9 (cf. below) makes clear the statement and the following parable: the verse speaks of *Keep thy soul* in connection with teaching others, *teach them to thy sons.*

13. In other words, if you keep Torah, you keep your own life. Cf. ARNB, p. 77.

CHAPTER 25

1. This statement is not clear. Perhaps the thought is, *despite* his (*evil*) impulse; but the reading of the text hardly permits this. Cf. ARNS, p. 79, n. 2; ARNB, p. 72. [The text seems clear if "his impulse," *yiṣro*, is here understood in the neutral sense of "his instinct" or "his disposition." J.O.]

2. Text, *rabbi;* Professor Ginzberg suggested reading *rabbenu* ("our master").

3. Cf., however, *Mabo*, p. 158.

4. Cf. *Mabo*, p. 159.

5. I.e. the hour of death.

6. The omitted passage reads: *"And he expired and died, and was gathered to his people;* it says also." This verse occurs nowhere in reference to Moses (but cf. Gen. 25: 8, 17; 35: 29; 49: 33). Cf. ARNS, p. 79, n. 15. Whatever the original reading of ARN at this point, the passage as a whole has obviously been added as further reflection on the subject of punishment of the wicked and reward of the righteous in Gehenna and Paradise respectively.

7. The Hebrew words for "face" (*panim*) and "back" (*'aḥor*) carry the overtones of "present" and "future," respectively.

8. On the association of Ps. 92 with the world to come see also above, p. 12. The homily is based on the similarity between the word used in Ezek. (*hegeh*) and that in Ps. (*higgayon*).

9. R. Johanan b. Zakkai at the time of his death.

10. According to Moore (2, 347 f.) the reference is to the Messiah, identified

with Hezekiah; Ginzberg (in Moore, *3*, 201 f.), on the other hand, suggests that since Hezekiah was a scholar, R. Johanan "thought of Hezekiah coming to meet him at his entrance on the better life."

11. Resuming the statements by Ben 'Azzai interrupted by the story of the death of Johanan b. Zakkai and the homily on Exod. 33:23 and Ezek. 2:10.

12. Cf. ARNS, p. 80, n. 17 (see also addenda to ARNS, pp. 146, 159) for the reading "idle conversation."

13. See above, Ch. 2, n. 4.

14. The text adds *le-šamayyim*, but the word does not occur in *Exempla*, p. 86. Having neglected to light the Sabbath lamp at the proper time, R. Eliezer feared that Hyrcanus would light it later, which is a mortal offense. See also G. Allon in *Tarbiz*, VII, p. 136.

15. See Jastrow, p. 1511, *s.v. šĕḇuṭ*.

16. Because he had been put under the ban some time before then. See PJT, pp. 30 ff.

17. Cf. above, Ch. 19, n. 10.

18. See above, p. 94 and n. 9, *ad loc.*

19. Literally, "blood." Professor Ginzberg suggested that perhaps *libbo* ("his heart") was the original reading.

20. See Lev. 12:2.

21. Exod. 22:17.

22. Cf. PJT, pp. 50 f. On the planting of cucumbers see also ARNB, p. 130.

23. A utensil or garment is susceptible to uncleanness only after it is ready for use, not in an unfinished state. And R. Eliezer maintained that so long as the shoe is still on the shoe last, even if it is ready for wear, it is regarded as being in an unfinished state; hence it is not susceptible to uncleanness.

24. The last word out of his mouth, in reply to one of the questions, was "clean," "pure"; see n. 25 below.

25. For he was no longer under the ban.

26. II Kings 2:12.

27. I.e. R. 'Aḳiba had many questions which would now go unanswered.

28. PA 4:2.

29. Because of the expense or sacrifice it may have entailed.

30. Cf. Saadia, p. 211.

31. PA 4:2.

32. Cf. the commentary of Elijah b. Abraham and Aknin, SM, p. 110. See, however, BY, *ad loc.*, and Azulai, 249a.

33. Cf. above, Ch. 10, p. 59.

34. The upper story had no permanent stairs and could be reached only by a ladder on the ground floor; the occupants of the upper story had to depend on those below them (L.G.).

35. The expression refers to (hypocritical?) scholars. Cf., however, ARNB, p. 73.

CHAPTER 26

1. See Finkelstein, *Akiba*, pp. 111, 329, n. 38; cf. Aknin, SM, p. 98; ARNB, pp. 71 f.

2. Cf. PA 3:13.

3. Literally, "come." Cf. ARNB, pp. 71 f.

4. Text, *ḳnym*. For the reading adopted, *ḳonam*, cf. ARNS, p. 82, n. 5; AT, *1*, 272, n. 5. The statement seems to say that one ought not to be the kind of person who is always attending banquets, because gradually he will become a burden to people, his presence will be resented, and to get rid of him they will finally take an oath (*ḳonam*) against his company; thus in the end he will be eating of what has been forbidden him. (I am indebted to Professor Lieberman for the explanation of this sentence.)

5. [In many instances where a doubt prevails as to whether a given prohibition does or does not apply, no liability for transgression ensues. However, in the above saying Rabbi 'Aḳiba seems to caution that one should avoid beforehand being faced with such a situation. J.O.]

6. I.e. as though he were buried where the Generation of the Flood—that is to say, the wicked—met with disaster. Cf. P. Běraḳot 4: 1, 7b; see *Legends, 5,* 202.

7. This sentence is not clear; Professor Lieberman suggests that perhaps the original reading was "among the wicked," and in abbreviated form the consonants in the MS were misread as "in the Land of Israel."

8. For the conception underlying this statement see HJP, pp. 161 ff. Mid. Tan., p. 58, reads "in Jerusalem."

9. See the story above, p. 71.

10. PA 2: 5 (in Hillel's name), with some variants and additions. Cf. also ARNB, p. 72.

11. See also below, Ch. 29, p. 122; ARNB, p. 81. The last clause in our passage is perhaps independent of the preceding one, thus: "moreover, they do not begin where they left off."

12. Cf. addenda to ARNS, p. 146.

13. See Ginzberg, *Commentary,* English introd., p. 24. Cf. below, Ch. 28, p. 116.

14. See, however, *Mabo,* p. 161.

15. Circumcision.

16. See *Aspects,* p. 220, n. 8.

17. I.e. knowledge of the Torah, scholarship.

18. PA 3: 11 (with some variants and omissions); cf. ARNB, p. 87. Cf. Klausner, *From Jesus to Paul* (New York, 1943), pp. 600 ff.

19. "Negative commandments" would seem to apply only to the first three of the following series.

20. Cf. the preceding note. Perhaps whatever properly should not be done is here intended by "negative commandments."

21. Literally, "If a man died and left a son who had not learned Torah from his father but went and learned Torah from others, such a one (i.e. the son) seeks flattery."

22. Text, Eliezer.

23. Two meaningless words in the text at this point: "destroys faces" (?). Perhaps we have here a reference to carved reliefs, as would seem to be suggested by BY, *ad loc.* See also TA, *1,* 336 f., n. 484; n. 24 below.

24. The entire clause is not clear, the word translated "step" being the same as that translated "lintel" in the immediately preceding clause (and "threshold" in the following one); but though the passage is badly preserved, the point of R. Eleazar's teaching is obvious: one ought always to be humble.

CHAPTER 27

1. PA 4: 6; cf. ARNB, p. 68.

2. It is characteristic of this treatise to associate Torah with God (cf. Introduction, p. xxii); hence the proof text.

3. Such may perhaps be the meaning of the rather ambiguous reading, and R. Joshua b. Korḥah's statement in the next paragraph may be an explanation of R. Papias' saying. On the expression "horses and chariots of Pharaoh" cf. Exod. 14: 9.

4. Cf. also AT, *1,* 319, n. 3.

5. Above, translated "steed."

6. Cf. PA 4: 5, and see ARNB, p. 68.

7. PA 2: 16 (in R. Tarfon's name), with some variants and additions; cf. ARNB, p. 84.

8. Text, Eliezer.

9. See Ginzberg, *Tamid* (in JJLP, p. 35, n. 4).

10. Cf. HJP, p. 94, n. 87.

11. Astronomy and geometry.

12. PA 3: 18. Cf. ARNB, p. 84.

13. Text, "The *halakot* and the (laws of) purity." The reading in Aknin, SM, p. 138, has been adopted by the translator.

14. I.e. liberal entertainment of strangers.

15. Literally, "making"; see further the next note.

16. Literally, "and their establishment." The clause is not clear.

17. Cf. below, Ch. 30, p. 123.

18. Cf. PA 2: 15 f.; ARNB, p. 84.

19. I.e. the study of Torah.

20. Literally, "filled."

21. Text, Eliezer. Cf. ARNB, p. 76; GS, *1,* 340.

22. See GS, *1,* 340, 366.

23. PA 4: 12.

24. In that he addressed him as *lord.*

25. The passage seems to reflect a general economic deterioration in the Holy Land. See also RB, p. 67. The passage however may be intended as a comment on Eleazar b. Shammua"s statement, i.e. because the Sages did not honor their students and characterized them by disrespectful terms ("straw, chaff"), in the end there remained not even "chaff" in Transjordan—there ceased to be students there altogether (SHY, *1,* 113, n. 2).

CHAPTER 28

1. On the connection of this verse with Babylonia see Nahmanides on Num. 32: 42 and Tosafot in B. Ḳiddušin, 49b, top; see also Ruth Rabba 5: 5. Zech. 5: 9 ff. is interpreted by the Rabbis (cf. e.g. B. Sanhedrin, 24a) to refer to hypocrisy (and arrogance); ARN takes v. 11 to suggest that in *the land of Shinar* (i.e. Babylonia) the house of hypocrisy was built, that is, principally located.

2. Cf. Lucian, *Essays in Portraiture Defended, 27.*

3. Cf. above, p. 112 and n. 13, *ad loc.*

4. Cf. ARNB, p. 70.

5. ARNS, "Rabbi."

6. I.e. by exacting taxes and offering the people amusements Rome is able to *exist* ('*oķeleṭ*) (L.G.). However, see *Toleḏoṭ*, p. 341.

7. Cf. ARNB, p. 68, and Aknin, SM, p. 134.

8. Cf. ARNB, p. 71.

9. Cf. PA 2:4; ARNB, p. 67.

10. Cf. PA 2:4 and commentators, *ad loc.*; ARNB, p. 67.

11. Cf. PA 2:7.

12. Text for this last clause is ambiguous.

13. Cf. GJP, p. 75, n. 68.

14. Cf. ARNB, p. 129.

15. Because it is fixed in the wall or structure.

16. Cf. MTS, p. 37 and n. 4.

17. Cf. Moore, 2, 244.

18. Cf. Jastrow, p. 91, *s.v. Isṭraṭa.*

CHAPTER 29

1. As to circumstances which might change the nature of his vow.

2. PA 4:18 (with some variants and omissions); cf. ARNB, p. 73.

3. The saying is not altogether clear (although rabbinic sources often speak of various activities of the heart). Here probably activities of the "heart" refer to intellectual functions; cf. AT, 2, 427, n. 4; see also Azulai, 252b.

4. Cf. PA 4:10; ARNB, p. 73.

5. Text, "lions, wolves, leopards, panthers," etc. Cf. ARNS, p. 87, n. 6. Professor Ginzberg called my attention to the order in M. Sanhedrin 1:4 and Ginzberg, *Commentary, 1,* 221 f.

6. Literally, "and busies himself with."

7. Perhaps here, too, the reading should be "one order, or two or three," etc.

8. Cf. PA 3:4; ARNB, p. 75.

9. Literally, "and does not open his mouth with words of the Torah."

10. Literally, "if the afterbirth of his mother."

11. See also the MSS reading (ARNS, p. 87, n. 15); our text varies slightly.

12. Text, Eliezer.

13. *Miṣwa;* ARNB, 34, p. 76, reads "for the sake of Heaven."

14. Cf. *Legends, 3,* 360 f.

15. By implication the verse includes Pharaoh, who will come down to beseech Moses.

16. Cf. ARNB, p. 76.

17. Cf. *Legends, 2,* 374.

18. Cf. TG Onkelos on Num. 33:3.

19. "Saith the Lord" does not occur in MT.

20. According to T. Yom Hakkippurim 5:8, repentance and the Day of Atonement atone for a third of man's sins, sufferings atone for a third, and the day of death wipes out the rest.

21. Cf. below, Ch. 39, p. 162. See *Aspects,* p. 308; Moore, *1,* 507-34, 546 ff.

22. They are thus responsible for the profaning of God's name. See also above, p. 112.

23. Cf. MBR, p. 192, n. 17; but see the reading in MHG, Gen., ed. Margulies, p. 20.

24. Cf. PA 4: 15 (R. Mattiah ben Heresh); ARNB, p. 75.

25. Text, "strive not to see him; sit in the company of scholars." MHG, *op. cit.*: "and strive to be seen in the company of scholars." The translation follows tentative reading suggested by Professor Ginzberg (cf. reading of Oxford MS in ARNS, p. 89, n. 32).

26. PA 4: 15; ARNB, p. 75. Cf. GJP, pp. 146 f.

CHAPTER 30

1. PA 4: 9 (with some variants); cf. ARNB, p. 82. Our text reverses the order of the clauses; but cf. ARNS, p. 89, n. 1.

2. Cf. above, p. 114.

3. See Lev. 5: 17 and for the example which follows, Lev. 5.

4. If the sin offering was beyond his means.

5. So R. Tarfon in the Mishnah, *Kĕriṭoṭ* 5: 2.

6. It is a basic rabbinic principle that divine goodness exceeds divine severity, that the measure of divine love is greater than the measure of justice (cf. also Enelow, English introduction, *Mishnat R. Eliezer*, pp. 49 ff.). And the statements which follow below illustrate that from the nature of punishment for transgression it is clear that much more certain and much greater proportionally will be the reward for good deeds performed.

7. See Num. 35: 9 ff.

8. Num. 35: 26 f.

9. See Deut. 19: 15.

10. Deut. 19: 16 ff.

11. Since according to the law *two* witnesses are required, perhaps the meaning is *one pair* of witnesses.

12. So addenda to ARNS, p. 147.

13. According to this view, Jacob did not believe his sons at all, Joseph's wagons notwithstanding. Only through the return of the Holy Spirit did he learn that Joseph was alive. Professor Ginzberg, however, suggested that we have here an independent homily in explanation of the expression "And the spirit of Jacob . . . revived."

14. Literally, "as though (his grave) had been dug and he had been buried."

CHAPTER 31

1. Cf. PA 5: 1; ARNB, p. 90.

2. See Ps. 33: 6. Ten times the word *wayyomer*, "and (God) said," occurs in connection with Creation, nine in Gen. 1 and once in Gen. 2: 18. Cf. Moore, *1*, 415; *3*, 126.

3. I.e. what may one learn from this? PA amplifies: "Could it not have been created by *one* utterance?"

4. ARNS adds "of Israel," without sufficient support from the sources; cf. *Legends*, *5*, 67.

5. Genesis uses the plural form in this instance.

6. Cf. ARNB, p. 22.

7. So addenda to ARNS, p. 147.

8. Translation uncertain; note the commentators, *ad loc.*

9. The verse in Isaiah is taken as a description of what was written in the book of the generations of Adam.

10. Cf. *Legends*, *5*, 82, n. 27.

11. See *Legends*, *7*, *s.v.* "Nine hundred and seventy-four."

12. See above, p. 67 and n. 21, *ad loc.*

13. Literally, "earth"; cf. AT, *1*, 365, n. 1.

14. Cf. *Legends*, *5*, 64 f.; JE, *8*, 544.

15. Literally, "openings, fissures" (cf. shs, p. 458), perhaps in the sense of "informers"; cf. *Thesaurus*, *12*, 6209. See also n. 16 below.

16. For other interpretations of this statement cf. Jastrow, *s.v. korṣin*, pp. 1343 f.; Bacher in REJ, *37*, 301 f.

17. Literally, "man's nose."

18. Rashi in B. Šabbaṭ, 151b: "the forehead is the smoothest and brightest part of the face."

19. Text, "man's urine"; cf. ARNS, p. 92, n. 16.

20. Text, "man's tears"; see the previous note.

21. In B. 'Arakin, 15b, the lips are described as one of the walls of the tongue.

22. Cf. B. 'Arakin, 15b, where the teeth are described as a wall (here doorway) of the tongue.

23. "Firmament": literally, "stretched out, spread flat," and so is the tongue.

24. Like the stars in the firmament, the cheeks stand out in the face; see commentators on Lev. R. 18: 1.

25. Cf. Cant. 4: 4.

26. Uplifted arms are like a mast.

27. See addenda to ARNS, p. 147. Cf. *Legends*, *5*, 245 (top).

28. Cf. Cant. 7: 8.

29. Cf. below, Ch. 33, p. 131.

30. Note the remark of the Tosafists in B. Nazir, 51a, that the flesh at the heel is so thick as to be lifeless, i.e. insensitive (L.G.). Is there an echo in our passage perhaps of "Achilles' heel"?

CHAPTER 32

1. PA 5: 2 (with substantial variants and omissions); cf. ARNB, p. 92.

2. Including Adam and Noah.

3. See Gen. 6: 3. According to this view God fixed two time limits for the Generation of the Flood, the first being 120 years and the second seven days of grace; cf. *Legends*, *1*, 153 f.; *5*, 174 f.

4. Cf. Kadushin, RM, pp. 147 f. and notes, *ad loc.*

5. Cf. *Aspects*, pp. 315 f.

6. Cf. *Legends*, *1*, 154.

7. Literally, "until I have given them double their reward." For the doctrine involved see above, p. 58 and note, *ad loc.;* below, Ch. 39, p. 162.

8. See the parable of the lame and the blind in Moore, *1,* 487 f.

9. Here taken in the sense of "lust, appetite," i.e. the evil impulse.

10. I.e. my evil impulse has been completely subdued; see Rashi on the verse in B. Bĕrakot, 61b.

11. I.e. the evil impulse.

12. So also according to several ancient versions. Our text, however, reads in accordance with MT: *"my."*

13. Cf. Moore, *3,* 148; see also *Aspects,* Ch. 15.

14. Notice the plural; hence, the homily seems to infer, there are two "judges," the two impulses.

15. Cf. *Aspects,* p. 243.

16. I.e. when do I put off passing sentence on the wicked?

17. Then judgment is immediate.

18. The word for "take stock" is the same as for "judge"; and R. 'Akiba is here applying the thought of measure for measure: God will show as little kindness as they have shown humility.

19. R. Judah the Prince.

20. To judge them severely.

CHAPTER 33

1. PA 5: 2 (with substantial variants); cf. ARNB, p. 93.

2. Exclusive of Noah.

3. This is not to be taken literally.

4. [Apparently, taken here to refer to the Written and the Oral Law; see above, p. 80 J.O.]

5. Cf. above, p. 128.

6. On the application of the verse to Abraham cf. Yalkut on Ps. 16: 7.

7. Once he had given away the money as a gift, Abraham would not take it back but would make the litigants share what he had at first given to the defendant for repayment if necessary.

8. Text, incorrectly, "charity and justice."

9. Text, "he would take out a *mina* of his own and give it to him. But if it was not so, he would say to them: 'Divide the sum between you and depart in peace.' " The restoration is based on a reading adduced in addenda to ARNS, p. 147.

10. PA 5: 3 (with some variants); cf. ARNB, p. 94.

11. See Gen. 12: 1 f., 10.

12. See Gen. 21: 10, 22: 1 ff.

13. See Gen. 12: 11 ff., 21: 10.

14. See Gen. 14: 13 ff.

15. See Gen. 15.

16. See Gen. 15: 7; *Legends, 1,* 198 ff.

17. See Gen. 17: 9 ff., 23 f.

18. Cf. PA 5: 4; ARNB, p. 94.

19. See Exod. 7: 19 f., 8: 1 ff., 8: 13 f., 8: 20, 9: 6, 9: 10, 9: 23 ff., 10: 13 ff.,

10: 22 f., 12: 29 f. This sentence is perhaps a doublet of the last clause in the previous paragraph. Cf. also ARNB, p. 94.

20. Cf. PA 5: 4; ARNB, p. 94. These miracles are described below, pp. 133 ff.

21. Perhaps a doublet, or variant, of the preceding sentence; cf., however, ARNB, p. 94.

22. Cf. *Mabo*, p. 167.

23. Text, *wyhm;* cf. II Sam. 22: 15 (*ḳere*).

24. Cf. ARNB, pp. 99 f.

25. MT (so too ARN, *editio princeps*): *"with his own rods."*

26. The homily is based on the Hebrew words *neḳabim* ("holes, hollows, tunnels") and *naḳabta* ("thou hast stricken through"); the picture the homilist has in mind is that of tunnels being hollowed out in the sea; cf. e.g. Maimonides on PA 5: 4; Aknin, SM, p. 149; and on "tunnel" see the *Siloam Inscription,* in A. Reifenberg, *Ancient Hebrew Arts* (New York, 1950), p. 23.

27. I.e., 12 paths were cut through the waters for the 12 tribes.

28. Though for Israel the bed of the sea was dry, when the Egyptians stepped into it, it turned into clay; cf. *Legends, 3,* 22. Perhaps, on the other hand, the meaning is "Make the floor of the sea soft to walk on."

29. Perhaps the meaning is that the sea was as wide open as the wilderness, so that passing through would be easy for the great multitude.

30. Against which the pursuing Egyptians would be dashed to death; cf. *Legends, 3,* 22. Perhaps, however, the meaning is "Make the floor of the sea like a stone-paved highway."

31. Israel now demanded that the waters which had already been transformed into protecting walls be made like flasks (lit., wine skins, leather bottles), which would provide them with sustenance on their way. For a different application of the flask image see Meḳilta, ed. Lauterbach, 2, 51.

32. See above, n. 27. Thus the paths were made dry and passable.

33. Cf. Rashi on Isaiah, *ad loc.*

34. See, however, TG on Isaiah, *ad loc.;* on the verb translated "lapped up" cf. TG on Isaiah, *ad loc.;* TG Jonathan on Num. 22: 4.

35. Cf. above, p. 121 and n. 17, *ad loc.*

CHAPTER 34

1. Cf. PA 5: 4; ARNB, pp. 98 f.; see also above, p. 54.

2. *'Arabah,* "an arid region."

3. See Judg. 17: 1 ff. The connection of this incident with Arabah is not clear. In B. Sanhedrin, 103b, "the idol of Micah" is connected by R. Johanan with Zech. 10: 11; cf. Rashi, *ad loc.;* perhaps our statement should therefore be put in connection with the comment on "Over against Suph."

4. Literally, Sea of Suph.

5. See Num. 21: 5. The word "Tophel" is taken here in the sense of *tiflah,* "frivolity, slander."

6. See Num. 16. Professor Ginzberg suggested that Laban, literally "white," is here associated with Korah, whose consonants *ḳrh* are read as *ḳereaḥ,* "baldheaded," hence "white."

7. See Num. 11. Perhaps the mention of Hazeroth at the end of the account of

the quail incident (Num. 11: 35) suggests the association of this trial with the place. Cf. Tg. Jonathan on Num. 11: 35.

8. See Num. 11: 1 ff.

9. See Exod. 16: 4 ff., 17: 7.

10. See Num. 11: 4 ff., 34. But cf. n. 7 above.

11. See Exod. 32. *Di-zahab* is taken in the sense of *dai zahab,* "enough gold." Although it is not clear what the ten trials are (cf. above, nn. 7, 10), and although Di-zahab is quoted presumably as one of the ten trials, it seems that the homilist does not take it as one of the ten; cf. the comment on *In the wilderness.*

12. Cf. ARNB, p. 100 f.

13. My Lord.

14. The Tetragrammaton.

15. See Exod. 3: 14.

16. See Exod. 6: 3.

17. (Lord of) Hosts; e.g. Isa. 44: 6.

18. Because the term is applied to human beings, R. Yose objects to its being an appellation of God.

19. Cf. ARNB, p. 101.

20. E.g. II Kings 23: 24.

21. E.g. II Chron. 34: 3.

22. E.g. Lev. 19: 4.

23. E.g. Isa. 27: 9.

24. E.g. II Chron. 24: 18.

25. E.g. I Sam. 15: 23.

26. The inverted *nun;* see MT, *ad loc.;* HJP, pp. 38 ff.

27. R. Simeon b. Gamaliel suggests that the marks indicate that the verses are not in their proper place in Scripture.

28. I.e. since a passage marked off by the letter N has just been discussed, another passage, where the N occurs in a peculiar way, is adduced.

29. In MT the *n* in Manasseh (*mnšh*) is suspended. If it is omitted, the remaining consonants are the same as those for Moses: *mšh.*

30. See Exod. 18: 3; I Chron. 23: 15.

31. The wicked king; cf. II Kings 21.

32. No textual peculiarity is involved in Zech. 4: 14, but the following homily seems to have been added because of an association of ideas. Thus: Gershom was rejected from succeeding his father because his conduct was improper; because of their improper conduct the priests have been rejected in favor of the Messiah. See also MV, 117 f.

33. This psalm has been taken to refer to the Messiah. Cf. Epistle to the Hebrews, Chs. 5–7.

34. Actually MT merely has the ' of *y'r* (wood) suspended. "River" would be *y'r,* ' taking the place of the '. Like the verse in Judges above, the present verse possesses a textual peculiarity which occasions homiletical comment.

35. Cf. *Legends,* 5, p. 294, n. 162.

36. [Suggesting a tradition whereby *y'r* was the *Kĕṯib,* with *y'r* as the *Qĕre.* J.O.]

37. I.e. in the Pentateuch. Cf. MT for all passages cited. The dots indicate (see below, p. 139) that the reading in the text was held to be doubtful and that the dotted words or letters were perhaps to be omitted altogether or have their position

in the verse changed. Here the dots are taken to suggest various homiletical (midrashic) comments, as a signal to something unusual. On the subject see the references to Blau, pp. 6–34, in the notes that follow, and HJP, pp. 43 ff. Cf. also ARNB, pp. 97 f.

38. Properly the dot should be over the *ḳ*, since this is the crucial letter. If *ḳ* was miswritten for *h*, the word would be *u-ḥeneha*, "and her"; and the verse should then be taken to say, "The Lord judge between me and her," i.e. Hagar.

39. I.e. between him and her, Abraham and Sarah. According to this view the true reading is held to be *u-ḥenehem*, that is: (*The Lord judge between me*) *and them*.

40. More likely the dots should properly be placed over the word *'yh*, "where is." But the letters now dotted suggest to the homilist the word *'yw*, pronounced *'ayyô*, that is, "where is he," thus implying that the angels inquired after the whereabouts of Abraham also.

41. See Gen. 19:35.

42. The whole word *bḳwmh* should properly be dotted to indicate that of her lying down he was unaware, but not of her getting up.

43. For the probable original significance of the dotting of *wyšḳhw* see Blau, pp. 22 f.; HJP, pp. 45 f.

44. The sign of the accusative preceding the word *flock*.

45. With the accusative sign omitted the verse suggests to the homilist that the *brethren went off to feed* (i.e. to make merry), while leaving *their father's flock in Shechem*. See further, however, Blau, pp. 23 ff.

46. Cf. Blau, pp. 9 f.

47. I.e. the duty to offer the Second Passover is incumbent upon him who on the 14th of Nisan was merely outside the Temple court (no less than upon those who were prevented from offering the First Passover by uncleanness or by being on *a journey afar off*). On the probable original reading of the verse and the dotting, however, cf. Blau, pp. 25 ff.

48. If the letter *r* of *'šr* is removed, the remaining consonants can represent the word for "man" (*'š*), and the homilist suggests that the verse be understood to say, *and women even unto Nophah, men unto Medeba* (*perished*). See further Blau, p. 29.

49. So our text, which seems to say that the word *w-'šrwn* (in the phrase *w-'šrwn 'šrwn*) is to be dotted. In MT the dot occurs only on the second *w* of *w-'šrwn*. See Blau, p. 15.

50. On the reading of our text cf. Blau, pp. 15, 17.

51. On the probable original location of the dots in this verse see Blau, pp. 30 ff.

52. The bracketed addition, missing in ARNA, has been restored on the basis of ARNB, p. 98.

53. That is, why didst thou include these "doubtful" passages?

54. The word for "she," "it" (Hebrew *hy'*), is for the most part written in the Pentateuch as *hw'*, which is also the rendering of the word for "he." Only in the following instances is the word for "she" or "it" rendered as *hy'*, i.e. with a *y* rather than a *w*.

55. Actually MT does not read the *she* (*be taken in the act*) as *hy'*; on the other hand, the same verse does read *she* (*being defiled*) with a *y*.

56. Note that only ten instances have been cited. Cf. ARNB, pp. 101 f., and the reading cited in OD, 2, 624 f.

57. See Moore, *1*, 435.

58. On Gog and Magog see *Legends*, 7, 191. Note that only nine descents (including the one to take place in the future) are listed. Cf. ARNB, pp. 96 f.

59. The verse is referred to God who, when Israel ("the brawling woman in a wide house" of the latter half of the verse) sinned, withdrew from their midst.

60. Text, *lašebet;* MT: *šebet*.

61. On what causes God to withdraw from the world see *Aspects*, pp. 33, 224.

62. Cf. ARNB, p. 95.

63. See Obad. 1.

64. See Num. 12: 7.

65. See Isa. 49: 5.

66. See Isa. 6: 8.

67. See Am. 7: 12.

68. See Ezek. 3: 17.

69. See I Sam. 9: 9.

70. See Joel 3: 1.

71. See Jer. 1: 5.

72. See Ps. 90: 1.

73. I.e. prophecy. Cf. ARNB, p. 95.

74. See Micah 2: 4.

75. See Hab. 2: 6.

76. See Ezek. 17: 2.

77. See Jer. 5: 13.

78. See Isa. 6: 9.

79. So our text, *tif'eret;* perhaps miswritten for *ḥaṭṭafah* ("sermon," see Am. 7: 16); cf. ARNS, p. 103, n. 42.

80. See Ezek. 37: 10.

81. See Mal. 1: 1.

82. See Ezek. 6: 2.

83. See Isa. 22: 1.

84. See Isa. 35: 10.

85. See Isa. 65: 18.

86. See Isa. 35: 10.

87. See Job 41: 14.

88. See Esth. 8: 15.

89. See Isa. 32: 13.

90. See I Chron. 16: 27.

91. See Jer. 33: 9.

92. See I Chron. 16: 32.

93. Cf. ARNB, pp. 121 f.

CHAPTER 35

1. Cf. PA 5: 5; ARNB, pp. 103 ff.; see also below, p. 145.

2. The lesser sacrifices could be eaten anywhere in Jerusalem.

3. In consequence of an earthquake.

4. Cf. Isa. 49: 20.

5. Cf. PA 5: 5. Note that only eight miracles are listed in the ARNA version of these miracles; cf. the list of ARNB. See also *Mabo*, pp. 89 ff.

6. On the following passage cf. ARNB, pp. 107 f.; B. Baba Ḳamma, 82b. See Finkelstein in AMJV (Heb. section), pp. 351 ff.; S. Bialoblotzki in AA, pp. 27 ff.

7. See Lev. 14: 34 f. Verse 34 reads, "When ye come into the land . . . which I give to you for a possession." To none of the tribes, however, was Jerusalem given as a possession. Cf. below, p. 144.

8. See Deut. 21: 1 ff. Verse 1 reads, "If one be found slain in the land which the Lord . . . giveth thee to possess it." Cf. preceding note.

9. Cf. Num. 19: 14; Bialoblotzki, pp. 31 f.

10. See above, p. 36. According to B. Baba Ḳamma, 82b, there is no reason for this; it was merely a tradition. See, however, Bialoblotzki, p. 35.

11. See Bialoblotzki, pp. 35 f.

12. I.e. one who renounces idolatry in order to acquire limited citizenship in Palestine (see Moore, *1*, 339 ff.). Cf. PTP, 134 ff.; Bialoblotzki, pp. 40 f.

13. Cf. II Kings 22: 14 ff. On Huldah see *Legends, 6,* 69, 249 f. Cf. Bialoblotzki, pp. 36 ff.

14. Southeast of the city. In other words the uncleanness was given passage into the outskirts of Jerusalem. We must assume that the cubic space of the tunnel was at least one handbreadth; otherwise, according to rabbinic law, the uncleanness would penetrate perpendicularly upward and render those who passed over the grave unclean (for they would then be regarded as "overshadowing"; cf. preceding n.). If, on the other hand, there is a cubic space of a handbreadth, we do not say that the uncleanness penetrates upward; it can then pass through the tunnel, out to the river Kidron. Cf. TR, *2,* 135.

15. According to B. Baba Kamma, 82b, because of the foul air that would spread after the use of fertilizer and because of weeds. Cf. Bialoblotzki, pp. 33 f. See also Josephus, *Contra Apionem,* I, 199.

16. They might defile hallowed things with the food they gather from refuse. On pigs, B. Baba Kamma, 82b, tells a story very much like that told by Josephus, Antt, XIV, ii, 1.

17. See Deut. 21: 18 ff.

18. Jerusalem was national territory; cf. above, n. 7; Bialoblotzki, p. 31.

19. Cf. Bialoblotzki, p. 30.

20. Only the structure on the ground, not the ground itself, could belong to an individual; cf. preceding note.

21. Cf. Bialoblotzki, pp. 28, 29 f.

22. From the pilgrims who come for the festivals; cf. Bialoblotzki, pp. 28 ff.

23. Cf. Finkelstein in AMJV, pp. 355, 360.

24. Cf. reference in n. 22 above.

25. See below, n. 27.

26. So *editio princeps,* and cf. HJP, p. 145, n. 8; n. 27 below. ARNS reads *mṣrym* ("Egyptian"?).

27. Jerusalem's residents extended to the pilgrims every hospitality for which the guests did not pay. In order to show their gratitude, however, the guests resorted to an interesting evasion (*ha'āramah*): often they had at their disposal large sums of second-tithe money, use of which was limited to the purchase of food, and then only in Jerusalem. If with such money an animal is bought, only the flesh is subject to second-tithe sanctity, not the hide (M. Ma'āśer Šeni 1: 3). Taking advantage of this law the pilgrims would deliberately buy animals whose hides were worth more than their flesh. This, which is obviously an "evasion" of the intent of the second-tithe law, the Mishnah finally legalized, for it states (*ibid.*) that second-tithe sanctity applies to the flesh only, even if the animal's hide is more valuable than its flesh. The guests left such hides as gifts for their hosts, and the latter could then trade with the hides profitably everywhere. To make the hides so valuable, the animals were no doubt painted in some way (on adorning of animals cf. HJP, pp. 145 f.) and the painted hides brought higher prices than ordinary hides. (I am indebted to Professor Saul Lieberman for the interpretation and understanding of this passage.) Note that more than ten things are said of Jerusalem in our passage.

28. Cf. *Legends, 6,* 156, n. 926.

29. Cf. Finkelstein in AMJV, pp. 367 f.

30 When the Land was being allotted.

31. Jericho was to belong to that tribe on whose lands the Temple was later to be built.

32. Until the Temple was built.

33. I.e. Jericho.

34. Ambiguous. BY, *ad loc.*, takes it as a reference to the Sages; Professor Ginzberg suggested that it refers to Joshua and his colleagues.

35. From the verse in I Chron. 2: 55 the homilist derives the identification of Kenites and Rechabites; and a tradition preserved in several sources (cf. e.g. MRS, p. 92) associates I Chron. 4: 23 with the Rechabites.

36. Cf. I Chron. 4: 23, *There they dwelt, occupied in the king's work.*

37. Though proselytes, they became God's people. The expression *'am lammakom* (God's people), Professor Ginzberg said, is strange and very likely corrupt.

38. Paraphrase of I Chron. 4: 9 (L.G.).

39. God gave him the good disciples he hoped for. Cf. *Legends, 3,* 75 f.; 6, 29; see also PTP, p. 189.

40. Cf. PA 5: 5; ARNB, pp. 105 f.

41. Cf. HJP, pp. 174 ff.

42. High Priest in 17–18 C.E.

43. Ishmael thus became unclean. Cf. TA, *1,* 251.

44. Cf. the story in Antt, XVII, vi, 4.

45. Cf. Epstein, SLC, pp. 34 f.

46. Render *piggul;* for the term, cf. e.g. Lev. 7: 18, 19: 7 f.; and for examples, cf. M. Zebahim 2: 2–5; 4: 1; 6: 7; and Menahot 2: 3. Among other things, improper intentions of the priest would render an offering *piggul.*

47. See Lev. 23: 10 ff.

48. Lev. 23: 17.

49. Lev. 24: 5 ff.

50. Lev. 6: 21.

51. Thus they did not clutter up the Sanctuary.

52. This is the tenth miracle, and what follows are variations on this theme.

53. *nikfafim.*

54. I.e. Jerusalem.

CHAPTER 36

1. Professor Obermann suggests that a heading like "FIVE groups of men shall neither live nor be brought to judgment," in keeping with the style of this entire section, must have been accidentally omitted by an early copyist of ARN. Cf. *Mabo,* pp. 106 f. Perhaps, however, the list included originally even more than the five "groups" now in our text; see M. Sanhedrin 10: 3–4 and T. Sanhedrin 13: 1–2, 6 ff. For a recent discussion of the meaning and ambiguities of the eschatological concepts in our chapter see *Mabo,* pp. 212 ff.

2. That is, the men of Sodom shall neither rise at the time of the Resurrection nor be sentenced to punishment at the Final Judgment which is to take place then.

3. See above, p. 68 and n. 25, *ad loc.;* cf. T. Sanhedrin 13: 8.

*. I.e. they will be included among those who are sentenced to punishment.

5. Note the description of the Sodomites in Gen. 13:13.

6. Literally, "Minors, children of wickedness." *Editio princeps* reads: "Minors, children of the wicked," and cf. Rashi on Isa. 44:5. See, however, the readings in T. Sanhedrin 13:1 and B. *ibid.*, 110b. Presumably ARN is here referring to Jewish, and not Gentile, children.

7. *Root* and *branch* are here taken as symbol for the young child.

8. Cf. T. Sanhedrin 13:1 and B. *ibid.*, 110b. The verb *ba'im* may, however, be taken to stand for "brought to judgment," as in R. Joshua's previous statement; but in that event "judgment" need not be understood as an unfavorable sentence, as the following discussion suggests.

9. I.e. the wicked himself will be punished, not his children.

10. The wicked.

11. Cf. the reading in T. Sanhedrin 13:1; B. *ibid.*, 110b; Rashi, *ad loc.*

12. Cf. n. 8 above.

13. It is not clear how this is derived from the verse. On the expression "young children of the wicked" cf. above, n. 6.

14. So *editio princeps*; ARNS: "true proselytes"; see GJP, pp. 83 f.

15. Cf. AT, *1*, 136 f. and nn., *ad loc.*

16. Cf. T. Sanhedrin 13:9 and see above, n. 8; but note how R. Joshua is quoted below (p. 149) in his reply to R. Eliezer.

17. Cf. AT, *1*, 135 f. and nn., *ad loc.*

18. Cf. T. Sanhedrin 13:10 and B. *ibid.*, 110b.

19. The Generation of the Wilderness so made its covenant; cf. Exod. 24:4–8.

20. See Num. 13 f.

21. The next two paragraphs stand in reverse order in our text; see ARNS, p. 108, n. 6.

22. Resuming the order of the text; see preceding note.

23. Professor Ginzberg called my attention to KU, p. 87, for the meaning of "day" (*yom*) as "sun." Cf. the commentary in M. Sanhedrin 10:3, ed. Albeck (p. 204); Ruth Rabba 7:15 and David Luria, *ad loc.*

24. Cf. Moore, 2, 369, and MV, pp. 77 ff.

25. See n. 28 below.

26. Text doubtful; cf. MS reading in ARNS, p. 108, n.*8.

27. Perhaps this refers back to the discussion of the Generation of the Wilderness.

28. Neither this nor the preceding paragraph is clear to me. Cf. the suggestion by Schechter, ARNS, p. 108; AT (Hebrew), *1*, 100 f.; and the translator's note, *ibid.*

29. Cf., however, the reading suggested by Elijah Wilna in ARNS, p. 108, n. 9.

30. "No share in the world to come" is hardly to be taken literally (cf. Ginzberg, JBL, *41*, 121, n. 17). The point being made is that the occupations of such people lend themselves easily to error or abuse. One who is judge in his own city, said Professor Ginzberg, is in danger of being partial to his relatives and friends.

31. Cf. below, Ch. 41, p. 173.

32. Cf. Prayer of Manasseh in Apocrypha, ed. Charles, *1*, 620 ff.

33. The Tetragrammaton, YHWH.

34. I.e. using the holy book for secular music.

35. Referring to magical healing practices by incantation; cf. JMS, pp. 120 f.

36. Cf. Moore, 2, p. 388.

37. Possibly the condemnation here is of the scholar who will not teach others; see ARNS, p. 109, n. 16.

CHAPTER 37

1. Cf. ARNB, p. 120.

2. Literally, "Superior to them all He created the firmament"; "to them all" is either not to be taken literally or perhaps to be omitted entirely (cf. MS reading in ARNS, p. 109, n. 1): a copyist may have misunderstood the word "superior" to mean "higher."

3. So too ARNB, p. 120. Our text has "evil winds," i.e. evil spirits.

4. Hebrew.

5. The various types of Pharisee here described (cf. ARNB, p. 124) represent what the Rabbis would call "pharisaic plagues," insincere, dishonorable pretenders. On the subject see Moore, 2, 188–95. The meaning for none of the terms is clear and is conjectural even in the Talmud. All that can be said with certainty is that such imitation Pharisees are strongly condemned by the Rabbis.

6. According to P. Běrakot 9: 7, 14b, one who carries his good works on his shoulders (i.e. is ostentatious), so that all may see how worthy he is. B. Soṭah, 22b, has another explanation.

7. Probably this is the same as one of the types (nikfi) described in P. Běrakot as one who says suddenly to his fellow, "Excuse me a moment, I have some religious duty to perform." B. Soṭah has another explanation.

8. If this is the same as the type listed in the other sources as kyzy, kyzyy, kyz'y, kwzy, according to P. Běrakot he is one who calculates; for each fault he carries out some good work and thus hopes to cancel his misdeeds. Another explanation in B. Soṭah. [Cf. other variants in the nomenclature of the SEVEN classes of Pharisees in Ibn Shāhīn's (Arabic) Book of Comfort (ed. J. Obermann, New Haven, 1933), pp. 107 f. and the notes ad. loc. J.O.]

9. Different readings and interpretations are furnished by the other sources. Professor Obermann suggests that the unintelligible word in our text is perhaps a doublet of the preceding mkṣw'y.

10. Translation conjectural. Perhaps the clause represents a doublet or gloss or variant of the unintelligible clause which follows. See n. 11 below.

11. Two meaningless words (mḥwptw 'š'ny) occur in the text, which may be a misreading of the phrase in B. Soṭah, "what is my duty that I may do it," i.e. the Pharisee who ostentatiously asks what is expected of him.

12. Translation conjectural. Literally, "Pharisee (i.e. separated) from the impulse (?)."

13. This may mean "merely from fear of God." Professor Obermann suggests that the phrase may mean "from fear of men."

14. Cf. ARNB, p. 119.

15. See JE, 3, 460.

16. Literally, "rebuke"; i.e., were it not for the limits set by God on nature it would continue to expand. Cf. PRE, ch. 5 ("were it not for God's rebuke the waters would have flooded the universe"); Legends, 5, 16 f., n. 43.

17. Cf. MTJM, pp. 72 ff.

18. Since the proof text speaks only of four (out of the seven) qualities, R.

Elijah Wilna substitutes "faithfulness" for "wisdom" and after the Hosea verse quotes Ps. 85: 11; cf. ARNS, p. 110, n. 7.

19. Cf. *Legends, 5,* 10 f.

20. The Latin *velum;* cf. Jastrow, *s.v. wilon.*

21. Gen. 1: 8.

22. Ps. 78: 23.

23. Isa. 63: 15.

24. Deut. 26: 15.

25. I Kings 8: 39.

26. Ps. 68: 5. On the functions of the various heavens cf. *Legends, 1,* 9; *5,* 10 f.

27. Cf. ARNB, p. 119.

28. Gen. 1: 1.

29. Gen. 2: 5.

30. Jer. 10: 11.

31. Josh. 4: 18.

32. Gen. 1: 10.

33. Isa. 18: 3.

34. Ps. 49: 2.

35. A play on words.

36. Very likely the text should read, "Why was it called Abode?"; cf. ARNS, p. 110, n. 10; BY, *ad loc.* See n. 37 below.

37. This is no doubt a play on the Hebrew word for "abode," *heled.* The commentators associate the image with the behavior of the weasel (Heb. *huldah*), which is said to hide things in the earth and to leave them there. Cf. HJP, p. 72. Much is obviously wanting in the text, since we would expect an explanation for each of the terms used for "earth"; cf. ARNB, p. 119. On the seven earths see *Legends, 1,* 10.

38. Cf. *Aspects,* pp. 175 ff.

39. Cf. above, p. 7, and n. 29, *ad loc.* An inference *a minori ad maius* or *vice versa.*

40. An inference by analogy, from congruent biblical expressions. See HJP, pp. 59 ff.

41. Deducing from one biblical passage a regulation applicable to a number of biblical passages which are related to each other.

42. A deduction (see n. 41 above) based on two biblical passages.

43. Determining the general by means of the particular which follows it.

44. Determining the particular by means of the general which follows it.

45. An inference from something similar in another passage.

46. See Strack, pp. 93 f., 285 ff. Cf. JR, *26,* 268 f.

47. Such undoubtedly is the meaning of the text; cf. the reading in ARNB, p. 110; Professor Lieberman calls my attention to P. Ḥagigah 1: 8, 76d. ARNS: "of what he has not heard he says: 'I have not heard'; and he is not ashamed and acknowledges what is true."

48. PA 5: 7 (with some minor variants); cf. ARNB, pp. 110 f.

49. Note Moses' speech in Lev. 10: 16 ff.

50. Cf. Lev. 10: 19: *And if I had eaten of the sin offering today, would it have been well-pleasing in the sight of the Lord?*

51. The two following paragraphs (put into parentheses in ARNS) partially

interrupt the exposition of PA 5: 7. The passage was doubtless added at this point because the story about Aaron in Lev. 10 had been cited, and a comment on another verse in that biblical passage is therefore introduced. The expression "similarly" in our text is not clear, and may be due either to an erroneous duplication of the same expression at the beginning of the paragraph after next ("The same applies," below, p. 156) or to a misreading of the source from which the passage was taken.

52. So our text; not in MT.

53. Out of courtesy on festive occasions one turns first to the oldest in the group; when some rebuke is to be given, on the other hand, it is directed at the youngest.

54. The meaning of this sentence is not entirely clear. It probably refers to some statement illustrating that God, too, did not break into the speech of another; cf. the illustration in reference to Abraham in the next paragraph.

55. The remainder of this paragraph is unclear. This may well be a gloss explaining why God did not speak to Aaron (specifically in what connection is not clear; perhaps the reference is to the view that despite Lev. 10: 8, God did not speak directly to Aaron; see MHG, Lev., p. 197, and cf. Sifre Numbers, 117, 37a).

56. Another instance of not breaking into someone's speech.

57. Professor Ginzberg suggested reading "four"; cf. ARNS, p. 112, n. 15 (middle).

58. Cf. *Aspects*, p. 203.

59. Cf. *Legends*, 5, 287, n. 33.

60. How could the slaughter of these children make up for Benjamin's loss if he did not return, and would Jacob want this! MT reads, *And Reuben said unto his father, saying*, etc.

61. In Gen. 32: 18 f., when Jacob instructs his servant what he is to say on meeting Esau, Jacob anticipates certain questions and provides answers in the proper order. Thus, *Whose art thou?* is the first question, and the first answer is *Thy servant, Jacob's.*

62. This is not clear. ARNB, p. 112, reads "Rebecca"; cf. the conversation in Gen. 24: 23 ff.

63. Cf. Gen. 29: 4 ff.

64. This verse seems pointless in the present connection, unless we assume that the homilist wishes to suggest that by implication Moses agreed with what the Lord said. ARNB, p. 112, more aptly quotes Lev. 10: 20.

CHAPTER 38

1. PA 5: 8 (with a goodly number of variants); cf. ARNB, pp. 113 ff. According to ARNS, p. 115, n. 12, the seven classes of transgression are neglect of (1) tithes; (2) heave offerings; (3) dough offering; (4) other priestly gifts; (5) gleanings, forgotten sheaf, and corners; (6) delay of justice (but see below, n. 7); and (7) idolatry, unchastity, and bloodshed.

2. As a result of devastation by war and brigands.

3. Cf. PA 5: 8; ARNB, p. 115. See Lev. 19: 9 f., 23: 22; Deut. 14: 28 f., 24: 19 ff.

4. So *editio princeps;* ARNS: *biškunaṭ*, which is either a misprint in our text (for *baššěkunah?*) or an abbreviation of *biškunaṭo*.

5. A form of oath.

6. PA 5:8; cf. ARNB, p. 114.

7. I.e. render a decision not in accord with the accepted law. The story which follows is perhaps meant to illustrate this point (and not "delay of justice"), but the application ought not to be pressed too literally. Cf. HUCA, *19*, 112 ff.

8. On the identity of these Sages (in this story) cf. the suggestion by Finkelstein, in ELM, pp. 29 ff. See also *Mabo*, pp. 100 f.

9. On the idiom "eat, drink, and recite a blessing in the name of Heaven," cf. above, p. 47.

10. Cf. SSA, 202 f.

11. The position of Naśi (cf. above, Ch. 10, n. 8) was held by descendants of Hillel; see above, p. 79 and n. 9, *ad loc.*

12. Literally, "the word."

13. So *editio princeps*. Our text: "I know, I would know."

14. This is a reference to the fatal revolt under Bar Kokhba in 132–35 (cf. JE, *2*, 505 ff.). See also Cassius Dio, *Roman History*, 69:14, on the great number of casualties.

15. Cf. above, n. 13.

16. PA 5:9; cf. ARNB, p. 115.

17. The following paragraph is misplaced in our text; see below, n. 19. Cf., however, the reading of this passage and the maxim in Aknin, SM, pp. 160 f.

18. This passage, wanting in our text, has been restored on the basis of Numbers Rabba 7:10.

19. There follows in our text the section on "For unchastity"; cf. n. 17 above. On the whole homily see *Aspects*, pp. 222 ff.

CHAPTER 39

1. I.e. he sins and repents, sins and repents.

2. I.e. he persists in his sin; cf. Azulai, 265a.

3. According to *Aspects*, p. 329, n. 3, this may mean, "The generation by itself is righteous, but is caused to sin by his criminal example." See, however, the first interpretation in BY, *ad loc.*

4. See above, Ch. 29, p. 122; cf. *Aspects*, pp. 328 f., Moore, *2*, 108 f.

5. Perhaps translate, "was not granted Adam"; cf. addenda to ARNS, p. 162, and see n. 6 below.

6. Cf. MTJM, p. 364, n. 130. The statement in our text is not altogether clear; but according to Professor Ginzberg, there can be no doubt that it is based on a concept prevailing in the mysticism of the Geonic period in which *děmuṭ*, "likeness," i.e. *děmuṭ haššěkinah,* "likeness (image) of the Shekinah," plays an important part; cf. Hekaloṭ, Ch. 6 (BHM, *2*, 44). The meaning of the sentence is that if it were not for the "fall of man," he would be able to understand and grasp all secrets of Creation, by means of understanding the "likeness of the Shekinah." Cf. ARNS, p. 116, n. 2. See also CA, p. 28.

7. Cf. PA 3:15 ("he" is R. 'Akiba); AT, *1*, 279 f.; but cf. also ARNB, p. 123. See Moore, *1*, 454 ff.

8. Cf. PA 3:16 ("he" is R. 'Akiba; but see ARNB, p. 135).

9. [Perhaps: ALL THAT LIVE. J.O.]

10. Cf. ARNB, p. 123.

11. So *editio princeps* (cf. AT, *1*, 336, n. 3); text, "atones up to."

12. Cf. above, pp. 121 f.; Moore, *1*, 507 ff.

13. Cf. ARNB, p. 123.

14. Cf. above, p. 58, and the saying of R. Eliezer bar Zadok below in this chapter. On the last clause cf. ARNS, p. 118, n. 5.

15. Perhaps R. Eliezer, son of R. Yose the Galilean; cf. ARNB, p. 123.

16. Cf. Job 1:21.

17. PA 3:14 (with several additions and with R. 'Aḳiḇa as authority); cf. ARNB, p. 124.

18. The Torah.

19. Num. 23:24.

20. Jud. 14:6.

21. Gen. 49:9.

22. Isa. 30:6.

23. Ps. 91:13.

24. Job 28:8. Cf. ARNB, p. 122.

25. Gen. 3:1. [The first name, *naḥaš*, is omitted in our text by haplography. J.O.]

26. Num. 21:8.

27. Exod. 7:9.

28. Jer. 8:17.

29. Isa. 30:6.

30. Ps. 140:4. Cf. ARNB, p. 122.

31. II Sam. 12:25.

32. Eccl. 1:1.

33. Prov. 30:1.

34. Prov. 31:1. [The first name, "Solomon," is omitted in our text by haplography J.O.]

CHAPTER 40

1. Cf. Moore, 2, 92.

2. Cf. above, p. 54 and n. 16, *ad loc.*

3. Cf. PA 5:18; ARNB, p. 125.

4. Cf. above, pp. 121 f. and notes, *ad loc.*

5. PA 5:10; ARNB, p. 126.

6. So PA and ARNB; our text, incorrectly: "Mine is thine and thine is mine."

7. See further below, p. 172 and note 21, *ad loc.;* and Abrahams in SG, 2, 647 ff.

8. Cf. ARNB, p. 129, and see PA 5:12. Cf. *Mabo*, p. 98.

9. Cf. ARNB, p. 129, and see PA 5:14 and ARNB, p. 126.

10 Literally, "one draws near (the sage) and sits down."

11. Literally, "has a portion (of reward)."

12. PA 5:15 (with some deviations); cf. ARNB, p. 127.

13. So *editio princeps;* the reference seems to be to the wicked disciple. Our text reads, "them"; see n. 14 below.

14. See Jastrow, p. 1357, col. 2. Professor Ginzberg was inclined to the belief that three classes of disciples are spoken of, to wit: (1) *Ḳeren* (Horn), (2) *Naḳuḇ* (perforated), and (3) *Ḳiṭṭu'ah*, i.e. "headless" (cf. *Legends, 6,* 95, n. 526).

15. Cf. Finkelstein, *Akiba*, pp. 114, 306; *Mabo*, pp. 99 f., 183 f., and Allon in *Tarbiz* (1950), p. 94, n. 41.

16. Cf. above, p. 26 (view of School of Shammai).

17. Cf. Allon, *op. cit.*

18. Professor Ginzberg suggested that perhaps some word like *mazziḳim* ("demons, evil powers") should be added to the text; Professor Obermann suggests that possibly *middot* is merely an early miswriting for *makkot*, "afflictions, plagues."

19. Text, "wolves, lions, leopards, bears, panthers," etc.; cf. ARNS, p. 128, n. 13.

20. Cf. *Flora, 1*, 70.

21. Cf. ARNB, p. 128.

22. This is not clear.

23. R. Eleazar ben Azariah was wealthy and of distinguished ancestry; cf. JE, 5, 97, col. 1.

24. In M. Baḅa Baṭra 10: 8, R. Ishmael speaks of "one who wishes to be wise" (L.G.).

25. Cf. Graetz, *2*, 428 f. See also above, p. 108.

26. I.e. Sages who were not ordained. Cf. ARNB, p. 129.

27. Ben 'Azzai was famous for his great devotion to study; he never married, he said, because he had given his life to the study of Torah.

28. Ben Zoma was famous as a preacher and interpreter of Scripture.

29. Cf. Graetz, p. 358. See also *Mabo*, p. 103.

30. Cf. ARNB, p. 128.

31. *Ibid.*

32. [We should supply here some such heading as "There are THREE things" (of which two are good for the wicked and one is good for the righteous); omission of the heading was no doubt due to the oversight of an early copyist. J.O.]

33. [Here, again, we should supply a heading to the effect that "THREE things" (should be avoided with respect to the Temple); the other two things are stated in B. Běraḳot, 54b; see ARNS, p. 128, n. 19. J.O.]

34. [Again a heading—such as "There are THREE things" (that should be observed by those who enter a privy)—would seem to have been omitted by a copyist. J.O.]

35. Professor Ginzberg suggested that very likely this is a reference to the use of a "pointer" while reading the Torah, as is still customary.

36. PA 5: 16; cf. ARNB, p. 131.

37. Literally, "thing"; the passage contrasts disinterested love with love directed toward something ulterior to itself.

38. II Sam. 13.

39. I Sam. 18.

40. PA 5: 17; cf. ARNB, p. 128.

41. The famous Sages.

42. Num. 16.

43. PA 4: 11 on the authority of R. Johanan Hassandělar; cf. ARNB, p. 128.

44. To receive the Commandments.

45. Gen. 11: 1 ff.

CHAPTER 41

1. The reading 'ole 'al, generally rendered "excels," occurs apparently in all the MSS of ARN; but the word 'ole does not appear in a number of PA texts (cf. e.g. Taylor, 2, 159 f., Aknin, SM, p. 126). Thus, "excels" not only is a doubtful rendering but is not borne out by the discussion in ARN which follows.

2. PA 4: 13; ARNB, pp. 130 f.

3. Aaron.

4. The Rabbis frequently compare the Torah to water: like water, the Torah is free and refreshing to all.

5. ARNS: "He said to him"; see n. 8 below.

6. ARNS: "with thee"; see n. 8 below.

7. ARNS: "thou hast neglected"; see n. 8 below.

8. So editio princeps and Oxford MS (ARNS, p. 130, n. 2, and cf. Ginzberg, Commentary, 1, 130). ARNS: "and thou didst engage." The story is really intended to emphasize the importance of Torah study (cf. Introduction above, p. xxii), compared to which, R. Simeon in effect declares, even so meritorious an act as visiting the sick is an "idle matter." Cf. Aknin, SM, pp. 126 f.; Toledot, pp. 314 f. and nn.

9. Cf. Gen. 35: 21. Probably to be identified with Geder, SE of Tiberias; see shv 1, 103.

10. Literally, "expounded."

11. After deducting the salary for the (poor) business manager (L.G.).

12. The bracketed words have obviously fallen out of the text (L.G.).

13. Literally, "weeping."

14. E.g. mustard. Literally, "fruits."

15. After bloodletting.

16. This term (Heb. ḥaber) refers to those who voluntarily undertake to observe punctiliously certain laws, especially those of cleanness and uncleanness. On the subject see Moore, 2, 76, 159; JE, 6, 121 ff.; cf. Lieberman in JBL (1952), pp. 199 ff.

17. Because of its uncleanness.

18. They stray into other people's premises and then cause damage.

19. Cf. above, p. 111, on the injunction against breaking bread with a priest who is an 'am ha-'areṣ; on the undependability of the 'am ha-'areṣ see the story above, p. 71. See further below, n. 21.

20. Cf. Lieberman in JBL (1952), p. 203.

21. The term is here applied specifically to those who are neglectful in observing the rules of cleanness and uncleanness and the regulations governing tithes. See also the reference above, Ch. 40, n. 7; RLGT, pp. 3 ff.

22. The following seems to be a fifth requirement; see, however, TR, 1, 64.

23. [For the "Articles of Associateship" and the separatism between the Associates and the "common people" in terms of cleanness and uncleanness see Maimonides, The Book of Cleanness (tr. H. Danby, YJS, 8), 237 ff. and the notes ad loc.; also ibid., pp. xii ff. J.O.]

24. The writing on the Tables of the Commandments which Moses broke; see

Exod. 32: 19 and cf. above pp. 20 ff. The two bracketed paragraphs, omitted in our text, have been restored on the basis of ARNB, p. 130; cf. ARNS, p. 133, n. 19.

25. This verse is taken to refer to the Torah in several talmudic passages.

26. PA 5: 20, ARNB, p. 133.

27. Cf. Ps. 2: 11 (L.G.).

28. On the restoration of the bracketed passage, cf. ARNS, p. 133, n. 21.

29. On the scholar compared to a sponge see above, p. 165; on a vessel coated with pitch, p. 74.

30. On the "funnel" see above, p. 166.

31. On this image cf. Mekilta, ed. Lauterbach, 2, 51.

32. On this subject see *Legends*, *3*, 48; *4*, 320 f.; *6*, 19, n. 112.

33. The Tables which Moses broke, Exod. 32: 19. Cf. *Legends*, *3*, 158; *6*, 65, n. 331.

34. Exod. 16: 33.

35. With which Moses anointed the sacred implements; cf. Lev. 8.

36. Cf. Exod. 4: 17.

37. Num. 17: 23.

38. Obviously more than five objects are listed. No doubt variant traditions and glosses are reflected in our passage; e.g. some take the "rod" to be Moses' rod, some take it to refer to Aaron's staff, etc.

39. They were in charge of preparing the incense in the Temple.

40. Exod. 25: 23.

41. Exod. 25: 31.

42. Exod. 26: 31.

43. Exod. 28: 36.

44. These objects were said to have been brought to Rome by Titus after his triumph over Judaea in the first century. See Josephus, *War*, VII, v, 5; VI, viii, 3.

45. Cf. above, p. 32. Professor Ginzberg suggested that at the opening of this paragraph some general statement like "FIVE things were said in regard to a bride: she is to be bathed, anointed, outfited, danced with, and have her praises sung," probably should be added; and that the story about R. Ṭarfon probably is given as illustration of such conduct, though the term "have her praises sung," *ḳillus*, is here wanting.

46. See above, p. 151. The five kings are the three mentioned above and Solomon and Jehoiakim. As to Solomon, P. Sanhedrin 10: 2, 29b, quite clearly shows that some counted him among the wicked kings; and likewise Jehoiakim (B. Sanhedrin, 103b). Later, however, one shied from mentioning Solomon among the wicked kings and all five names had to be left out (L.G.).

47. Cf. above, p. 151.

48. Literally, "shall be purged, refined" (note the verse from Zech. in the following paragraph). Those altogether righteous are immediately sentenced to their reward, those altogether wicked are immediately sentenced to their doom; cf. B. Rosh Ha-Shana, 16b–17a, and T. Sanhedrin 13: 3. [Cf. Koran 56: 7 ff. J.O.]

49. On this term see S. Lieberman in JQR, *35*, 15, n. 99.

50. So our text, which is evidently difficult. Schechter (ARNS, p. 134, n. 25, end) suggests that the verse be omitted at this point and added below as a proof text for the view of the School of Hillel. However, the brief comment on Ps. 116: 4 may be an exclamation either by R. Yose or the editor of ARN that he may be

spared such a fate (for he—either R. Yose or the editor—probably did regard himself as belonging to the large group of "betwixt and between").

51. In the flames of Gehenna. For the meaning of the reading adopted (ARNS, p. 134, n. 25) cf. Ginzberg in Moore, *3*, 198, and TR, *2*, 161. ARNS: "and break through, bubble forth" (?).

52. The third group, i.e. those betwixt and between.

53. I.e. the dead.

54. MT: *me.*

55. On this subject see Moore, *2*, 318, and *3*, 198.

56. PA 6: 11.

57. According to Maimonides the reference is to Israel. But it is also possible that the reference is to God, and the expression *his righteousness* may be taken in the sense of *his charity,* i.e. God's conferring a bounty on Israel.

58. With this paragraph it is customary to conclude the recital of each chapter of PA.

ABBREVIATIONS

AA—*Alei Ayin: The Salman Schocken Jubilee Volume*, Jerusalem, 5708-5712 [1948-52]

AC—Alexander Kohut, *Aruch completum*, 8 vols. Vienna, 1926

AET—Wilhelm Bacher, *Die aelteste Terminologie der juedischen Schriftauslegung*, Leipzig, 1899

Aknin, SM—R. Joseph b. Jehuda, *Sepher Musar, Kommentar zum Mischnatraktat Aboth*, ed. Wilhelm Bacher, Berlin, 1910

AMJV—*Alexander Marx Jubilee Volume*, New York, 1950

Antt—Josephus, *Antiquities*

ARN—*'Aḅot ḍĕ-Rabbi Naṯan*

ARNA—*Version A* of ARN

ARNB—*Version B* of ARN

ARNS—Solomon Schechter's ed. of ARN, Vienna, 1887

Aspects—Solomon Schechter, *Some Aspects of Rabbinic Theology*, New York, 1909

AT—Wilhelm Bacher, *Agada der Tannaiten*, 2 vols. Strassburg, 1890-1903

Azulai—Hayyim Joseph David Azulai, *Sefer Kikkar la-'Aḍen*, Livorno, 1801

B.—Babylonian Talmud

BHM—*Beṯ ha-Midrasch*, ed. Adolph Jellinek, Jerusalem, 1938

Blau—Ludwig Blau, *Masoretische Untersuchungen*, Strassburg, 1891

BY—*Binyan Yĕhošua'*, commentary by R. Joshua Falk on ARN in the regular eds. of the Babylonian Talmud

CA—*Commentarius in Aggadot*, by R. Azriel of Gerona, ed. Jesaia Tishbi, Jerusalem, 1945

CPB—Israel Abrahams, *A Companion to the Authorized Daily Prayer Book*, London, 1922

Deut. R.—Deuteronomy Rabba

DM—Zachariah Frankel, *Darke ha-Mishnah*, Warsaw, 1923

DR—*Midrash Debarim Rabbah*, ed. Saul Lieberman, Jerusalem, 1940

DS—*Diḳduḳe Soferim*, Raphael Rabinowitz, Munich, 1868

ELM—*Essays and Studies in Memory of Linda R. Miller,* ed. Israel Davidson, New York, 1938

Essai—J. Derenbourg, *Essai sur l'histoire et la géographie de la Palestine,* Paris, 1867

Exempla—Moses Gaster, *The Exempla of the Rabbis,* London, 1924

Finkelstein, *Akiba*—Louis Finkelstein, *Akiba,* New York, 1936

Flora—Immanuel Löw, *Die Flora der Juden,* 2 pts., Vienna and Leipzig, 1924–26

Gen. R.—Genesis Rabba

Ginzberg, *Commentary*—Louis Ginzberg, *A Commentary on the Palestinian Talmud,* New York, 1941

GJP—Saul Lieberman, *Greek in Jewish Palestine,* New York, 1942

Graetz—H. Graetz, *History of the Jews,* Philadelphia, 1891

GS—Louis Ginzberg, *Genizah Studies,* 2 vols. New York, 1928–29

Ha-Perushim—Louis Finkelstein, *Ha-Perushim ve-Anshe Keneset ha-Gedolah,* New York, 1950

HJP—Saul Lieberman, *Hellenism in Jewish Palestine,* New York, 1950

HTR—*Harvard Theological Review*

HUCA—*Hebrew Union College Annual*

HYKP—Saul Lieberman, *Hayerushalmi Kiphshuto,* Jerusalem, 1934

Jastrow—Marcus Jastrow, *A Dictionary of the Targumim, the Talmud Babli and Yerushalmi, and the Midrashic Literature,* New York and Berlin, 1926

JBL—*Journal of Biblical Literature*

JC—Salo Wittmayer Baron, *The Jewish Community,* Philadelphia, 1942

JE—*Jewish Encyclopedia*

JJLP—*Journal of Jewish Lore and Philosophy,* 1919

JMC—Louis M. Epstein, *The Jewish Marriage Contract,* New York, 1927

JMS—Joshua Trachtenberg, *Jewish Magic and Superstition,* New York, 1939

J.O.—Julian Obermann

JQR—*Jewish Quarterly Review*

JR—*Journal of Religion*

KU—*Kitbe Ugarit,* ed. Harold Louis Ginsberg, Jerusalem, 1936

Legends—Louis Ginzberg, *Legends of the Jews,* 7 vols. Philadelphia, 1909–38

Lev. R.—Leviticus Rabba

L.G.—Louis Ginzberg

LGJV—*Louis Ginzberg Jubilee Volume,* New York, 1945

LW—Samuel Krauss, *Griechische und lateinische Lehnwörter,* 2 pts. Berlin, 1898–99

M.—Mishnah

Mabo—Louis Finkelstein, *Mabo le-Massektot Abot ve-Abot d'Rabbi Natan,* New York, 1950

MBR—*Midraš Berešit Rabbati,* ed. Ch. Albek, Jerusalem, 1940

MHG—Midrash ha-Gadol

MHM—R. Israel ibn al-Nakawa, *Menorat Ha-Maor,* ed. H. G. Enelow, New York, 1929–32

Mid. Tan.—*Midrash Tannaim zum Deuteronomium,* ed. D. Hoffmann, Berlin, 1909

MLBT—Louis B. Epstein, *Marriage Laws in the Bible and the Talmud,* Cambridge, Mass., 1942

MMKJV—*Mordecai M. Kaplan Jubilee Volume,* New York, 1953

Moore—George Foot Moore, *Judaism in the First Centuries of the Christian Era,* 3 vols. Cambridge, Mass., 1927–40

MRS—*Mechilta de-Rabbi Simon b. Jochai,* ed. D. Hoffmann, Frankfurt a.M., 1905

MT—Masoretic Text

MTJM—Gershom G. Scholem, *Major Trends in Jewish Mysticism,* Jerusalem, 1941

MTS—Boaz Cohen, *Mishnah and Tosefta Shabbat,* New York, 1935

MV—Joseph Klausner, *Die messianischen Vorstellungen des juedischen Volkes im Zeitalter der Tannaiten,* Heidelberg, 1903

Num. R.—Numbers Rabba

OD—David Solomon Sassoon, *Ohel Dawid,* 2 vols. London, 1932

OT—Max Kadushin, *Organic Thinking,* New York, 1938

P.—Palestinian Talmud

PA—Pirḳe 'Aḅot

Pauly-Wissowa—*Real-Encyclopaedie der classischen Altertumswissenschaft*

PJT—Ben Zion Bokser, *Pharisaic Judaism in Transition,* New York, 1935

PRE—*Pirḳe Rabbi Eliezer, with the Commentary of R. David Luria,* Warsaw, 1852

PTP—Bernard J. Bamberger, *Proselytism in the Talmudic Period,* Cincinnati, 1939

RB—Michael Avi-Yonah, *Bime Roma u-Bizantiyon,* Jerusalem, 1946

REJ—*Revue des études juives*

RLGT—C. G. Montefiore, *Rabbinic Literature and Gospel Teachings,* London, 1930

RM—Max Kadushin, *The Rabbinic Mind,* New York, 1952

RR—*Review of Religion*

Saadia—Saadia Gaon, *The Book of Beliefs and Opinions,* trans. Samuel Rosenblatt, New Haven, 1948 (YJS, *I*)

SG—C. G. Montefiore, *Synoptic Gospels,* 2 vols. London, 1927

shs—Ibn Ḡanâḥ, *Sepher Haschoraschim,* ed. Bacher, Berlin, 1896

shy—*Sefer hayyišuḅ,* ed. Samuel Klein, Vol. *I,* Jerusalem, 5699 (1939)

shya—*Sepher hajaschar,* ed. Lazarus Goldschmidt, Berlin, 1923

sj—Solomon Schechter, *Studies in Judaism,* Philadelphia: first series, reprinted 1938; second series, 1908; third series, 1924

SLC—Louis M. Epstein, *Sex Laws and Customs in Judaism,* New York, 1948

SPG—Israel Abrahams, *Studies in Pharisaism and the Gospels,* Cambridge: first series, 1917; second series, 1924

SSA—Adolf Büchler, *Studies in Sin and Atonement in the Rabbinic Literature of the First Century,* London, 1928

Strack—Hermann L. Strack, *Introduction to the Talmud and Midrash,* Philadelphia, 1931

T.—Tosefta

TA—Samuel Krauss, *Talmudische Archaeologie,* 2 vols. Leipzig, 1910–12

Taylor—C. Taylor, *Sayings of the Jewish Fathers,* 2 vols. Cambridge, 1877–1900

Tg—Targum

Thesaurus—Elieser ben Iehuda, *Thesaurus totius hebraitatis et veteris et recentioris,* Jerusalem, 1948

Tolĕdoṯ—Gedaliahu Allon, *Tolĕdoṯ Hayyĕhudim be-'Ereṣ Yiśra'el,* Tel Aviv, 1952

TR—Saul Lieberman, *Tosefeth Rishonim,* 4 pts. Jerusalem, 1937–39

Wertheimer—*Batei Midrashot,* ed. S. A. Wertheimer, 2 vols. Jerusalem, 1950–53

Yalḵuṭ—*Yalḵuṭ Šim'oni,* Warsaw edition

YJS—Yale Judaica Series

CHAPTERS OF THE FATHERS

(*PIRKE 'ABOT*)

translated by

HERBERT DANBY

ACKNOWLEDGMENT

It is the editor's pleasant duty to express indebtedness to the Clarendon Press, Oxford, and to Mrs. H. Danby for their courtesy in approving the reprinting here of Herbert Danby's translation of *The Chapters of the Fathers,* in *The Mishnah* (Oxford, Clarendon Press, 1933), pp. 446–461.

CHAPTERS OF THE FATHERS

I. 1. Moses received the Law from Sinai and committed it to Joshua, and Joshua to the elders, and the elders to the Prophets; and the Prophets committed it to the men of the Great Synagogue. They said three things: Be deliberate in judgment, raise up many disciples, and make a fence around the Law.

2. Simeon the Just was of the remnants of the Great Synagogue. He used to say: By three things is the world sustained: by the Law, by the [Temple-] service, and by deeds of loving-kindness.

3. Antigonus of Soko received [the Law] from Simeon the Just. He used to say: Be not like slaves that minister to the master for the sake of receiving a bounty, but be like slaves that minister to the master not for the sake of receiving a bounty; and let the fear of Heaven be upon you.

4. Jose b. Joezer of Zeredah and Jose b. Johanan of Jerusalem received [the Law] from them. Jose b. Joezer of Zeredah said: Let thy house be a meeting-house for the Sages and sit amid the dust of their feet and drink in their words with thirst.

5. Jose b. Johanan of Jerusalem said: Let thy house be opened wide and let the needy be members of thy household; and talk not much with womankind. They said this of a man's own wife: how much more of his fellow's wife! Hence the Sages have said: He that talks much with womankind brings evil upon himself and neglects the study of the Law and at the last will inherit Gehenna.

6. Joshua b. Perahyah and Nittai the Arbelite received [the Law] from them. Joshua b. Perahyah said: Provide thyself with a teacher and get thee a fellow[-disciple]; and when thou judgest any man incline the balance in his favour.

7. Nittai the Arbelite said: Keep thee far from an evil neighbour and consort not with the wicked and lose not belief in retribution.

8. Judah b. Tabbai and Simeon b. Shetah received [the Law] from them. Judah b. Tabbai said: Make not thyself like them that would influence the judges; and when the suitors stand before

thee let them be in thine eyes as wicked men, and when they have departed from before thee let them be in thine eyes as innocent, so soon as they have accepted the judgement.

9. Simeon b. Shetah said: Examine the witnesses diligently and be cautious in thy words lest from them they learn to swear falsely.

10. Shemaiah and Abtalion received [the Law] from them. Shemaiah said: Love labour and hate mastery and seek not acquaintance with the ruling power.

11. Abtalion said: Ye Sages, give heed to your words lest ye incur the penalty of exile and ye be exiled to a place of evil waters, and the disciples that come after you drink [of them] and die, and the name of Heaven be profaned.

12. Hillel and Shammai received [the Law] from them. Hillel said: Be of the disciples of Aaron, loving peace and pursuing peace, loving mankind and bringing them nigh to the Law.

13. He used to say: A name made great is a name destroyed, and he that increases not decreases, and he that learns not is worthy of death, and he that makes worldly use of the crown shall perish.

14. He used to say: If I am not for myself who is for me? and being for mine own self what am I? and if not now, when?

15. Shammai said: Make thy [study of the] Law a fixed habit; say little and do much, and receive all men with a cheerful countenance.

16. Rabban Gamaliel said: Provide thyself with a teacher and remove thyself from doubt, and tithe not overmuch by guesswork.

17. Simeon his son said: All my days have I grown up among the Sages and I have found naught better for a man than silence; and not the expounding [of the Law] is the chief thing but the doing [of it]; and he that multiplies words occasions sin.

18. Rabban Simeon b. Gamaliel said: By three things is the world sustained: by truth, by judgement, and by peace, as it is written, *Execute the judgement of truth and peace* (Zech. 8:16).

II. 1. Rabbi said: Which is the straight way that a man should choose? That which is an honour to him and gets him honour from men. And be heedful of a light precept as of a weighty one, for thou knowest not the recompense of reward of each precept; and reckon the loss through [the fulfilling of] a precept against its reward, and the reward [that comes] from transgression against its loss. Consider three things and thou wilt not fall into the hands of transgression: know what is above thee—a seeing eye and a hearing ear and all thy deeds written in a book.

2. Rabban Gamaliel the son of R. Judah the Patriarch said: Excellent is study of the Law together with worldly occupation, for toil in them both puts sin out of mind. But all study of the Law without [worldly] labour comes to naught at the last and brings sin in its train. And let all them that labour with the congregation labour with them for the sake of Heaven, for the merit of their fathers supports them and their righteousness endures for ever. And as for you, [will God say,] I count you worthy of great reward as though ye [yourselves] had wrought.

3. Be heedful of the ruling power for they bring no man nigh to them save for their own need: they seem to be friends such time as it is to their gain, but they stand not with a man in his time of stress.

4. He used to say: Do his will as if it was thy will that he may do thy will as if it was his will. Make thy will of none effect before his will that he may make the will of others of none effect before thy will.

5. Hillel said: Keep not aloof from the congregation and trust not in thyself until the day of thy death, and judge not thy fellow until thou art come to his place, and say not of a thing which cannot be understood that it will be understood in the end; and say not, When I have leisure I will study: perchance thou wilt never have leisure.

6. He used to say: A brutish man dreads not sin, and an ignorant man cannot be saintly, and the shamefast man cannot learn, and the impatient man cannot teach, and he that engages overmuch in trade cannot become wise; and where there are no men strive to be a man.

7. Moreover he saw a skull floating on the face of the water and

he said unto it, Because thou drownedst they drowned thee and at the last they that drowned thee shall be drowned. He used to say: The more flesh the more worms; the more possessions the more care; the more women the more witchcrafts; the more bondwomen the more lewdness; the more bondmen the more thieving; the more study of the Law the more life; the more schooling the more wisdom; the more counsel the more understanding; the more righteousness the more peace. If a man has gained a good name he has gained [somewhat] for himself; if he has gained for himself words of the Law he has gained for himself life in the world to come.

8. Rabban Johanan b. Zakkai received [the Law] from Hillel and from Shammai. He used to say: If thou hast wrought much in the Law claim not merit for thyself, for to this end wast thou created. Five disciples had Rabban Johanan b. Zakkai, and these are they: R. Eliezer b. Hyrcanus, and R. Joshua b. Hananiah, and R. Jose the Priest, and R. Simeon b. Nathaniel, and R. Eleazar b. Arak. Thus used he to recount their praise: Eliezer b. Hyrcanus is a plastered cistern which loses not a drop; Joshua b. Hananiah— happy is she that bare him; Jose the Priest is a saintly man; Simeon b. Nathaniel is fearful of sin; Eleazar b. Arak is an ever-flowing spring. He used to say: If all the Sages of Israel were in the one scale of the balance and Eliezer b. Hyrcanus in the other, he would outweigh them all. Abba Saul said in his name: If all the Sages of Israel were in the one scale of the balance and with them Eliezer b. Hyrcanus, and Eleazar b. Arak was in the other, he would outweigh them all.

9. He said to them: Go forth and see which is the good way to which a man should cleave. R. Eliezer said, A good eye. R. Joshua said, A good companion. R. Jose said, A good neighbour. R. Simeon said, One that sees what will be. R. Eleazar said, A good heart. He said to them: I approve the words of Eleazar b. Arak more than your words, for in his words are your words included. He said to them: Go forth and see which is the evil way which a man should shun. R. Eliezer said, An evil eye. R. Joshua said, An evil companion. R. Jose said, An evil neighbour. R. Simeon said,

He that borrows and does not repay. He that borrows from man is as one that borrows from God, for it is written, *The wicked borroweth and payeth not again but the righteous dealeth graciously and giveth* (Ps. 37:21). R. Eleazar said, An evil heart. He said to them: I approve the words of Eleazar b. Arak more than your words for in his words are your words included.

10. They [each] said three things. R. Eliezer said: Let the honour of thy fellow be dear to thee as thine own, and be not easily provoked, and repent one day before thy death; and warm thyself before the fire of the Sages, but be heedful of their glowing coals lest thou be burned, for their bite is the bite of a jackal and their sting the sting of a scorpion and their hiss the hiss of a serpent, and all their words are like coals of fire.

11. R. Joshua said: The evil eye and the evil nature and hatred of mankind put a man out of the world.

12. R. Jose said: Let the property of thy fellow be dear to thee as thine own; and fit thyself for the study of the Law, for [the knowledge of] it is not thine by inheritance; and let all thy deeds be done for the sake of Heaven.

13. R. Simeon said: Be heedful in the reciting of the *Shema'* and in the *Tefillah;* and when thou prayest make not thy prayer a fixed form, but [a plea for] mercies and supplications before God, for it is written, *For he is gracious and full of compassion, slow to anger, and plenteous in mercy, and repenteth him of the evil* (Joel 2:13); and be not wicked in thine own sight.

14. R. Eleazar said: Be alert to study the Law and know how to make answer to an unbeliever; and know before whom thou toilest and who is thy taskmaster who shall pay thee the reward of thy labour.

15. R. Tarfon said: The day is short and the task is great and the labourers are idle and the wage is abundant and the master of the house is urgent.

16. He used to say: It is not thy part to finish the task, yet thou art not free to desist from it. If thou hast studied much in the Law much reward will be given thee, and faithful is thy taskmaster who shall pay thee the reward of thy labour. And know

that the recompense of the reward of the righteous is for the time to come.

III. 1. Akabya b. Mahalaleel said: Consider three things and thou wilt not fall into the hands of transgression. Know whence thou art come and whither thou art going and before whom thou art about to give account and reckoning. 'Whence thou art come' —from a putrid drop; 'and whither thou art going'—to the place of dust, worm, and maggot; 'and before whom thou art about to give account and reckoning'—before the King of kings of kings, the Holy One, blessed is he.

2. R. Hanina the Prefect of the Priests said: Pray for the peace of the ruling power, since but for fear of it men would have swallowed up each other alive. R. Hananiah b. Teradion said: If two sit together and no words of the Law [are spoken] between them, there is the seat of the scornful, as it is written, *Nor sitteth in the seat of the scornful* (Ps. 1:1). But if two sit together and words of the Law [are spoken] between them, the Divine Presence rests between them as it is written, *Then they that feared the Lord spake one with another: and the Lord hearkened, and heard, and a book of remembrance was written before him, for them that feared the Lord and that thought upon his name* (Mal. 3:16). Scripture speaks here of 'two'; whence [do we learn] that if even one sits and occupies himself in the Law, the Holy One, blessed is he, appoints him a reward? Because it is written, *Let him sit alone and keep silence, because he hath laid it upon him* (Lam. 3:28).

3. R. Simeon said: If three have eaten at one table and have not spoken over it words of the Law, it is as though they had eaten of the sacrifices of the dead, for it is written, *For all tables are full of vomit and filthiness without God* (Is. 28:8). But if three have eaten at one table and have spoken over it words of the Law, it is as if they had eaten from the table of God, for it is written, *And he said unto me, This is the table that is before the Lord* (Ezek. 41:22).

4. R. Hananiah b. Hakinai said: He that wakes in the night or that walks alone by the way and turns his heart to vanity, is guilty against his own soul.

5. R. Nehunya b. Ha-Kanah said: He that takes upon himself the yoke of the Law, from him shall be taken away the yoke of the kingdom and the yoke of worldly care; but he that throws off the yoke of the Law, upon him shall be laid the yoke of the kingdom and the yoke of worldly care.

6. R. Halafta b. Dosa of Kefar Hanania said: If ten men sit together and occupy themselves in the Law, the Divine Presence rests among them, for it is written, *God standeth in the congregation of God* (Ps. 82:1). And whence [do we learn this] even of five? Because it is written, *And hath founded his group upon the earth* (Am. 9:6). And whence even of three? Because it is written, *He judgeth among the judges* (Ps. 82:1). And whence even of two? Because it is written, *Then they that feared the Lord spake one with another: and the Lord hearkened, and heard* (Mal. 3:16). And whence even of one? Because it is written, *In every place where I record my name I will come unto thee and I will bless thee* (Ex. 20:24).

7. R. Eleazar b. Judah of Bartotha said: Give unto him what is his for thou and what thou hast are his; and it is written in [the Scripture concerning] David, *For all things come of thee, and of thine own have we given thee* (I Chron. 29:14).

8. R. Jacob said: If a man was walking by the way and studying and he ceased his study and said, 'How fine is this tree!' or 'How fine is this ploughed field!' the Scripture reckons it to him as though he was guilty against his own soul.

9. R. Dosethai b. Yannai said in the name of R. Meir: He that forgets one word of his study, the Scripture reckons it to him as though he was guilty against his own soul, for it is written, *Only take heed to thyself, and keep thy soul diligently, lest thou forget the words which thine eyes saw* (Deut. 4:9). Could this be even if his study was too hard for him? Scripture says: *And lest they depart from thy heart all the days of thy life*; thus he is not guilty

against his own soul unless he sits and puts them away from his heart.

10. R. Hanina b. Dosa said: He whose fear of sin comes before his wisdom, his wisdom endures; but he whose wisdom comes before his fear of sin, his wisdom does not endure. He used to say: He whose works exceed his wisdom, his wisdom endures; but he whose wisdom exceeds his works, his wisdom does not endure.

11. He used to say: He in whom the spirit of mankind finds pleasure, in him the spirit of God finds pleasure; but he in whom the spirit of mankind finds no pleasure, in him the spirit of God finds no pleasure. R. Dosa b. Harkinas said: Morning sleep and midday wine and children's talk and sitting in the meeting-houses of the ignorant people put a man out of the world.

12. R. Eleazar of Modiim said: If a man profanes the Hallowed Things and despises the set feasts and puts his fellow to shame publicly and makes void the covenant of Abraham our father, and discloses meanings in the Law which are not according to the *Halakah,* even though a knowledge of the Law and good works are his, he has no share in the world to come.

13. R. Ishmael says: Be swift [to do service] to a superior, and kindly to the young, and receive all men cheerfully.

14. R. Akiba said: Jesting and levity accustom a man to lewdness. The tradition is a fence around the Law; Tithes are a fence around riches; vows are a fence around abstinence; a fence around wisdom is silence.

15. He used to say: Beloved is man for he was created in the image [of God]; still greater was the love in that it was made known to him that he was created in the image of God, as it is written, *For in the image of God made he man* (Gen. 9:6). Beloved are Israel for they were called children of God; still greater was the love in that it was made known to them that they were called children of God, as it is written, *Ye are the children of the Lord your God* (Deut. 14:1). Beloved are Israel, for to them was given the precious instrument; still greater was the love, in that it was made known to them that to them was given the precious

instrument by which the world was created, as it is written, *For I give you good doctrine; forsake ye not my Law* (Prov. 4:2).

16. All is foreseen, but freedom of choice is given; and the world is judged by grace, yet all is according to the excess of works [that be good or evil].

17. He used to say: All is given against a pledge, and the net is cast over all living; the shop stands open and the shopkeeper gives credit and the account-book lies open and the hand writes and every one that wishes to borrow let him come and borrow; but the collectors go their round continually every day and exact payment of men with their consent or without their consent, for they have that on which they can rely; and the judgement is a judgement of truth; and all is made ready for the banquet.

18. R. Eleazar b. Azariah said: If there is no study of the Law there is no seemly behaviour, if there is no seemly behaviour there is no study of the Law; if there is no wisdom there is no fear [of God], if there is no fear [of God] there is no wisdom; if there is no knowledge there is no discernment, if there is no discernment there is no knowledge; if there is no meal there is no study of the Law, if there is no study of the Law there is no meal. He used to say: He whose wisdom is more abundant than his works, to what is he like? To a tree whose branches are abundant but whose roots are few; and the wind comes and uproots it and overturns it, as it is written, *He shall be like a tamerisk in the desert and shall not see when good cometh; but shall inhabit the parched places in the wilderness* (Jer. 17:6). But he whose works are more abundant than his wisdom, to what is he like? To a tree whose branches are few but whose roots are many; so that even if all the winds in the world come and blow against it, it cannot be stirred from its place, as it is written, *He shall be as a tree planted by the waters, and that spreadeth out his roots by the river, and shall not fear when heat cometh, and his leaf shall be green; and shall not be careful in the year of drought, neither shall cease from yielding fruit* (Jer. 17:8).

19. R. Eleazar Hisma said: [The rules about] Bird-offerings and the onset of menstruation—these are essentials of the *Hala-*

koth; but the calculations of the equinoxes and gematria are but the savoury dishes of wisdom.

IV. 1. Ben Zoma said: Who is wise? He that learns from all men, as it is written, *From all my teachers have I got understanding* (Ps. 119: 99). Who is mighty? He that subdues his [evil] nature, as it is written, *He that is slow to anger is better than the mighty, and he that ruleth his spirit than he that taketh a city* (Prov. 16: 32). Who is rich? He that rejoices in his portion, as it is written, *When thou eatest the labour of thy hands happy shalt thou be, and it shall be well with thee* (Ps. 128: 2). *Happy shalt thou be*—in this world; *and it shall be well with thee*—in the world to come. Who is honoured? He that honours mankind, as it is written, *For them that honour me I will honour, and they that despise me shall be lightly esteemed* (I Sam. 2: 30).

2. Ben Azzai said: Run to fulfil the lightest duty even as the weightiest, and flee from transgression; for one duty draws another duty in its train, and one transgression draws another transgression in its train; for the reward of a duty [done] is a duty [to be done], and the reward of one transgression is [another] transgression.

3. He used to say: Despise no man and deem nothing impossible, for there is not a man that has not his hour and there is not a thing that has not its place.

4. Levitas of Jabneh said: Be exceeding lowly of spirit, for the hope of man is but the worm. R. Johanan b. Baroka said: He that profanes the name of Heaven in secret shall be requited openly: in profaning the Name it is all one whether it be done unwittingly or wantonly.

5. R. Ishmael his son said: He that learns in order to teach is granted the means to learn and to teach; but he that learns in order to perform is granted the means to learn and to teach, to observe and to perform. R. Zadok says: Keep not aloof from the congregation, and make not thyself like them that seek to influence the judges. Make them not a crown wherewith to magnify thyself or a spade wherewith to dig. And thus used Hillel to say:

He that makes worldly use of the crown shall perish. Thus thou mayest learn that he that makes profit out of the words of the Law removes his life from the world.

6. R. Jose said: He that honours the Law is himself honoured by mankind; and he that dishonours the Law shall himself be dishonoured by mankind.

7. R. Ishmael his son said: He that shuns the office of judge rids himself of enmity and theft and false swearing; and he that is forward in giving a decision is foolish, wicked, and arrogant.

8. He used to say: Judge not alone, for none may judge alone save One. And say not, 'Receive ye my opinion', for it is for them to choose and not for thee.

9. R. Jonathan said: He that fulfils the Law in poverty shall in the end fulfil it in wealth; and he that neglects the Law in wealth shall in the end neglect it in poverty.

10. R. Meir said: Engage not overmuch in business but occupy thyself with the Law; and be lowly in spirit before all men. If thou neglectest the Law many things neglected shall rise against thee; but if thou labourest in the Law He has abundant reward to give thee.

11. R. Eliezer b. Jacob says: He that performs one precept gets for himself one advocate; but he that commits one transgression gets for himself one accuser. Repentance and good works are as a shield against retribution. R. Johanan the Sandal-maker said: Any assembling together that is for the sake of Heaven shall in the end be established, but any that is not for the sake of Heaven shall not in the end be established.

12. R. Eleazar b. Shammua said: Let the honour of thy disciple be as dear to thee as thine own and as the honour of thy companion, and the honour of thy companion as the fear of thy teacher, and the fear of thy teacher as the fear of Heaven.

13. R. Judah said: Be heedful in study, for an unwitting error in study is accounted wanton transgression. R. Simeon said: There are three crowns—the crown of the Law, the crown of the priesthood, and the crown of kingship; but the crown of a good name excels them all.

14. R. Nehorai said: Wander afar to a place of the Law; and say not that it will follow after thee or that thy companions will establish it in thy possession; and lean not upon thine own understanding.

15. R. Yannai said: It is not in our power to explain the well-being of the wicked or the sorrows of the righteous. R. Mattithiah b. Heresh said: Be first in greeting every man; and be a tail to lions and be not a head to jackals.

16. R. Jacob said: This world is like a vestibule before the world to come: prepare thyself in the vestibule that thou mayest enter into the banqueting hall.

17. He used to say: Better is one hour of repentance and good works in this world than the whole life of the world to come; and better is one hour of bliss in the world to come than the whole life of this world.

18. R. Simeon b. Eleazar said: Appease not thy fellow in the hour of his anger, and comfort him not while his dead lies before him, and question him not in the hour of his vow, and strive not to see him in the hour of his disgrace.

19. Samuel the Younger said: *Rejoice not when thine enemy falleth, and let not thine heart be glad when he is overthrown, lest the Lord see it and it displease him, and he turn away his wrath from him* (Prov. 24:17 f.).

20. Elisha b. Abuyah said: He that learns as a child, to what is he like? To ink written on new paper. He that learns as an old man, to what is he like? To ink written on paper that has been blotted out. R. Jose b. Judah of Kefar ha-Babli said: He that learns from the young, to what is he like? To one that eats unripe grapes and drinks wine from his winepress. And he that learns from the aged, to what is he like? To one that eats ripe grapes and drinks old wine. Rabbi said: Look not on the jar but on what is in it; there may be a new jar that is full of old wine and an old one in which is not even new wine.

21. R. Eleazar ha-Kappar said: Jealousy, lust, and ambition put a man out of the world.

22. He used to say: They that have been born [are destined] to

die, and they that are dead [are destined] to be made alive, and they that live [after death are destined] to be judged, that men may know and make known and understand that he is God, he is the Maker, he is the Creator, he is the Discerner, he is the Judge, he is the Witness, he is the Complainant, and it is he that shall judge, blessed is he, in whose presence is neither guile nor forgetfulness nor respect of persons nor taking of bribes; for all is his. And know that everything is according to the reckoning. And let not thy [evil] nature promise thee that the grave will be thy refuge: for despite thyself wast thou fashioned, and despite thyself wast thou born, and despite thyself thou livest, and despite thyself thou diest, and despite thyself shalt thou hereafter give account and reckoning before the King of kings of kings, the Holy One, blessed is he.

V. 1. By ten Sayings was the world created. And what does the Scripture teach thereby? Could it not have been created by one Saying? But this was to requite the ungodly which destroy the world that was created by ten Sayings, and to give a goodly reward to the righteous which sustain the world that was created by ten Sayings.

2. There were ten generations from Adam to Noah, to show how great was his longsuffering, for all the generations provoked him continually until he brought upon them the waters of the Flood. There were ten generations from Noah to Abraham, to show how great was his longsuffering, for all the generations provoked him continually until Abraham our father came and received the reward of them all.

3. With ten temptations was Abraham our father tempted, and he stood steadfast in them all, to show how great was the love of Abraham our father.

4. Ten wonders were wrought for our fathers in Egypt and ten at the Sea. Ten plagues did the Holy One, blessed is he, bring upon the Egyptians in Egypt and at the Sea. With ten temptations did our fathers tempt the Holy One, blessed is he, in the wilderness, as it is written, *Yet have they tempted me these*

ten times and have not hearkened to my voice (Num. 14:22).

5. Ten wonders were wrought for our fathers in the Temple: no woman miscarried through the smell of the flesh of the Hallowed Things; and no flesh of the Hallowed Things ever turned putrid; and no fly was seen in the shambles; and the High Priest never suffered a pollution on the Day of Atonement; and the rains never quenched the fire of the wood-pile [on the Altar]; and no wind prevailed over the pillar of smoke; and never was a defect found in the *Omer* or in the Two Loaves or in the Shewbread; [and the people] stood pressed together yet bowed themselves at ease; and never did serpent or scorpion do harm in Jerusalem; and no man said to his fellow, *The place is too strait for me* (Is. 49:20) that I should lodge in Jerusalem.

6. Ten things were created on the eve of Sabbath between the suns at nightfall: the mouth of the earth, the mouth of the well, the mouth of the she-ass, the rainbow, and the manna and the rod and the Shamir, the letters and the writing and the Tables [of stone]. Some say also: The evil spirits and the sepulchre of Moses and the ram of Abraham our father. Some say also: The tongs made with tongs.

7. There are seven marks of the clod and seven of the wise man. The wise man does not speak before one that is greater than he in wisdom; and he does not break in upon the words of his fellow; and he is not hasty in making answer; he asks what is relevant and makes answer according to the *Halakah;* and he speaks on the first point first and on the last point last; and of what he has heard no tradition he says, 'I have not heard'; and he agrees to what is true. And the opposites of these are the marks of the clod.

8. Seven kinds of retribution come upon the world for seven classes of transgression. If some give tithe and some do not give tithe, there comes famine from drought: some suffer hunger while some have enough. If [all] resolved that they would not give tithe there comes famine from tumult and drought. And if they will not set apart Dough-offering there comes an all-consuming famine. Pestilence comes upon the world because of crimes deserving of the death-penalties enjoined in the Law that

are not brought before the court; and because of [the transgressions of the laws of] the Seventh Year produce. The sword comes upon the world because of the delaying of justice and the perverting of justice; and because of them that teach the Law not according to the *Halakah*.

9. Noisome beasts come upon the world because of false swearing and the profaning of the Name. Exile comes upon the world because of idolatry and incest and the shedding of blood; and because of [neglect of the year of] the Release of the land. At four periods pestilence increases: in the fourth year and in the seventh year and in the year after the seventh year and at the end of the Feast [of Tabernacles] every year. 'In the fourth year'—because of [neglect of] Poorman's Tithe in the third year; 'in the seventh year'—because of [neglect of] Poorman's Tithe in the sixth year; 'in the year after the seventh year'—because of [transgressing the laws of] Seventh Year produce; 'and at the end of the Feast of [Tabernacles] every year'—because of wrongfully withholding the dues of the poor.

10. There are four types among men: he that says, 'What is mine is mine and what is thine is thine'—this is the common type, and some say that this is the type of Sodom; [he that says,] 'What is mine is thine and what is thine is mine'—he is an ignorant man; [he that says,] 'What is mine is thine and what is thine is thine own'—he is a saintly man; [and he that says,] 'What is thine is mine, and what is mine is mine own'—he is a wicked man.

11. There are four types of character: easy to provoke and easy to appease—his loss is cancelled by his gain; hard to provoke and hard to appease—his gain is cancelled by his loss; hard to provoke and easy to appease—he is a saintly man; easy to provoke and hard to appease—he is a wicked man.

12. There are four types of disciple: swift to hear and swift to lose—his gain is cancelled by his loss; slow to hear and slow to lose—his loss is cancelled by his gain; swift to hear and slow to lose—this is a happy lot; slow to hear and swift to lose—this is an evil lot.

13. There are four types of almsgivers: he that is minded to give but not that others should give—he begrudges what belongs to others; he that is minded that others should give but not that he should give—he begrudges what belongs to himself; he that is minded to give and also that others should give—he is a saintly man; he that is minded not to give himself and that others should not give—he is a wicked man.

14. There are four types among them that frequent the House of Study: he that goes and does not practise—he has the reward of his going; he that practises but does not go—he has the reward of his practising; he that goes and also practises—he is a saintly man; he that neither goes nor practises—he is a wicked man.

15. There are four types among them that sit in the presence of the Sages: the sponge, the funnel, the strainer, and the sifter. 'The sponge'—which soaks up everything; 'the funnel'—which takes in at this end and lets out at the other; 'the strainer'—which lets out the wine and collects the lees; 'the sifter'—which extracts the coarsely-ground flour and collects the fine flour.

16. If love depends on some [transitory] thing, and the [transitory] thing passes away, the love passes away too; but if it does not depend on some [transitory] thing it will never pass away. Which love depended on some [transitory] thing? This was the love of Amnon and Tamar. And which did not depend on some [transitory] thing? This was the love of David and Jonathan.

17. Any controversy that is for God's sake shall in the end be of lasting worth, but any that is not for God's sake shall not in the end be of lasting worth. Which controversy was for God's sake? Such was the controversy of Hillel and Shammai. And which was not for God's sake? Such was the controversy of Korah and all his company.

18. He that leads the many to virtue, through him shall no sin befall; but he that leads the many to sin, to him shall be given no means for repentance. Moses was virtuous and he led the many to virtue; the virtue of the many depended on him, as it is written, *He executed the justice of the Lord and his judgements with Israel*

CHAPTERS OF THE FATHERS 247

(Deut. 33: 21). Jeroboam sinned and he led the many to sin; the sin of the many depended on him, as it is written, *For the sins of Jeroboam which he sinned and wherewith he made Israel to sin* (I Kings 15: 30).

19. He in whom are these three things is of the disciples of Abraham our father; but [he in whom are] three other things is of the disciples of Balaam the wicked. A good eye and a humble spirit and a lowly soul—[they in whom are these] are of the disciples of Abraham our father. An evil eye, a haughty spirit, and a proud soul—[they in whom are these] are of the disciples of Balaam the wicked. How do the disciples of Abraham our father differ from the disciples of Balaam the wicked? The disciples of Abraham our father enjoy this world and inherit the world to come, as it is written, *That I may cause those that love me to inherit substance and that I may fill their treasuries* (Prov. 8: 21). The disciples of Balaam the wicked inherit Gehenna and go down to the pit of destruction, as it is written, *But thou, O God, shalt bring them down into the pit of destruction; bloodthirsty and deceitful men shall not live out half their days* (Ps. 55: 23).

20. Judah b. Tema said: Be strong as the leopard and swift as the eagle, fleet as the gazelle and brave as the lion to do the will of thy father which is in heaven. He used to say: The shameless are for Gehenna and the shamefast for the garden of Eden. May it be thy will, O Lord our God and the God of our fathers, that the Temple be built speedily in our days, and grant us our portion in thy Law with them that do thy will.

21. He used to say: At five years old [one is fit] for the Scripture, at ten years for the Mishnah, at thirteen for [the fulfilling of] the commandments, at fifteen for the Talmud, at eighteen for the bride-chamber, at twenty for pursuing [a calling], at thirty for authority, at forty for discernment, at fifty for counsel, at sixty for to be an elder, at seventy for grey hairs, at eighty for special strength, at ninety for bowed back, and at a hundred a man is as one that has [already] died and passed away and ceased from the world.

22. Ben Bag-Bag said: Turn it and turn it again for everything

is in it; and contemplate it and grow grey and old over it and stir not from it for than it thou canst have no better rule.

23. Ben He-He said: According to the suffering so is the reward.

VI. KINYAN TORAH: [These things] have the Sages taught in the language of the Mishnah. Blessed is he that made choice of them and their Mishnah!

1. Rabbi Meir said: He that occupies himself in the study of the Law for its own sake merits many things, and, still more, he is deserving of the whole world. He is called friend, beloved [of God], lover of God, lover of mankind; and it clothes him with humility and reverence and fits him to become righteous, saintly, upright, and faithful; and it keeps him far from sin and brings him near to virtue, and from him men enjoy counsel and sound knowledge, understanding and might, for it is written, *Counsel is mine and sound knowledge, I am understanding, I have might* (Prov. 8:14). And it gives him kingship and dominion and discernment in judgement; to him are revealed the secrets of the Law, and he is made like to a never-failing spring and like to a river that flows ever more mightily; and he becomes modest, longsuffering, and forgiving of insult; and it magnifies him and exalts him above all things.

2. R. Joshua b. Levi said: Every day a divine voice goes forth from mount Horeb, proclaiming and saying, 'Woe to mankind for their contempt of the Law!' For he that occupies himself not in the study of the Law is called 'reprobate' (*NaZuF*), as it is written, *As a golden ring in the snout* (Nezem Zahab b'aF) *of a swine, so is a fair woman without discretion* (Prov. 11:22). And it is written, *And the tables were the work of God, and the writing was the writing of God, graven* (haruth) *upon the tables* (Exod. 32:16). Read not *haruth* but *heruth* (freedom), for thou findest no freeman excepting him that occupies himself in the study of the Law; and he that occupies himself in the study of the Law shall be exalted, for it is written, *From Mattanah to Nahaliel, and from Nahaliel to Bamoth* (Num. 21:19).

3. He that learns from his fellow a single chapter or a single

Halakah or a single verse or a single expression or even a single letter, must pay him honour, for so we find it with David, king of Israel, who learned only two things from Ahitophel, but called him his teacher, his companion, and his familiar friend; for it is written, *But it was thou, a man mine equal, my companion and my familiar friend* (Ps. 55: 13). And is there not here an inference from the less to the greater?—if David king of Israel, who learned but two things from Ahitophel, called him his teacher, his companion, and his familiar friend, how much more then must he that learns from his fellow a single chapter or a single *Halakah* or a single verse or a single expression or even a single letter pay him honour! And 'honour' is naught else than 'the Law', for it is written, *The wise shall inherit honour* (Prov. 3: 35), and *The perfect shall inherit good* (Prov. 28: 10); and 'good' is naught else than 'the Law', for it is written, *For I give you good doctrine; forsake ye not my Law* (Prov. 4: 2).

4. This is the way [to get thee knowledge] of the Law. Thou shalt eat bread with salt *and thou shalt drink water by measure* (Ezek. 4: 11), and on the ground shalt thou sleep and thou shalt live a life of trouble the while thou toilest in the Law. If thou doest thus, *Happy shalt thou be and it shall be well with thee* (Ps. 128: 2); *happy shalt thou be*—in this world; *and it shall be well with thee*—in the world to come.

5. Seek not greatness for thyself and covet not honour. Practise more than thou learnest; and crave not after the tables of kings, for thy table is greater than their table and thy crown than their crown; and faithful is thy taskmaster who shall pay thee the reward of thy labour.

6. Greater is [learning in] the Law than priesthood or kingship; for kingship is acquired by thirty excellences and the priesthood by twenty-four; but [learning in] the Law by forty-eight. And these are they: by study, by the hearing of the ear, by the ordering of the lips, by the understanding of the heart, by the discernment of the heart, by awe, by reverence, by humility, by cheerfulness; by attendance on the Sages, by consorting with fellow-students, by close argument with disciples; by assiduity, by

[knowledge of] Scripture and Mishnah; by moderation in business, worldly occupation, pleasure, sleep, conversation, and jesting; by longsuffering, by a good heart, by faith in the Sages, by submission to sorrows; [by being] one that recognizes his place and that rejoices in his lot and that makes a fence around his words and that claims no merit for himself; [by being one that is] beloved, that loves God, that loves mankind, that loves well-doing, that loves rectitude, that loves reproof, that shuns honour and boasts not of his learning, and delights not in making decisions; that helps his fellow to bear his yoke, and that judges him favourably, and that establishes him in the truth and establishes him in peace; and that occupies himself assiduously in his study; [by being one] that asks and makes answer, that hearkens and adds thereto; that learns in order to teach and that learns in order to practise; that makes his teacher wiser, that retells exactly what he has heard and reports a thing in the name of him that said it. Lo, thou hast learnt that he that tells a thing in the name of him that said it brings deliverance unto the world, for it is written, *And Esther told the king thereof in Mordecai's name* (Esth. 2:22).

7. Great is the Law, for it gives life to them that practice it both in this world and in the world to come, as it is written, *For they are life unto those that find them, and health to all their flesh* (Prov. 4:22); and it says, *It shall be health to thy navel and marrow to thy bones* (Prov. 3:8); and it says, *She is a tree of life to them that lay hold upon her, and happy is everyone that retaineth her* (Prov. 3:18); and it says, *For they shall be a chaplet of grace unto thine head, and chains about thy neck* (Prov. 1:9); and it says, *She shall give to thine head a chaplet of grace, a crown of glory shall she deliver to thee* (Prov. 4:9); and it says, *For by me thy days shall be multiplied and the years of thy life shall be increased* (Prov. 9:11); and it says, *Length of days is in her right hand; in her left hand are riches and honour* (Prov. 3:16); and it says, *For length of days, and years of life, and peace, shall they add to thee* (Prov. 3:2).

8. R. Simeon b. Judah in the name of R. Simeon b. Yohai said: Beauty and strength and riches and honour and wisdom and old

age and grey hairs and children are comely to the righteous and comely to the world, for it is written, *The hoary head is a crown of beauty; it shall be found in the way of righteousness* (Prov. 16:31); and it says, *The glory of young men is their strength and the beauty of old men is the hoary head* (Prov. 20:29); and it says, *The crown of the wise is their riches* (Prov. 14:24); and it says, *Children's children are the crown of old men; and the glory of children are their fathers* (Prov. 17:6); and it says, *Then the moon shall be confounded and the sun ashamed; for the Lord of hosts shall reign in mount Zion and in Jerusalem, and before his elders shall be glory* (Is. 24:23). R. Simeon b. Menasya said: These seven qualities which the Sages have reckoned as comely to the righteous were all of them fulfilled in Rabbi and in his sons.

9. R. Jose b. Kisma said: I was once walking by the way and a man met me and greeted me and I returned his greeting. He said to me, 'Rabbi, from what place art thou?' I answered, 'I come from a great city of Sages and scribes'. He said to me, 'If thou wilt dwell with us in our place I will give thee a thousand thousand golden *denars* and precious stones and pearls'. I answered, 'If thou gavest me all the silver and gold and precious stones and pearls in the world I would not dwell save in a place of the Law'. And thus it is written in the Book of Psalms by David, king of Israel, *The Law of thy mouth is better unto me than thousands of gold and silver* (Ps. 119:72). Moreover at the time of a man's departure, neither silver nor gold nor precious stones nor pearls go with him, but only [his knowledge of] the Law and good works; for it is written, *When thou walkest, it shall lead thee; when thou sleepest, it shall watch over thee; and when thou awakest it shall talk with thee* (Prov. 6:22). *When thou walkest it shall lead thee* —in this world; *when thou sleepest, it shall watch over thee*—in the grave; *and when thou awakest, it shall talk with thee*—in the world to come. And it says, *The silver is mine, and the gold is mine, saith the Lord of hosts* (Haggai 2:8).

10. Five possessions did the Holy One, blessed is he, take to Himself in his world; and these are they: the Law is one possession, and the heaven and earth are one possession, Abraham is

one possession, Israel is one possession, and the Temple is one possession. Whence [do we learn this of] the Law? Because it is written, *The Lord possessed me in the beginning of his way, before his works of old* (Prov. 8:22). Whence [do we learn this of] heaven and earth? Because it is written, *The heaven is my throne, and the earth is my footstool; what manner of house will ye build unto me and what place shall be my rest* (Is. 66:1)? And it says, *O Lord, how manifold are thy works! In wisdom hast thou made them all: the earth is full of thy riches* (Ps. 104:24). Whence [do we learn this of] Abraham? Because it is written, *And he blessed him, and said, Blessed be Abram of God Most High, possessor of heaven and earth* (Gen. 14:19). Whence [do we learn this of] Israel? Because it is written, *Till thy people pass over, O Lord, till the people pass over which thou hast gotten* (Ex. 15:16). And it says, *Unto the saints that are in the earth, and the excellent in whom is all my delight* (Ps. 16:3). Whence [do we learn this of] the Temple? Because it is written, *The place, O Lord, which thou hast made for thee to dwell in; the sanctuary, O Lord, which thy hands have established* (Ex. 15:17). And it says, *And he brought them to the border of his sanctuary, to this mountain, which his right hand had gotten* (Ps. 78:54).

11. Whatsoever the Holy One, blessed is he, created in his world, he created it only for his glory, as it is written, *Everything that is called by my name and that I have created, I have formed it, yea, I have made it* (Is. 43:7). And it says, *The Lord shall reign for ever and ever* (Ex. 15:18).

R. Hananiah b. Akashya said: The Holy One, blessed is he, was minded to grant merit to Israel; therefore hath he multiplied for them the Law and commandments, as it is written, *It pleased the Lord for his righteousness sake to magnify the Law and make it honourable* (Is. 42:21).

INDEX 1

Passages Quoted

GENESIS

LEVITICUS

NUMBERS

DEUTERONOMY

JOSHUA

THE FATHERS
JUDGES

I SAMUEL

II SAMUEL

II KINGS

ISAIAH

JEREMIAH

EZEKIEL

INDEX 1

THE FATHERS

PSALMS

PROVERBS

INDEX 1

8: 30 f., 127
8: 34, 29
9: 2, 25
10: 2, 31
10: 19, 100
11: 30, 142
12: 16, 154
13: 13, 101
13: 14, 143
16: 32, 101
17: 28, 100
21: 9, 141
21: 19, 142

21: 22, 101
21: 24, 99
22: 22 f., 159
23: 5, 172
24: 30 f., 104
25: 1, 5
25: 7, 110
25: 21 f., 85
26: 13 f., 97
27: 2, 61
27: 14, 62
28: 17, 164
30: 32, 62

JOB

1: 8, 22
1: 21, 76
3: 1 ff., 156 f.
3: 2, 157
3: 25, 58
4: 1, 157
8: 1, 157
11: 1, 157
14: 19, 41
21: 13, 130
21: 14, 130

25: 6, 93
28: 11, 42
28: 13–15, 66
28: 17, 104
28: 22, 66
31: 1, 24
31: 17, 47
31: 20, 47
32: 1, 157
32: 6 f., 156

CANTICLES

1: 6, 95
1: 8, 88
1: 9, 113
4: 15, 136

7: 3, 17
7: 11, 6
7: 12–13, 6

RUTH

1: 1, 4

LAMENTATIONS

3: 23, 15

3: 28, 51

ECCLESIASTES

4: 1, 68
4: 8, 69

4: 9, 50
4: 14, 83

THE FATHERS

INDEX 1

INDEX 2 *

Authorities

* This index lists the names of Sages either as the authorities to whom dicta and statements are attributed or as subjects of anecdotes, homilies and interpretations.

INDEX 3

Subjects

Aaron: and Moses, 4, 54, 64 f., 115, 155 f.; sons of, 4, 57, 76, 156, 189, 232; in tent of meeting, 19; punished for slander, 54; disciples of, 63; as peacemaker, 63 f.; and Pharaoh, 121; at Di-zahab, 137; and Messiah, 137 f.; not numbered among Levites, 139; death of, 65; staff of, 173, 220

Abel, 126, 177

Abihu, 156

Abiram, 95

Abraham: burnt offering of, 14; treatment of the poor, 47; led men under Shekinah, 68; and ministering angels, 72; ten generations from Noah to, 131, 243; ten trials of, 132, 243; and Hagar, 138; burial of, 150; one of three Patriarchs, 153; when praying in behalf of men of Sodom, 156; justice and charity of, 131 f.

Absalom, 151

Abstinence, as a hedge about vows, 111

Abtinas, House of, 173

Adam, 8–16; hedge about the words of, 8 ff.; creation of, 11, 13; named animals, 13; made burnt offering, 14; born circumcised, 23; worked in Garden of Eden before eating, 60; sons of, 76; book of generations of, 126; ten generations from, to Noah, 129, 243. *See also* Eve

Africans, flat feet of, 79

Agada, 49, 185; study of, 74, 118

Age to come. *See* World to come

Agur, 163

Ahab, 57, 151

Ahaziah, 57, 151

Ahitophel, 151, 249; his hankering for greatness, 173

Almighty. *See* God

Altar: Titus at, 9; built by Adam, 14; removed by Hezekiah, 22; burial under, 111; Shekinah withdrew from Temple court to, 141; pillar of smoke, 146, 244

'Am ha-'areṣ, 86, 97, 98 f., 111, 112, 164, 172, 219, 233, 238, 245. Cf. 219, n.23

Amnon, 57, 168, 246

Amram, 55

Angels: man little lower than, 20; treatment of those who wished to release a prisoner, 51; of death, 65 f., 128; names of, 67; Abraham to, 72; smote Assyrians, 114. *See also* Ministering angels

Anger, 78 f., 119, 235, 242, 245

Animals, 11; naming of, 13; saintliness of, 53, 186, 242, 247; no evil impulses in, 85

Anointing, rite of, 3, 175

Anointing oil, 3, 173

Apostates, 86

Holy of Holies, 145, 146, 168, 183
Holy One, blessed be He. *See* God
Holy Spirit, 125, 142
Holy tongue (Hebrew language), 153, 213
Holy Writings, 5; hedge about the words of, 8, 25; types of, 167
Honor, 241, 249; of fellow men, 78, 235, 240; hedge about, 111
Horeb, 54, 136, 248
Hospitality, 47, 144, 231
"Hosts," 137. *See also* God
Huldah, the prophetess, 143
Humility, 48, 101, 240, 241, 247, 248, 249; hedge about, 111
Hyrcanus (father of R. Eliezer), 43, 44; (son of R. Eliezer), 107

Idolatry, 26 f., 112, 215; David and, 111; names of contempt for, 137; punishment for, 160, 163, 245
Immersion pool, 94, 108
Impulses, good and evil, 82 ff., 75, 105, 193; evil, 27, 75, 86, 95, 101; judgment of, 130, 205
Inference, 7, 24; by Moses, 19, 21; from Job, 24; from Gabriel, 24; by 'Aḳiḇa, 41; concerning spies, 54; from Miriam, 55; by heathen, 81; from measure of reward, 123 f.; from particular to general and vice versa, 86, 154
Informers, 86
Isaac, 153
Isaiah, Book of, when seen in a dream, 167
Ishmael, 73
Ishmael b. Ḳimḥiṯ: suffered uncleanness on day of atonement, 146; his mother beheld two of her sons serving as High Priests, 146
Israel: Torah given to, 4; and Balaam, 7; and work, 60 f.; rulers of, 61; peace in, 63 f., 67; number named Aaron in, 64; enemies requited by seventy-two letter name, 73; at time of exile to Babylon, 97; and golden calf, 96; redemption of, 98; leaving land of Pharaoh, 121; in Egypt, 132; at Red Sea, 113, 133 ff.; in wilderness, 136; enemies of, likened to boars, 138; called "alive," 142; those who surname themselves by name of, 148; punishment for unchastity, 160 f.; called children of God, 162, 238; assembly before Mt. Sinai, 168; returned to place of origin, 172
Israel, Land of: admonition not to leave, 111, 112; those buried in, 111; wisdom of, 116; called "living," 142
Ithamar, son of Aaron, 156

Jabez, 145
Jacob: born circumcised, 23; Holy spirit came to, 125; those who call themselves by name of, 148; one of three Patriarchs, 153; sons of, 125; death of, 188
Jamnia, 36, 77, 192
Jedidiah, 163
Jehoshaphat, 57
Jeremiah, born circumcised, 23
Jeremiah, Book of, when seen in a dream, 167
Jericho, 145, 211